No Country for Old Men

From Novel to Film

Edited by
Lynnea Chapman King
Rick Wallach
Jim Welsh

THE SCARECROW PRESS, INC.
Lanham • Toronto • Plymouth, UK
2009

Published by Scarecrow Press, Inc.
A wholly owned subsidary of The Rowman & Littlefield Publishing Group, Inc.
4501 Forbes Boulevard, Suite 200, Lanham, Maryland 20706
http://www.scarecrowpress.com

Estover Road, Plymouth PL6 7PY, United Kingdom

British Library Cataloguing in Publication Information Available

Library of Congress Cataloging-in-Publication Data

No country for old men : from novel to film / [text and editing] Lynnea
Chapman King, Rick Wallach, Jim Welsh.
    p. cm.
  Includes bibliographical references and index.
  ISBN 978-0-8108-6729-1 (pbk. : alk. paper) — ISBN 978-0-8108-6730-7 (ebook)
  1. McCarthy, Cormac. No country for old men. 2. McCarthy, Cormac—Film
and video adaptations. 3. No country for old men (Motion picture) 4. Film
adaptations—History and criticism. I. King, Lynnea Chapman, 1967– II.
Wallach, Rick. III. Welsh, Jim, 1938–
  PS3563.C337 N638 2009
  813'.54—dc22
                                                                2009012063

Printed in the United States of America

Contents

Preface: Too Smart for Mainstream Media?

Lynnea Chapman King

I twice viewed *No Country for Old Men* in the theater, and on both occasions after the final image of Tommy Lee Jones had cut to black, there were audible exclamations from the patrons around me: "That's it?" "What happened?" This twelfth film by Joel and Ethan Coen evoked the same response that the brothers' films have been eliciting for over two decades: stunned silence, confusion, disappointment, and perhaps even hostility or disgust from viewers accustomed to tidily packaged cinematic narratives, but drawn to a Coen film by a clever trailer or a favorite actor. The public regularly weighs in on Coen films on blogs, around water coolers, and over post-viewing dinner or drinks; academia, however, has not been as enthusiastic. Scholarly criticism of the Coens has been relatively scant despite the multiple awards and nominations earned by their films, although more recently the Coens have become subject to increasing critical attention.

With this newfound critical interest in mind, I organized a forum on the Coen brothers at the twenty-ninth annual meeting of the Southwest/Texas Popular Culture Associations in Albuquerque, New Mexico, in February of 2008, anticipating that academics might be interested in some spontaneous Coen analysis. I was pleasantly surprised when a number of McCarthy scholars attended, ready to offer their perspectives on the adaptation of *No Country for Old Men*. Also in attendance were Jim Welsh, founder of *Literature/Film Quarterly*, and Rick Wallach, of the Cormac McCarthy

Society and the *Cormac McCarthy Journal*, who have joined me in coediting
this collection. The forum's vigorous discussion yielded analyses of various
perspectives: *No Country for Old Men* as post–September 11 commentary;
its treatment of social codes, myth, gender, geography, hairstyles; and its
indebtedness to Flannery O'Connor. This collection grew out of that forum,
combined with essays originally appearing in the spring 2005 issue of the
Cormac McCarthy Journal and subsequently revised significantly for this
volume. The essays divide into analyses of the novel, collected in chapters
1–6, and those dedicated to the film, in chapters 7–15. There is, of course,
overlap in both directions.

Rick Wallach's introduction explores the cinematic qualities of McCarthy's novel by addressing the cinematic subject and the spectator's identification, or lack thereof, with that subject. Wallach also considers Ed Tom
Bell's voice in both the novel and the film, a topic that recurs throughout these analyses, as he contrasts Bell's moral arguments with Anton
Chigurh's determinism. Javier Bardem, who portrayed Anton Chigurh
in the film, has commented in interviews that Chigurh is a symbol of
fate, whose code dictates irrevocable action, as opposed to Bell's moral
conservatism symbolizing tradition, the law, and Christian morality.
Accordingly, Linda Woodson devotes her chapter to the competing discourses of moral responsibility and determinism in the characters of Bell
and Chigurh, a competition she traces throughout McCarthy's fiction. In
fact, several other essays note similarities between *Blood Meridian*'s Judge
Holden and Anton Chigurh, particularly in terms of their shared worldviews. The stripped-down style of *No Country for Old Men*, however, is
a departure for McCarthy, as readers familiar with his previous works
will be aware. Steven Frye offers an explanation for this shift, turning
our attention to the title of the novel and the poem from which it origi-
nates: W. B. Yeats's "Sailing to Byzantium." Frye's analysis of the poem
and its corresponding application to the novel predicate his observation
that McCarthy's marked stylistic departure provides the reader with two
worlds: that of Bell's interior consciousness, whose folksy regional dialect
will be more familiar to McCarthy's readers, and the objective world of
the third person narrative, which is artless, spare, and consistent with the
bleak country of the Yeats poem.

Moving from the novel's poetic antecedents to its reception, David
Cremean challenges critics' designation of Bell as the voice of a "conservative" McCarthy, using Joseph Campbell's concept of the mythic hero
to trace the evolution of Bell and Llewelyn Moss, who undergo, respectively, an inner quest and a journey of action. Cremean notes McCarthy's
"all stories are one" approach to literature, which John Vanderheide
further considers as he offers *No Country for Old Men* as an allegory for
all McCarthy's novels. The pilgrim Bell, he suggests, moves from power-

lessness to empowerment in an allegory of renunciation of capitalism and the nihilism that accompanies it. Like Vanderheide, John Cant examines the allegorical nature of Ed Tom Bell as aged father and voice of the novel, discussing the Oedipal myth in McCarthy's work prior to *No Country* as well as its absence in this novel. Cant argues that although this work is not Oedipal, it's much more difficult to say what *No Country* actually is. In the DVD bonus material for the film, members of the cast and crew offer their opinions as to how one might label this narrative: horror, crime, Western, noir, even comedy at times. This search for genre is echoed by readers and viewers alike: What do we "call" this work? Through what lens should we view it? Robert Jarrett concludes the initial portion of this anthology by considering the novel's multiple generic conventions, focusing on the popular misapprehension of *No Country* as a thriller and exploring its possible alternate generic designations.

Jim Welsh introduces the second half of this collection, bridging the previous analyses of the novel and the forthcoming examinations of the film as he weaves together many of the threads that run through this volume: the complexities of adaptation theory and practice; issues of genre, allegory, fidelity, intertextuality; and the place of this film in the Coen canon. Because this film is an adaptation, antecedents figure prominently in discussions in these chapters: poetic, mythic, cinematic, and literary. Patricia Tyrer and Pat Nickell consider the film as a revisionist Western, viewing Ed Tom Bell, Anton Chigurh, and Llewelyn Moss as descendants of their generic ancestors. Their approach is extended by Scott Covell, who deems Chigurh a postmodern Western nemesis. Covell explores Chigurh's villainous cinematic and literary predecessors, measuring his credentials against Western badmen and *Blood Meridian*'s Judge and "the kid." Chigurh's lack of generic convention extends to his physical appearance, as is appropriate for a postmodern villain, and Sonya Topolnisky examines the costuming of Chigurh, Moss, and Bell, demonstrating that "in art, as in life, clothing signifies" within the genre of Western cinema. Topolnisky further discusses the costumes in light of viewer expectations for the genre as well as Bell's perspective on the relationship between attire and his views of right and wrong, thus returning us to the issues of morality introduced by Wallach and Woodson.

Audiences perceive the American West stereotypically as a man's world and as a by-product of that world, Western films rely heavily on masculine dominance. These assumptions are challenged by two chapters on gender: in the first, Stacey Peebles considers the males of *No Country for Old Men* against the masculine ideal in Westerns, noting that these three men operate within but also in opposition to generic conventions and offering an alternative to masculine authority in the Western. Erin K. Johns then examines the masculine systems of law, nature, and fate as espoused by Bell, Moss, and Chigurh, arguing for the role of women within those systems as sites of resistance to them. Johns then extends her discussion of gender to the Coens' work more broadly, pointing out such critiques of gender systems in other Coen films as well. Dennis Cutchins focuses on a system of a different sort, the religious worldviews of McCarthy and the Coen brothers. He discusses the narrative gaps in the film's treatment of Moss's death and the implications of the changes from novel to film. Exploring the role of grace in determining agency and meaning in the film, Cutchins anticipates Dennis Rothermel, who considers Schopenhauer's assertion that great art confronts the meaning of life. Like Bell, the film viewer must "[search] for what's important in the story"—in life—a process that earns this story, claims Rothermel, the designation of great art.

This process of searching is a common theme of Coen films, as their projects overtly invite speculation, challenge their viewers, and encourage nonpassive cinematic experiences. My students and I are endlessly seeking the "key" to Coen films, and in our penultimate chapter, Jason Landrum suggests that *No Country for Old Men* could be that key. Landrum undertakes a reception study of the Coens' films from *Blood Simple* through *No Country*, and then utilizes patterns in Coen criticism to demonstrate the impact of excess on the spectator and the position of *No Country* within the Coen oeuvre. Landrum demonstrates that popular reviewers have trivialized most of the Coen Brothers' films because of their alleged "excesses," a presumed coldness and inhumanity toward their peculiar characters, and a refusal of the filmmakers to explain their work to the clueless in parody interviews. Landrum offers a new and different model for critical evaluation in order to help correct this trend. We close the collection with an interview with Roger Deakins, long-time Coen collaborator and the cinematographer for the adaptation of *No Country for Old Men*. Deakins offers his perspectives on this film, the Coens, the Western, and the role of film in society.

The goal of the Albuquerque Coen forum was to provide opportunity for an exchange of ideas on a burgeoning topic, and the Coen brothers offer us many such opportunities with each new film, raising unanswered, perhaps unanswerable questions: What are we to do with the Landlord's performance piece in *The Big Lebowski*? Why does a pivotal scene in *The Man Who Wasn't There* contain a flying saucer? Was Chigurh indeed behind the door when Ed Tom Bell walked into that hotel room? The discussion continues, and we are pleased to be a part of it.

Acknowledgments

We would especially like to acknowledge Stephen Ryan, our most patient and cooperative editor, for his contributions to and continuing support of this project. We are appreciative, as well, for the enthusiasm and assistance of the Cormac McCarthy Society.

Introduction: Dialogues and Intertextuality: *No Country for Old Men* as Fictional and Cinematic Text

Rick Wallach

To consider a film and its parental work of fiction together is to imagine a dialogue going on between two mediums. This imagining, as the articles in this collection demonstrate, consists of more than a mere comparison of paired narratives. We ask how the text *informs* the film and vice-versa. Do details of character and action in one medium clarify (or obscure) something about motives or sequences of events in the other? In what ways does the film differ from the novel, and why does it differ when it does? It's commonplace for avid cinema goers to avoid reading the book to avoid cluttering their perceptions of the film, and even more commonly, lovers of the novel avoid seeing the film because they don't think that the cinema version will do justice to the book. "The book was better" is perhaps the single most ubiquitous critical pronouncement in all of American culture. Surely, Hollywood has given us ample reasons for our popular critical fatalism. One need look no further than *Dune* (1984) or *Captain Corelli's Mandolin* (2001)[1] for classic examples of sources badly served by their cinematic versions. Nevertheless, if you've read the novel without having seen the film, or seen the film without having read the book, what additional dimensions of meaning remain unexplored in either one, or, to put it another way, what interpretive opportunities have we missed?

In the case of *No Country for Old Men* we can—and indeed we should—view this dialogue between the novel and the film as an extension of the relations of the novel with the rest of Cormac McCarthy's canon. *No Country for Old Men* (2005) extends McCarthy's long preoccupation with theatrical and cinematic modes of representation. Aside from his two published plays, *The Stonemason* (1994b) and *The Sunset Limited* (2006), he has also authored one produced film drama, *The Gardener's Son*, written for the PBS Visions series in 1976, published in book form in 1996. *No Country for Old Men* was itself originally conceived as a film script some-time during the 1980s; McCarthy rewrote it as a novel perhaps a decade and a half later—to then have it rescripted by the Coen Brothers into an Academy Award–winning film.[2]

Aside from McCarthy's dramatic texts, any number of critical studies and reviews regard his novels—in their scenaristic grandeur, intricate descriptions of places and settings, and schematized melodramatic excesses—as "cinematic." How so? Certainly, his descriptions of terrain are carefully plotted to enhance the reader's visualization of the landscape. In this passage from *Blood Meridian* (1985), sweeping vistas of the Badlands at night repeatedly cut back, film-like, to close-ups of the riders traversing them, close enough so that the reader can "hear" the sounds made by the bits in the horses' mouths and the creaking of their saddle leather:

> Crossing those barren gravel reefs in the night they seemed remote and without substance. Like a patrol condemned to ride out some ancient curse. A thing surmised from the blackness by the creak of leather and the chink of metal . . . and they traveled under the cape of the wild mountains upon a broad soda plain with dry thunder to the south and rumors of light. Under a gibbous moon horse and rider spanceled to their shadows on the snowblue ground and in each flare of lightning those selfsame forms rearing with a terrible redundancy behind them like some third aspect of their presence hammered out black and wild upon the naked grounds. (151–52)

Note especially how McCarthy uses nautical terms like "reefs," "cape," and "snowblue ground," and invokes the broadness of the plain upon which they ride, in contrast to the mountains around them, to impart an only partially conscious sense of the vastness and flatness of the sea. This dramatically enhances the sense of the riders' isolation and smallness upon the setting in which he has placed them.

Although the so-called cinematic qualities of his novels have become a given among his critics and reviewers, there hasn't really been much discussion of this intriguing assumption. The sole prior occasion for eliciting consideration of the cinematic dimensions of McCarthy's work was director Billy Bob Thornton's disappointing 2000 adaptation of the breakthrough bestseller *All the Pretty Horses* (1992). With its casting of thirty-something actors as the teenaged protagonists of the novel, its fa-mously butchered postproduction, and the acrimony between Thornton and his producers at Miramax Films, there was little about this adaptation to inspire discussion anywhere but in the gossip columns. There, Thornton's struggle with the Weinstein Brothers to keep as much of his labors as possible off the cutting room floor became legendary. "My contract—from now on, for the rest of my life—only says three words: kiss my ass," Thornton remarked in the wake of his dustup with his studio (Josyph 2000).

I wrote above of McCarthy's prior interest in the theatrical and cinematic and represented *No Country* as an extension of those interests. In the novel that I and not a few others still regard as his masterpiece, *Blood Meridian* (1985), theatrical or performance imagery is crucial to the story. The protagonist of *Blood Meridian*, "the kid," first encounters his terrifying nemesis Judge Holden during a revival tent meeting. The destinies of the members of the Glanton gang are cryptically set forth by an elaborately staged gypsy tarot card reading. Judge Holden's grand metaphor for the futility of human existence is also theatrical: "The truth about the world . . . is that anything is possible. Had you not seen it all from birth and thereby bled it of its strangeness it would appear to you for what it is, a hat trick in a medicine show, a fevered dream, a trance bepopulate with chimeras having neither analogue nor precedent, an itinerant carnival, a migratory tentshow whose ultimate destination after many a pitch in many a mudded field is unspeakable and calamitous beyond reckoning" (245).

The novel concludes with the killing of a crinoline-clad dancing bear upon a saloon stage. The judge's final words invoke the stage as well: "Hear me, man, he said. There is room on the stage for one beast and one alone. All others are destined for a night that is eternal and without name. One by one they will step down into the darkness before the footlamps" (331).

Anton Chigurh has impressed critics as Judge Holden's latterday incarnation. However, as classical myths posit a "golden age"—of whose heroes and demigods our contemporary heroes and villains are their bronze age simulacrums, operating at a diminished remove—Chigurh's character is proper to an ideological age rather than to a heroic or even to a philosophical one. Whereas the judge's oratory is always expansive, often anecdotal or parabolic, Chigurh's pronouncements are spare and direct. "You're asking that I make myself vulnerable, and that I can never do. I have only one way to live. It doesn't allow for special cases" (*No Country*, 259), Chigurh informs Carla Jean in response to her plea for clemency—just before shooting her. This is a statement of ideological rigidity punctuated, as all such statements ultimately are, by a calculated act of violence. It exemplifies none of the questioning posture of philosophy. Judge Holden's oratory is simultaneously inflected, parodied, and

reified—emptied, as it were, of resonance—by Chigurh's one-track pronouncements on the determinism of mortality. Compare, for example, the
judge's description of a game of mortal chance with Chigurh's description
of the same thing:

> Suppose two men at cards with nothing to wager save their lives. Who has
> not heard such a tale? A turn of the card. The whole universe for such a
> player has labored clanking to this moment which will tell if he is to die at
> that man's hand or that man at his. What more certain validation of a man's
> worth could there be? This enhancement of the game to its ultimate state
> admits no argument concerning the notion of fate. . . . In such games as have
> for their stake the annihilation of the defeated the decisions are quite clear.
> The man holding this particular arrangement of cards in his hand is thereby
> removed from existence. This is the nature of war, whose stake is at once the
> game and the authority and the justification. (*Blood Meridian*, 249)

In the now infamous "coin flip scene" in *No Country for Old Men*, the coin
toss has replaced the playing card draw:

> You need to call it, Chigurh said. I cant call it for you. It wouldnt be fair. It
> wouldnt even be right. Just call it.
>   I didnt put nothin up.
>   Yes you did. You've been putting it up your whole life. You just didnt
> know it. You know what the date is on this coin?
>   No.
>   It's nineteen fifty-eight. It's been traveling twenty-two years to get here.
> And now it's here. And I'm here. And I've got my hand over it. And it's
> either heads or tails. And you have to say. Call it.
>   I dont know what I stand to win. . . .
>   You stand to win everything, Chigurh said. Everything. (56)

Moreover, the descriptions of violence in *Blood Meridian* are often ame-
liorated by its elaborate choreography and vatic narrative voice. These
aesthetic baffles are replaced by a sparer, less baroque, much grittier
tone and a splitting of the narrative into two distinct voices in the more
recent novel. One of the odder aspects of Bell's monologue is that it is
retrospective, coexisting uneasily in the novel with the eidetic passages
taking place in a present tense. It is important to the maintenance of irony
between Bell's introspective monologues and the more or less objectively
narrated third-person passages that Bell knows so little about how or
why the "messes" get made, even when their solution depends wholly
upon his formidable powers of deductive speculation. He may be able to
reconstruct such episodes in part, but he is wholly unable to anticipate
the scene or moment of the next one. Similarly, he knows Chigurh only
by footprint and the unmistakable signature of his work, and reconstructs

him, perhaps a bit too grandly, as *"a true and living prophet of destruction"* (*No Country*, 4).

Retrospective or not, Bell's monologues preserve the state of partial ignorance in which the sheriff operates while the episodes he ruminates upon take place. One notable exception is that he realizes that he had been close enough to the killer to have been observed by him: "*I walked in front of those eyes once. I wont do it again*" (4). It is as if the natural order of spectatorship, already subverted by Bell's dearth of information, is finally upended by his realization that he had been the subject of "speculation" himself. This conundrum is reconstituted by the film when the sheriff visits the scene of Llewelyn Moss's death at the El Paso motel. Through the hole Chigurh's cattlegun has punched in the lock, the audience sees the temporarily cornered Chigurh, reflected in the doorknob on the opposite side of the door, warily regarding Bell's reflection in the outside doorknob. It is not clear that Bell sees this image, but the camera does. It is as if the camera that stood for Bell's gaze had been suddenly turned around to gaze at *him* through the eyes of his nemesis.[3] The film reconstitutes the dichotomy of the two texts of the novel for us as audience/narratee. We share in Bell's ignorance because we don't know how Chigurh disappears from the room without Bell spotting him.

Indeed, much of the text of *No Country for Old Men* has a cinematic, rather than strictly literary, quality. Of its two dominant narrative voices—that of the third-person narrator of the "action" passages and the interior monologues of Sheriff Bell—the former, albeit flatter and more formal, is distinctly eidetic, or visual. Thus, the eidetic form is ideally suited to an intertextuality more cinematic than literary. Its world is the world of *Traffic* (2000), *Pulp Fiction* (1994), even *The Day of the Jackal* (1973) and other super-hit-man films that capitalize on the lure of, and to no small degree romanticize, the millions of dollars to be made from drug dealing, sophisticated armaments, contract assassinations, steely psychopathic resolve, and "chase scenes." This narrative style is especially appropriate because popular, or kitsch, cinema has largely supplanted literature as the principal purveyor of myth to the denizens of late capitalist civilization. This, of course, is as much an ideological as it is an ontological problem of contemporary cinema. It was always an inescapable consequence of a popular cinema to subvert its own capacity to deglamorize the criminal mythos of the drug trade. Whatever moral intentionality might lay behind a script, it always yields to the exaggerations and inflations of the lens and the big screen. The mere act of magnification of the human form propagates an excess of credibility that print media cannot impart on a moment-to-moment basis. We as audience are always seduced into sympathy with criminal characters as they escape deadly situations and outwit civil authorities. To represent this illicit world otherwise would contravene the economic determinism of the kitsch culture that sustains the American cinema in the first place. Chigurh's apparent "invincibility"—his ability to take the hardest hits and to emerge, if not unscathed then at least undeterred—is no more nor less than the commercially heroic ethos of the star athlete "playing hurt" made a duskier sort of flesh. Perhaps nowhere does Chigurh's personality seem more a grotesquely noble cipher of sorts than the moment in the novel when he returns the drug money to the cartel chief who had lost it to Llewelyn Moss. It is not, we realize, simply greed that has motivated the killer. By excluding this scene from the film, the Coens represent Chigurh as a pure inflection of sports mania heroism. He is the triumphant competitor. Dare I say that like many of our most revered athletes, he appears to be motivated by greed after all? Despite his brutality and psycopathy, in an amoral popular ethos like ours he even seems more admirable than the "overmatched" Sheriff Bell. Whereas it has been the critical commonplace to seek the moral compass of both the novel and the film in Ed Tom Bell's reflections and conduct, McCarthy's (and the Coens') most lacerating commentary on contemporary American culture inheres less in the sheriff's pronouncements than in the stature that his nemesis achieves. This vicious irony exemplifies how comparing the film to its source discloses problems not readily apparent when one considers either medium alone.

Chigurh's stature-by-default has a further parallel in the bleak outlook evinced by Sheriff Bell's monologues in the novel. We cannot describe Bell's voice as a "privileged" narrative in the Bakhtinian sense of possessing an excess of seeing and knowing in comparison with his narratee. The eidetic narrative passages subvert such a privileged vantage at every turn. Much of what the third-person narrative conveys to *its* narratee is invisible to Bell. He may come across, and comment upon, the scenes of carnage described in the narrative ex post facto. "It's a mess, aint it Sheriff?" asks Wendell, surveying the remains of "that colossal goatfuck" (141) into which the narrative's pivotal drug deal has long since imploded. "If it aint," replies Bell, "it'll do till a mess gets here" (77), in one of the novel's (and the film's) most memorable turns of phrase.

Bell's moral outrage is uncompromised and unattenuated by the third-person narrative voice within which Chigurh's enunciations are nested, and even if it cedes tactical space to Chigurh's determinism, it never knowingly cedes *moral* ground. Unfortunately, though, Bell's voice *unknowingly* cedes quite a bit of it. Not only is that voice unequal to the details of the action occurring in the eidetic narrative; it also expresses Bell's inequality to their consequences. Even as it actively frames the moral arguments of the novel and opposes the amoral, deterministic philosophy enunciated by Chigurh, Bell's voice frequently expresses defeat before that very amorality. It is a defeat to which his narratee is treated at the very outset of the novel:

But there is another view of the world out there and other eyes to see it and that's
where this is goin. It has done brought me to a place in my life I would not of thought
I'd of come to. Somewhere out there is a true and living prophet of destruction and I
dont want to confront him. I have seen his work. I walked in front of those eyes once.
I wont do it again. . . . I think a man would have to put his soul at hazard [to confront
such evil]. And I wont do that. I think now that maybe I never would. (4)

Even as this novel is in fact a cinematic script *overwritten* by a literary
narration,[4] McCarthy employs rhetorical strategies that subvert the killer's eidetic or cinematic discursive authority and finally render it subject
to judgment by Bell's moral position even as Bell's confessions subvert
his own moral stature. The reader of *No Country for Old Men* is placed in
the not entirely comfortable position of knowing from the git-go that the
folksy gentleman who bares his soul so generously is also a phlegmatic de-
featist. By contrast, the cinema audience watches Bell's defeat take shape
slowly over the course of the narrative, and come to a head during his
heartbreaking visit to his paraplegic Uncle Ellis late in the film. The novel
thereby equivocates Bell's discourse from the outset in a way that the film
script, which dispenses with all but a small portion of Bell's monologue,
does not. Thus literature, which in the economic context of late capitalist
culture has been marginalized by comparison with cinema, remains not
merely a resource for the screen but also a vehicle for the deglamorization
of the cinematic ethos of romanticized brutality and greed.

In McCarthy's epic Border Trilogy (*All the Pretty Horses* [1992]; *The
Crossing* [1994a]; and *Cities of the Plain* [1998]) theatrical metaphors also
abound. The treatment of these metaphors in this series of novels directly
anticipates the problem of the dichotomy of the two opposed voices of
No Country for Old Men in both its fictional and cinematic modes. References to role-playing, choreography, puppetry, scripting, and stage
management usually signal questions about fate or destiny throughout
McCarthy's canon. As in the earlier *Blood Meridian*, staged spectacles figure importantly all three novels, including plays, operas, puppet shows,
dogpit fights, carnivals, concerts, and horse auctions. I have suggested
that the trilogy represents theatrical spectatorship as a master trope for all
forms of narrative (Wallach 2001, 21–36). I am, of course, cognizant that
significant differences obtain between the theater stage and the sound
stage. However, because the theatrical mode is contained within the cinematic I am going to make my own job easier by collapsing theatrical and
cinematic for the moment, distinguishing them when necessary.

The two most striking examples of pure or passive spectatorship in the
trilogy are John Grady Cole's viewing of a play in which his mother is
a character in *All the Pretty Horses*, and the traveling opera performance
of *I Pagliacci* seen by Billy Parham in *The Crossing*. Billy and John Grady
share an inability to understand or, perhaps more accurately, decode the

dramas that they witness. We can understand the interpretive problems experienced by the trilogy's protagonists as allegories of reading. A reader experiences the theatrical text differently from the audience, who sees motion or position where the reader has seen description and stage directions. Ingarden attempts to resolve this disparity by distinguishing between dialogue, which he calls *Haupttext* (primary text), and stage direction (for which we will substitute "shooting script" here), which he calls *Nebentext* (ancillary text). His division suggests "parallel signifying systems" of which "only the *Haupttext* is available to the spectators of a performance as a producer of meaning" while the directions in the script remain invisible to them (Ingarden 1973, 80).

As John Grady watches his mother perform in a play, he seems, paradoxically, to be searching out the marginal directions and notes of her play rather than listening to the dialogue: "Then the curtain rose and his mother came through a door onstage and began talking to a woman in a chair" (*Pretty Horses*, 21). The novel depicts John Grady as theatrical spectator as a device to foreground the difficulties such reconstructions always entail by, in effect, inverting the natural positions of reader and audience. "The drama is usually considered as a 'given,' offered to the spectator as a ready-structured whole through the mediation of the performance. The reality of the process is altogether different," observes Elam. "The effective construction of the dramatic world and its events is the result of the spectator's ability to impose order upon a dramatic content whose expression is in fact discontinuous and incomplete" (Elam 1993, 99). As his failure to comprehend his mother's play suggests, John Grady's ability to perform acts of narrative reconstitution is severely inhibited. Although he entertains "the notion that there would be something in the story itself to tell him about the way the world was or was becoming, there was not. There was nothing in it at all" (*Pretty Horses*, 21).

According to Aston and Savona, the "classical" mode of theatrical presentation, to which category the Oedipus cycle belongs, for example, "operates at the level of *Haupttext*: it consists almost entirely of dialogue." They distinguish this system from the "bourgeois" model, which "operates at both the level of the *Haupttext* and explicit *Nebentext* [but] much information continues to be offered in the intra-dialogic mode, both to counterpoint and supplement the extra-dialogic directions" (Aston and Savona 1991, 94). For Lucienne Goldmann, this is also the mode of dramatic representation that parallels the rise of the novel and exhibits a pronounced homology with other modes of representation and exchange in bourgeois culture (qtd. in Mayne 1993, 49–52). However, in a third possibility, the "radical" model, "the directions work to inscribe a form of theatricality that calls attention to its status *as* theatricality" (Aston and

Savona 1991, 94), thus subverting the complacent seamlessness with social institutions of the bourgeois model.

McCarthy plays all three of these formats against each other deftly,
constructing passages of dialogue that conform to the classical mode,
but which only expose Billy's and John Grady's dependence on the un-
perceived directions that conform to the bourgeois mode, and flagging
his use of both through explicit discussions of stagecraft like that offered
by the diva of *I Pagliacci* in *The Crossing* (*Crossing*, 228–31). The audience,
notes the diva, is blind to the forces that control the action upon the stage.
Like the baffled John Grady perched in the mezzanine above his mother's
stage, the spectator "cannot see that for the wearer of the mask nothing
is changed. The actor has no power to act but only as the world tells him.
Mask or no mask is all as one to him" (*Crossing*, 230). If John Grady is
stymied, Billy reduces the drama to the lowest common denominator of
his own experience: "The company was perhaps describing some adventures of their own in their travels and they sang into each other's faces
and wept and in the end the man in buffoon's motley slew another man
perhaps his rival with a dagger and young boys ran forward with the
curtain hems to draw them shut" (219). The problem is, at no time does
the narrator attribute these perceptions to Billy. Strictly speaking, based
on the text they remain the discourse of the narrator alone. It is as if the
narrator's somewhat befuddled conclusions have been projected upon
the scene while Billy, for his part, naïvely envisions the clown's makeup
as "warpaint."

Dianne Luce has shown that *I Pagliacci*, an opera about an opera company, "is a play within a play in which the fiction impacts reality and
reality is transformed to, represented in, or masked by fiction" (Luce 1999,
200). The members of the audience depicted *within* the dramatic context
of the opera are unaware that they are watching a real murder, thinking
it is only part of the play. They make the same error the narrator of *The
Crossing* appears to make, suggesting the play represents the troupe's
actual experiences, "perhaps describing some adventure of their own in
their travels" (219). This conundrum suggests the theatrical problem of
discrepant awareness. As Pfister notes,

> The discrepant awareness that separates dramatic figures and the audience
> is the result of two contradictory factors. First, the audience is always pres-
> ent as a group of spectators throughout the action, whereas the individual
> figures do not generally participate directly in more than just a part of it. . . .
> At the same time, the advance information held by the figures introduces an
> element of insecurity for the audience, because it can never know until the
> end whether a figure has articulated his or her advance information in full,
> or whether important pieces of information have been suppressed. These

two factors work against each other and bring about opposing structures of
discrepant awareness. (Pfister 1988, 50–51)[5]

Although this problem of discrepant awareness is clearly present in
McCarthy's text, his resort to the "radical mode" of representation further
complicates the problem. Even the narrator uses such equivocating tags
as "perhaps" to destabilize its own assertions or analyses; we may begin
to assess the reach of this contingency when we realize that it is not in
fact any specific narrative tag proffered by the narrator that directs us
to attribute its musings to John Grady or Billy as subject. As Goldmann
inferred, it is merely our bourgeois habit of reading, with its homologic
assumptions of narrative and subjective parity, which encourages us to
make the connection. In literal terms, the disparity between the narrator's
description of the clown as a clown and Billy's perception of the figure
as dressed in "warpaint" deeply problematizes the relationship between
the narration and Billy's putative consciousness. This dichotomy also suggests a number of theories of cinematic representation having to do with
the construction of the cinematic subject and the viewer's identification
or resistance to identification with that subject. As Mayne notes, theories
of spectatorship were an attempt to resolve this implicit resistance, much
as reader-response theory was an effort to resolve the narrator/reader
duality. Jean-Luis Baudry postulated the idea of the cinematic "apparatus" that "produces an ideological position through its very mechanics of
representation—i.e., the camera, editing, the immobile spectator situated
before the screen." As in our habits of reading and inferring, "ideology
is not imposed upon the cinema, it is always already implicated in it"
(Mayne 1993, 45).

If the narrative voice and the consciousness of the protagonist cannot finally be collapsed into one another as an even temporarily unified
subject (if, in fact, one is ranged against the other and both are riddled
with a deficit rather than with a surplus of "seeing and knowing"), such
an epiphany of disconnection recalls the Anti-Manifesto of Fernando Arrabal, founder of the Dada-influenced *théâtre panique*. Arrabal believes
that drama should combine "the mechanics of memory and the rules of
chance. The more the work of the artist is governed by chance, confusion,
the unexpected, the richer, the more stimulating, the more fascinating
it will be." He also insists "that actors should never inhabit their roles
comfortably" (qtd. in Carlson 1984, 458), which is surely borne out not
only by the narrator/subject duality, but also in the disjunction between
the social role and private role that Sheriff Bell in *No Country for Old Men*
has chosen for himself. Furthermore, *théâtre panique*'s Mexican cofounder,
filmmaker Alejandro Jodorowski, "condemns as misguided and hopeless
the tradition of trying to make 'permanent' an ephemeral art. Such an

attempt has led to an emphasis on text rather than on life, on mechanical repetition (never in fact achieved) rather than on improvisation, on fixed settings and architectural spaces rather than surroundings that can change with the life of the performance" (Carlson 1984, 459). The diva in *The Crossing* inflects precisely Jodorowski's suspicion of permanence when she expresses her weariness of being "killed night after night. It drains one's strength. One's powers of speculation" (*Crossing*, 229). Here, "speculation" may mean either assessment of probability, or the act of viewing, if not both, since the source of the opera's dramatic tension is that the viewer may not necessarily understand at what level of reality the action is progressing.

This subjective failure of "speculation" in the trilogy repeats itself over and over in the fictional *No Country for Old Men*. In the novel, the two distinct strains of narrative effectively simulate Ingarden's dichotomy of perception and predicate the alternative structure of the cinematic narrative as well. What is so interesting about all of these characters' narrative disquisitions is the question of for whom they are intended. Certainly, neither Sheriff Bell, Moss, nor Chigurh are equipped to think in such analytical terms. Bell often appears to be an utterly passive subject, like Baudry's immobile spectator. Nevertheless, it is crucial to note that in the novel the two narrators' constructions, Bell's included, are so positioned that the characters, who are the de facto speculating co-subjects of narration, must share their broken or compartmentalized gazes. To whom is Bell addressing himself? His unspecified narratee shares the limitations of what Bell sees or knows about the pursuit of Moss and, eventually, of Carla Jean by Chigurh, reconstructing the various episodes of flight and carnage in retrospect from the bits of evidence left behind. Within Bell's monologues, unlike the eidetic passages, this narratee is, like Bell, always arriving too late to be a true spectator of the action. In fact, upon closer inspection, it becomes clear that *Bell is not really narrating the events of the story at all*. He's telling his own story, and for the most part its relation to the flight of Moss/pursuit by Chigurh, and all the machinations of the opposing drug gangs are merely analogical or anecdotal at best.

In filmic terms, Christian Metz calls this condition "primary cinematic identification," wherein the spectator identifies with himself as the gaze of the camera [read: narrator] "which has looked before him at what he is now looking at and whose stationing determines the vanishing point. During the projection [read: narration] this camera is absent, but it has a representative consisting of another apparatus, called precisely 'a projector.' An apparatus the spectator has behind him, at the back of his head, that is, precisely where phantasy locates the 'focus' of all vision" (Metz 1974, 41–42). The film, on the other hand, by dispensing with all but the short initial voiceover drawn from Bell's first monologue effectively "liberates" Bell's narratee to accompany all of the characters and share their gazes of events *as they happen*.

What I've tried to do above is lay some structural groundwork for a multidimensional consideration of the uneasy and complex ways in which fictional texts and cinematic texts communicate with each other, and to review at the same time some of the extant critical tools for exploring those communications. What follows are extended and more specific interrogations of these often elusive and difficult relationships between kindred artistic media. Cormac McCarthy has made this just a little easier for us because his frequent recourse to both the imagery and borrowed structural affinities of cinematic and theatrical representation act as signposts. They direct our attention to where he addresses the problems such relationships suggest.

NOTES

1. I vividly recall reading an interview with *Corelli* director John Madden wherein the would-be assassin of Louis de Bernière's sublime novel of ideas declared that the book was really just a "love story"—and I just *knew* that he was going to butcher it. He did. Frank Herbert's epic series of science fiction novels, *Dune*, of course, has been through several execrable film iterations by now—David Lynch's 1984 version which, inexplicably, did not cost Kyle MacLachlan the rest of his career, and the nondescript 2000 television miniseries—and will doubtless have to endure several more.

2. As of this writing (January 2009), Cormac McCarthy's collected personal papers, manuscripts, and letters are being sorted and cataloged by the librarians at the Texas Writer's Collection at Texas State University in San Marcos. It may well be that within a few months the collection will be made available to critics and scholars, and we will have an opportunity to study McCarthy's original screenplay for *No Country for Old Men* and be able to compare it with both the novel and the Coen brothers' screenplay.

3. This reversal recalls the inversion of spectatorship that concludes the groundbreaking psychological thriller *Coming Apart* (1969), when the psychiatrist throws his camera in a fit of rage and frustration and shatters the mirror, whose reflection we suddenly realize is what we have been watching all along. Bell's situation in the novel is not unlike that of Rip Torn's disintegrating psychiatrist, even if their personalities are radically different.

4. McCarthy originally wrote this story as a screenplay, then went back years later and rewrote it as a novel. In its frequent, lengthy passages of dialogue, the resonances of the original text can be easily discerned.

5. And as my perspicacious readers have no doubt already realized, this concept itself owes a considerable debt to Bakhtin's notion of the narrator's "excess of seeing and knowing."

REFERENCES

Aston, Elaine, and George Savona. 1991. *Theatre as Sign-System: A Semiotics of Text and Performance*. London: Routledge.

Captain Corelli's Mandolin. 2001. Dir. John Madden. Universal Pictures.

Carlson, Marvin. 1984. *Theories of the Theater*. Ithaca, NY: Cornell University Press.

The Day of the Jackal. 1973. Dir. Fred Zinnemann. Warwick Film Productions.

Dune. 1984. Dir. David Lynch. De Laurentiis Entertainment Group.

Elam, Kier. 1993. *The Semiotics of Theater and Drama*. London: Routledge.

Ingarden, Roman. 1973. *The Literary Work of Art*. Trans. G. G. Grabowicz. Evanston: Northwestern University Press.

Josyph, Peter. 2000. "Filming *All the Pretty Horses*." On-camera interview with Billy Bob Thornton. Unpublished videotape from editor's private collection.

Luce, Dianne C. 1999. "The Road and the Matrix: The World as Tale in *The Crossing*." In *Perspectives on Cormac McCarthy*, ed. Edwin T. Arnold and Dianne C. Luce (revised edition), 195–220. Jackson: University Press of Mississippi.

Mayne, Judith. 1993. *Cinema and Spectatorship*. New York: Routledge.

McCarthy, Cormac. 1985. *Blood Meridian, or, The Evening Redness in the West*. New York: Alfred A. Knopf.

———. 1992. *All the Pretty Horses*. New York: Alfred A. Knopf.

———. 1994a. *The Crossing*. New York: Alfred A. Knopf.

———. 1994b. *The Stonemason: A Play in Five Acts*. Hopewell, NJ: Ecco Press.

———. 1998. *Cities of the Plain*. New York: Alfred A. Knopf.

———. 2005. *No Country for Old Men*. New York: Alfred A. Knopf.

———. 2006. *The Sunset Limited: A Novel in Dramatic Form*. New York: Vintage.

Metz, Christian. 1974. *Language and Cinema*. New York: Mouton de Gruyter.

Pfister, Manfred. 1988. *The Theory and Analysis of Drama*. Trans. John Halliday. Cambridge: Cambridge University Press.

Pulp Fiction. 1994. Dir. Quentin Tarantino. A Band Apart.

Traffic. 2000. Dir. Steven Soderbergh. Bedford Falls Productions.

Wallach, Rick. 2001. "Theater, Ritual and Dream in the Border Trilogy." *Southwestern American Literature* 27, no. 1 (Fall): 21–36.

1

✝

"You are the battleground": Materiality, Moral Responsibility, and Determinism in *No Country for Old Men*

Linda Woodson

Too often in south Texas, one reads headlines in regional papers like the *San Antonio Express-News* that demonstrate where the circumstances of *No Country for Old Men* (2005) have led on both sides of the border. The morning of October 2, 2005, brought this Associated Press news story: "Yet another cop gunned down in Nuevo Laredo" (26A). The details mirror the kinds of events that fill McCarthy's novel: a man suffering gunshot wounds drives himself to the hospital, a police officer arrives to question him, four gunmen come into the hospital, shoot and kill the officer, and carry the wounded man away. The story reports that "more than 135 people have been killed by violence in the city since January, . . . including 14 police officers." The numbers continue to rise. News stories of local *policia* engaged in drug trafficking, law-enforcement officers gunned down in the middle of a busy street, a *federale* killed in a shootout initiated by Nuevo Laredo officers also exist. On October 3, 2005, a headline in the *Express-News* reads, "Chief projects hope amid danger," a story about a newly appointed Nuevo Laredo police chief that includes the startling fact: "More than 40 city cops were arrested, and at the federal government's orders, the remaining 700 officers underwent a battery of psychological, technical, polygraph, and drug tests" (3B), with the result of barely three hundred remaining on the force. At least on the Mexican side of the border, the prediction of Sheriff Bell is clearly true: "*A crooked peace officer is just a damned abomination*" (*No Country*, 216) and "*He's ten*

times worse than the criminal. And this aint goin away" (216–17). Gloria
Anzaldúa, in *Borderlands/La Frontera* (1987), writes of this landscape both
metaphorically and literally in her poem "To live in the Borderlands
means you":

> Living in the Borderlands means you fight hard
> to resist the gold elixir beckoning from the bottle,
> the pull of the gun barrel,
> the rope crushing the hollow of your throat,
> In the Borderlands
> you are the battleground
> where enemies are kin to each other. (194)

Those who witness this battleground fueled by druglords' power struggles know to place the blame, as does Cormac McCarthy in *No Country
for Old Men*, clearly with those who demand the drugs; *"We're bein bought
with our own money"* (303), declares Sheriff Bell, but he points to a larger
malaise: *"There's always been narcotics. But people don't just up and decide to
dope theirselves for no reason. By the millions"* (303).

In this ominous location, with a materiality not seen in the earlier Border
Trilogy, a materiality exhibited in plot, character, setting, and language,
McCarthy continues to explore the challenge to moral responsibility from
"scientific discoveries about the form and implications of the laws of
nature" (Fischer and Ravizza 1998, 26), that he had begun in the earlier
fiction. The philosophical question being asked (though not answered),
becomes, "Is there a way to view ourselves as morally responsible agents
even if determinism were true?" Or as the Dueña Alfonsa asks in *All the
Pretty Horses* (1991): "If fate is the law then is fate also subject to that law?
At some point we cannot escape naming responsibility. It's in our nature"
(241).

In *Responsibility and Control*, John Martin Fischer and Mark Ravizza
(1998), define *causal determinism* as follows: "the thesis that, for any given
time, a complete statement of the facts about that time, together with a
complete statement of the laws of nature, entails every truth as to what
happens after that time" (14). I shall use that definition to inform this
chapter because the definition of *determinism* varies widely, and whether
or not it exists continues to be a subject of debate among physicists and
philosophers in the context of prominent physical theories, including classical mechanics, special relativistic physics, general relativity, and quantum mechanics. Even in theories of chaotic dynamical systems, it appears
to be difficult to decide if randomness arises from genuine stochasticity or
is governed by underlying deterministic laws (Hoefer 2003, 9). I also will,
from this point on, omit the word *causal* since philosophers debate what
causation is as well. The question of determinism is often addressed in

the Border fiction. In *All the Pretty Horses* it appears as, "In this headlong deficit the blood of multitudes might ultimately be exacted for the vision of a single flower" (282). In *The Crossing* (1994) the *ganadero* speaks of this concept to Billy, "You do not know what things you set in motion. . . . No man can know. No prophet foresee. The consequences of an act are often quite different from what one would guess" (202). In *No Country for Old Men* it is expressed more repeatedly: "Ever step you take is forever. You cant make it go away" (227); "And the shape of your path was visible from the beginning" (259); and "When you're called on like that you have to make up your mind that you'll live with the consequences. But you don't know what the consequences will be" (278)—just to offer a few examples. Fischer and Ravizza assert that while many contemporary physicists doubt that this concept is completely true, they do support the idea that although macroscopic events are not fully determined, they are very close to that (1998, 15). That may be overstating the situation; in fact in the *Stanford Encyclopedia of Philosophy*, Carl Hoefer asserts just the opposite: "Many physicists in the past 60 years or so have been convinced of determinism's falsity" (2003, 7), basing their ideas on the concept that the Final Theory will be a variation of quantum mechanics, and that quantum mechanics rules out determinism. Hoefer argues that these two concepts are both highly debatable, and that until sometime in the future when the features of the Final Theory are revealed, the argument for or against determinism will continue (7). The threat to moral responsibility remains the same in either case.

In the Border Trilogy, McCarthy's interrogation of the question begins with John Grady Cole's responsibility to Blevins and to the events at La Purisima, continues with Billy Parham's responsibility for the deaths of his parents and of Boyd, and concludes with Billy's responsibility for John Grady. In all of these instances, the question of moral responsibility concerns *omission*, something one failed to do that he later believes would have changed the course of events and their consequences. In an effort to achieve absolution, the one who believes he failed in his moral responsibility often seeks out an older, perhaps wiser person, to whom to confess in an act that mirrors the sacrament of penance of the Catholic Church.

In *All the Pretty Horses*, in spite of the Ozona judge's assurance earlier that he had faith in John Grady Cole's account of his possession of the horse (289), John Grady goes to the judge's home in the evening to confess that he doesn't feel "in the right about everything" (290). He begins by acknowledging his role in failing to live up to Don Hector's expectations of him: "And I was the one that brought it about. Nobody but me" (289). He then confesses killing the boy in the penitentiary. And finally, he confesses his lack of action in the death of Blevins: "The reason I wanted to kill him [the Mexican captain] was because I stood there and let him walk that boy out in the trees and shoot him and I never said nothin" (293). In each instance, like a priest, the judge functions as intermediary to absolution, although he reminds John Grady that it is really something between John Grady and "the good Lord" (293): "Son, he said, you strike me as somebody that maybe tends to be a little hard on theirselves" (291). In sharing his own story of how he became a judge, he speaks of determinism: "I think I just didn't have any choice. Just didn't have any choice" (292), but explains his own troubled conscience concerning the boy he sent to the electric chair (292). Finally he offers Cole a blessing and a charge for the future: "There's nothin wrong with you son. I think you'll get it sorted out" (293).

In *The Crossing*, Billy's sense of responsibility for his parents' death through his failure to warn them of the Indian's presence is never explicit. In the case of Boyd's death, however, he clearly feels he has neglected his moral responsibility. Quijada speaks of determinism: "The day is made up of what has come before" (387). When Quijada tells him, "Maybe you are the one who should have cared for him better" (386), Billy indicates that Boyd wasn't easy to care for; nevertheless, he later acknowledges his role in bringing Boyd to Mexico: "I don't think he even cared about the horses, but I was too dumb to see it" (387). In penance Billy vows to take Boyd back to "his own country" (387), but Quijada offers him absolution without that penalty by suggesting that Boyd is "where he is supposed to be" (387). Nevertheless, Billy makes the difficult journey, with Boyd's bones becoming something between reliquary and albatross.

After John Grady Cole's death, Billy confesses in the epilogue of *Cities of the Plain* (1998) his sense of responsibility using the same words that Quijada had said to him about his responsibility to Boyd, "I should of looked after him better" (263). In an attempt to alleviate Billy's guilt, or perhaps in an expression of his own, Mac responds, "We all should of" (263). And, again to help Billy with his guilt, Mac urges him, "Let it go, son" (264). The traveler that Billy meets many years later offers a statement of determinism: "The template for the world and all in it was drawn long ago. Yet the story of the world, which is all the world we know, does not exist outside of the instruments of its execution. Nor can those instruments exist outside of their own history" (287). And as to decision, the traveler speaks of its impossibility: "Yet there are no crossroads. Our decisions do not have some alternative. We may contemplate a choice but we pursue one path only. The log of the world is composed of its entries, but it cannot be divided back into them" (286).

In *No Country for Old Men*, the role of moral responsibility if determinism is true is interrogated in perhaps the most material landscape of McCarthy's writing. The story functions as homily without conclusion in which even the language itself shifts to a referential language that calls attention to that place rather than to itself. In much of the earlier Border fiction, the language often constructs a materiality of its own. These "lyrical effusions," as Steve Kellman (2005, 20) refers to them, take the reader to a different plane of reference, a narrativity that often turns in on itself for its referent. In *The Crossing*, we find an example of this in the description of the country seen by Billy as he rides the high country after the wolf's death:

> At the eastern escarpment he dismounted and led the horse along a shelf of gray rock. The scrub juniper that grew along the rim leaned in a wind that had long since passed. Along the face of the stone bluffs were old pictographs of men and animals and suns and moons as well as other representations that seemed to have no referent in the world although they once may have. He sat in the sun and looked out over the country to the east, the broad barranca of the Bavispe and the ensuing Carretas Plain that was once a seafloor and the small pieced fields and the new corn greening in the old lands of the Chichimeca where the priests had passed and soldiers passed and the missions fallen into mud and the ranges of mountains beyond the plain range on range in pales of blue where the terrain lay clawed open north and south, canyon and range, sierra and barranca, all of it waiting like a dream for the world   to come to be, world to pass. He saw a single vulture hanging motionless in some high vector that the wind had chosen for it.
> He saw the smoke of a locomotive passing slowly downcountry over the plain forty miles away. (135)

Here the text itself assumes the role of object. Compare that language to the obdurant language of the following passage after Bell's removal of the dead hawk from the road: "He stood there looking out across the desert. So quiet. Low hum of wind in the wires. High bloodweeds along the road. Wiregrass and sacahuista. Beyond in the stone arroyos the tracks of dragons. The raw rock mountains shadowed in the late sun and to the east the shimmering abscissa of the desert plains under a sky where raincurtains hung dark as soot all along the quadrant" (*No Country*, 45).

With a respect for the terrible potentiality of violence in the real borderlands where *No Country for Old Men* is set, McCarthy forgoes the lyrical language to create a place where reference points to that palpable violence. Here he creates what Foucault calls a "site of a fleeting articulation" (1977, 143), where the competing discourses of moral responsibility in the language of Sheriff Bell and of determinism in the language of Chigurh contradict, and yet within that contradiction is the very real place in which we all must reside. "All that exist are 'islands of determinism,'" Lyotard (1984, 59) argues in his theory of the local. As Daniel Punday describes this location in "Theories of Materiality and Location," "Contradictions between and within discourses can be analyzed at some locale, but such locations themselves arise out of the contradictions and clashes within the discourses" (1998, 1).

Some early reviewers have compared Anton Chigurh to the judge of *Blood Meridian*, as the fashioner of men's fate and the instrument of death. Chigurh, however, bears a much closer affinity to Flannery O'Connor's Misfit. Although both the judge and Chigurh are beyond good and evil, the judge functions as a hegemonic power in a pre-postmodern world. As he decides what to record, what to erase, in historical record, he mirrors the creation of patterns of logic in a trace that makes possible acts of aggression among groups, such as that exhibited by Manifest Destiny; in Foucault's words, he masters history (1977, 160). He is in the process of creating a "formal agenda of an absolute destiny" (*Blood Meridian*, 85):

> He sketched for the sergeant a problematic career of the man before them, his hands drafting with a marvelous dexterity the shapes of what varied paths conspired here in the ultimate authority of the extant—as he told them—like strings drawn together through the eye of a ring. He adduced for their consideration references to the children of Ham, the lost tribes of Israelites, certain passages from the Greek poets, anthropological speculations as to the propagation of the races in their dispersion and isolation through the agency of geological cataclysm and an assessment of racial traits with respect to climatic and geographical influences. (84–85)

And later, "Words are things. The words he is in possession of he cannot be deprived of. Their authority transcends his ignorance of their meaning" (85), that is, their materiality.

Chigurh, on the other hand, sees himself not as having the power to pull together the strings of an absolute destiny, but rather as an "instrument" (*No Country*, 57) of that which has already been determined. McCarthy's protagonists are often orphans: the kid, John Grady Cole, and Billy. In an ironic twist Chigurh is the orphan in *No Country for Old Men*. He exists outside of society and is of indeterminate origin and purpose. It is never fully clear why he involves himself in the hunt for Llewelyn Moss. Even his name is indeterminate in origin: if he is of Eastern European origin, one would have expected the use of a patronymic to make that clear, yet there is the fact of his Christian first name, Anton. As indeterminate as his origin is, nevertheless, he lives in a precise existence, though one seemingly outside of the text itself, as he moves in and out to execute with terrible purpose the end of its characters. Because he is so disciplined and because he functions, as Wells points out (*No Country*, 153), in his own version of a principled way—keeping his word and leaving no witnesses—he is readily identifiable with The Misfit, who, if he could have seen Christ crucified himself, would just as readily act under other principles. For example, Chigurh tells the proprietor at the filling station at Sheffield, "Anything can be an instrument" (*No Country*, 57) and then, "Small things. Things you wouldn't even notice. They pass from hand to hand. People don't pay attention. And then one day there's an accounting. And after that nothing is the same" (57). Later with Carla Jean, he speaks again of himself as instrument: "I had no say in the matter" (259).

The coin toss of both of these scenes is interesting and potentially misleading in its seeming reliance on chance. In Roman society it was used as a way of revealing already determined fate. There have been studies that show that identical behavior results in the coin toss if all conditions are precisely controlled and outside interferences are excluded (Hoefer 2003, 7). It is interesting that in neither case does the participant other than Chigurh know exactly what the toss is for or whether heads will be in their favor or his, or even if heads is the desired result. Further, in the incident at the filling station, readers only assume that it is a life-or-death toss based upon their knowledge of Chigurh as killer. Thus, the outcome is still fully hidden in the mind of Chigurh, and perhaps, like the Romans, he is waiting for revelation of determined fate. The man at the filling station says, "Well I need to know what it is we're callin here," and Chigurh responds, "How would that change anything?" (*No Country*, 56). The coin, like Chigurh, has become an instrument of determined consequence: "Its just a coin. For instance. Nothing special there. What could that be an instrument of? You see the problem. To separate the act from the thing. As if the parts of some moment in history might be interchangeable with the parts of some other moment. How could that be? Well, it's just a coin. Yes. That's true. Is it?" (57).

In the later incident Carla Jean questions the coin toss: "You make it like it was the coin. But you're the one" (*No Country*, 258) and "The coin didn't have no say. It was just you" (258). To which Chigurh replies, "Perhaps. But look at it my way. I got here the same way the coin did" (258). And later speaking of the inevitability of the results of the coin toss, he says, "I had no belief in your ability to influence a coin in your favor. How could you? A person's path through the world seldom changes and even more seldom will it change abruptly. And the shape of your path was visible from the beginning" (259).

Chigurh is a psychopath, but of a truly terrifying kind. Fischer and Ravizza define a *psychopath* as an individual of "coldness and detachment" (1998, 78), not moved at all by the suffering of his victims. In describing moral responsibility, they use two terms—*receptivity* and *reactivity*. To be receptive is to have "the capacity to recognize the reasons that exist" (69). To be reactive is to have "the capacity to *translate* reasons into choices (and then subsequent behavior)" (69). Fischer and Ravizza then distinguish two types of psychopaths: the first is mentally disordered and incapable of recognizing reasons for action that come from other individuals' rights (79); the second is not out of control, capable of being receptive to reasons, although not moral ones. Chigurh is the latter; he is not morally responsible, but rather he exists outside of moral responsibility altogether. For example, his reason for killing Carla Jean is that he has given his word to Moss that he would. Therein lay the principles that Wells has remarked upon: "You're asking that I make myself vulnerable and that I can never do. I have only one way to live. It doesnt allow for special cases" (*No Country*, 259).

Some early commentaries on *No Country for Old Men* have asserted that Sheriff Bell is the voice of an increasingly conservative McCarthy. For example, Madison Smartt Bell writes, "The new novel is organized around a conventional moral compass, mostly furnished by the good Sheriff Bell" (2005, 2). This perspective is easily embraced because Bell is given the foremost narrative voice in the interspersed first-person chapters. Rather I would suggest that Bell's voice is yet another part of the material body of the Border region, a balancing voice to the violence of the region, a piece of the "site of articulation." Neither he nor Chigurh is a fully believable character because each represents a position in the material discourse of the location. Certainly Bell represents the conservative mentality that is made visible in contemporary efforts of civilian Minutemen to guard the U.S.-Mexico border. He reflects those who, seeing their world change, try to make their old values fit that new world, and seeing the futility of a fit, often feel despair. But he also speaks for the possibility of moral responsibility in this setting, where he suggests that Satan may have come up with narcotics to *"bring the human race to its knees"* (*No Country*, 218). This conservative voice is not newly minted in McCarthy's fiction. It bears traces of the words of John Grady Cole's father: "People dont feel safe no more, he said. We're like the Comanches was two hundred years ago. We dont know what's goin to show up here come daylight" (*Pretty Horses*, 26). Bell's voice embodies the question each of us must ask if we accept the possibility of determinism, even if only in the sense of Lyotard's "islands of determinism": how do we act with moral responsibility in that world? Does moral responsibility even exist in that world? Bell's answer to those questions is clear, if ours is not: "*I think that when the lies are all told and forgot the truth will be there yet. It dont move about from place to place and it dont change from time to time*" (*No Country*, 123). In his seemingly naïve assertion that the loss of manners was a first cause of the violence around him, he is echoing what many contemporary psychologists are asserting, that the absence of manners in our world represents the placing of self-interest before the feelings of others, the impaired capacity to be reactive to moral reasons.

Sheriff Bell's admission of his "sin" of omission comes late in the book when he visits the home of Ellis, presumably in part, for just that purpose.

His behavior follows the same pattern we have seen earlier—admission of guilt to an older, perhaps wiser, and trusted individual, in an act that mirrors religious confession, and partial relief and absolution through the words of that individual. Bell has carried his burden of guilt for many years, since World War II. He reveals that he escaped in the middle of the night following a shelling of a house where he and his troops were holed up; Bell was thrown free and left, although he did not know if there were any survivors among his men (*No Country*, 274–75). His staying would have likely meant certain death. He was later given a commendation, which he tried to refuse because he did not believe he deserved it (275). Again, Bell's failure, like that of John Grady and Billy, is one of omission. The response from Ellis serves for partial absolution: "You didnt have no choice" (277), and later, "Well, in all honesty I cant see it bein all that bad. Maybe you ought to ease up on yourself some" (278). At the start of the next chapter, Bell tells the reader, "*He said I was bein hard on myself*" (281), an echo of the words of the judge to John Grady.

In *An Essay on Free Will*, Peter Van Inwagen states the incompatibility theory and gives the challenge to contemporary philosophy concerning free will and moral responsibility: "If we do not have free will, then there is no such thing as moral responsibility, therefore, since there is such a thing as moral responsibility, there is such a thing as free will. (Moreover, since free will is incompatible with determinism, determinism is false)" (1983, 21–22). Of course for most philosophers, the absence of moral responsibility would create an intolerable world, a world much like that inhabited by Chigurh, a world that reduces the meaning and value of our lives. As Susan Wolf describes that world in "The Importance of Free Will," "A world in which human relationships are restricted to those that can be formed and supported in the absence of the reactive attitudes is a world of human isolation so cold and dreary" (1993, 106). Those "reactive attitudes" are described as "admiration and indignation, pride and shame, respect and contempt, gratitude and resentment" (106).

Whereas contemporary philosophers recognize that we cannot be fully responsible for our actions (Strawson 1986, 312), many are addressing ways to understand how to overcome incompatibility. Fischer and Ravizza, in "Responsibility for Consequences," argue that although Borges's description of the future as a "garden of forking paths" is the more naturally appealing belief, nevertheless, given only one path into the future, we can still be held morally accountable (Fischer and Ravizza 1993, 347). It is an argument similar to theirs that McCarthy's Border fiction appears to support. Control is traditionally thought of as being necessary for moral responsibility; that is, a person has alternative possibilities and follows one path when another is fully in his power to follow (Fischer and Ravizza 1998, 20). To give up a belief in this sort of control, one would have to abandon behavior that represents our understanding of human life (25). Fischer and Ravizza argue that we don't really require that sort of control to retain moral responsibility. They distinguish between two kinds of control: regulative control and guidance control (1998, 31). Regulative control requires the ability to perform freely both an action and an alternative action. The kind of control that they argue for, guidance control, need not involve alternatives (33). In this sort of control an agent freely performs an action, whether or not the power to do something else exists. Moral responsibility is grounded in this kind of control. For clarity, let me share one of example from Fischer and Ravizza (1998, 32–38): Sally is driving a "driver instruction" automobile with dual controls. She comes to a corner and turns the car to the right. However, although Sally isn't aware of it, her driving instructor would have turned the car to the right, even if Sally had not performed that action. In this case Sally chooses freely and acts in accord with her choice just as if there was no intervener at all. The agent takes "the reasons to be sufficient," chooses "in accordance with the sufficient reasons," and acts "in accordance with the choice" (Fischer and Ravizza 1998, 41), a theory of reasons-responsiveness. Thus, agents "can be morally responsible, even though they are not free to do otherwise" (59).

In spite of contemporary physics' assertion that past, present, and future are probably illusory categories (Hoefer 2003, 16), most of us naturally tend to think of the past as "fixed" and out of our control and, therefore, that the actions of the past have determined the direction of the future, at least in the smaller "islands of determinism." Along the Texas-Mexico border, where *No Country for Old Men* takes place, the present violence of the drug wars is believed to be a product of past actions or omissions, of desires and demands, and as Sheriff Bell asserts, "*I know as certain as death that there aint nothing short of the second comin of Christ that can slow this train*" (*No Country*, 159). McCarthy shows us the alternatives for action, however, in the characters of Chigurh and Bell. As if to underscore their role as alternatives, he gives each a scene of interaction with the natural world: Bell gently moves the dead redtail hawk out of traffic so that its body won't be desecrated further (43), and Chigurh, seeing a large white bird, shoots at it to test his silencer (97). Believing fully, as Moss tells the hitchhiker, that "ever step you take is forever. You cant make it go away" (227), Chigurh represents the attitude in its extreme that releases responsibility and gives up reactive attitudes, that behavior that gives up all it means to us to be human. Bell, on the other hand, may not have had a real choice in his action to leave his troops, but because he perceives that he did, because he questions whether saving his own life is a right and sufficient reason for his failure to stay, he feels the guilt that, we understand, maintains his humanness. We may believe, like Ellis, that he is being too hard on himself; nevertheless, the moral responsibility is his.

While it is true that past actions—greed and insatiable desires for drugs—have brought about the unspeakable violence of the border region, McCarthy offers us two images—the water trough and Bell's dream—both toward the end of *No Country for Old Men*, that serve to remind us of reactive attitudes that define our humanness, to remind us that we can't accede to abjection. The image of the stone water trough (*No Country*, 307) is an example of hope that builds something durable in the face of unknown consequences, something that may withstand time regardless of the events of the future. That hope, combined with the power of love of Bell's dream of his father waiting for him, illustrates attitudes that allow us to retain the meaning and value of our lives. Sheriff Bell speaks for that hope: "But I would like to be able to make that kind of promise. I think that's what I would like most of all" (308).

As a homily on moral responsibility in a contemporary world, the Border fiction offers characters who exhibit varying degrees of their sense of responsibility. John Grady Cole, because of the circumstances and his character, is killed in the process of revenging Magdalena's death. Moss is motivated to return to the site of violence in order, perhaps, to take the wounded man a drink of water. These two demonstrate the possible ends of those who confront the instruments of determinism, should such exist. Bell demonstrates the choice of self-preservation and its subsequent guilt. And Chigurh represents the willingness to be the instrument itself. The reader is asked to be aware of the consequences of all of these grave decisions. If there is authorial voice regarding moral responsibility and determinism at all in the Border fiction, I believe that it is not the conservative voice of Sheriff Bell, but the voice of the *ganadero* as he speaks to Billy, "You must be sure that the intention in your heart is large enough to contain all wrong turnings, all disappointments. Do you see? Not everything has such a value" (*Crossing*, 202). And if there is an authorial voice on the possibility of retaining our humanity, it is the voice of the gypsy at the end of *The Crossing* who also speaks to Billy, the voice that urges us to live as if "the world was made new each day and it was only men's clinging to its vanished husks that could make of that world one husk more" (411).

REFERENCES

Anzaldúa, Gloria. 1987. *Borderlands/La Frontera: The New Mestiza*. San Francisco: Aunt Lute Books.

Bell, Madison Smartt. 2005. "Might of the Hunter." *Artforum*, June 1. www.high beam.com/doc/IP3-856297241.html.

Fischer, John Martin, and Mark Ravizza, S.J. 1993. "Responsibility for Conse-quences." In *Perspectives on Moral Responsibility*, ed. John Martin Fischer and Mark Ravizza, S.J., 322–47. Ithaca, NY: Cornell University Press.

———. 1998. *Responsibility and Control: A Theory of Moral Responsibility*. Cambridge: Cambridge University Press.

Foucault, Michel. 1977. *Language, Counter-Memory, Practice: Selected Essays and In-terviews*. Ed. Donald F. Bouchard. Trans. Donald F. Bouchard and Sherry Simon. Ithaca, NY: Cornell University Press.

Hoefer, Carl. 2003. "Causal Determinism." *The Stanford Encyclopedia of Philosophy*, January 23. Plato.stanford.edu/entries/determinism-causal.

Kellman, Steve. 2005. "All the Pretty Corpses." *Texas Observer* 97, no. 15 (July 22): 20–21.

Lyotard, Jean Francois. 1984. *The Postmodern Condition: A Report on Knowledge*. Trans. Geoff Bennington and Brian Massumi. Minneapolis: University of Min-nesota Press.

McCarthy, Cormac. 1985. *Blood Meridian, or, The Evening Redness in the West*. New York: Vintage.

———. 1991. *All the Pretty Horses*. New York: Vintage.

———. 1994. *The Crossing*. New York: Vintage.

———. 1998. *Cities of the Plain*. New York: Alfred A. Knopf.

———. 2005. *No Country for Old Men*. New York: Alfred A. Knopf.

O'Connor, Flannery. 1971. "A Good Man Is Hard to Find." In *The Complete Stories of Flannery O'Connor*, 117–33. New York: Farrar, Straus and Giroux.

Punday, Daniel. 1998. "Theories of Materiality and Location: Moving through Kathy Acker's *Empire of the Senseless*." *Genders Online Journal* 27: 1–23. www .genders.org/g27/g27_theories.html.

San Antonio Express-News. 2005a. October 2, 26A.

———. 2005b. October 3, 3B.

Strawson, Galen. 1986. *Freedom and Belief*. Oxford: Clarendon Press.

Van Inwagen, Peter. 1983. *An Essay on Free Will*. Oxford: Clarendon Press.

Wolf, Susan. 1993. "The Importance of Free Will." In *Perspectives on Moral Re-sponsibility*, ed. John Martin Fisher and Mark Ravizza, S.J., 101–18. Ithaca, NY: Cornell University Press.

2

✛

Yeats's "Sailing to Byzantium" and McCarthy's *No Country for Old Men:* Art and Artifice in the Novel

Steven Frye

McCarthy's *No Country for Old Men* will certainly elicit much discussion, especially regarding the notable stylistic departure from his previous works. The new novel is lean, sparse, at times terse, arguably vivid and evocative in terms of language and scenes. Some readers may find merit and even innovation in this approach to narrative. Others may note a lack of the complexity, lyricism, and beauty we often associate with McCarthy's prose. However, there is likely to be little disagreement that McCarthy's latest novel is quite dissimilar to those that precede it. The reason for this departure may be simple. Perhaps McCarthy has run his artistic course, and *No Country for Old Men* (2005), sadly, represents the diminution of his artistic powers. Or it could be that the author's motives are simply mercenary and careerist, insofar as we know that the novel was previously scheduled to be adapted into film. The first explanation seems implausible, since the shift in style is so studied, precise, and seemingly intentional, displaying still a strong sense of artistic control. The second motive partially explains, but only partially, since McCarthy's storied willingness to remain reclusive and to leave promotion to others makes a complete sell-out seem unlikely. Historically, he has simply valued the integrity of his art too highly. I want to at least explore the possibility that his selection of the title is not incidental, that his use of the first line of William Butler Yeats's poem "Sailing to Byzantium" (1983) bears in significant ways upon the meaning of the book. This poem contrasts the prosaic and sensual world of the here and now with the transcendent and timeless world of beauty in art, and the first line, "That is no country for old men," refers to an artless world of impermanence and sensual pleasure. I want to posit, somewhat tentatively, that the title is at least one key to the stylistic departure that characterizes the novel and that perhaps, if the novel is read in the context of the title, we might discover a motive behind its distinctiveness. The main narrative displays it seems (in contrast to the interior monologues of Sheriff Bell) a deliberate lack of artifice, or at least the appearance of such, and an intentional eschewing of the overtly lyrical and poetic qualities of the prose we associate with McCarthy. We might assume, then, given the themes and contrasts posited in "Sailing to Byzantium," that McCarthy is toying with the idea that an overly aestheticized prose is a problematic way to characterize a commonplace, transient, death-strewn world. On the surface this might seem to be an argument against the aesthetic that defines his previous novels, but McCarthy is ever the experimentalist, testing new ideas and approaches to see how they work. His experiment with a less lyrical style may in fact be a deliberate attempt to bring this style into line with his world. Given the Yeats poem's ultimate celebration of the fruits of artistic creation, we might also tease out some of the same contrasts in *No Country for Old Men*, which appear in the intimation of a realm outside the harsh country, and in a tonality of hope that is less present in his other works, especially in those preceding the Border Trilogy.

To explore these possibilities, we must first begin with the Yeats poem, in an attempt to clarify McCarthy's motivation for borrowing the title from the first line. The poem begins,

> That is no country for old men. The young
> In one another's arms, birds in the trees—
> Those dying generations—at their song,
> The salmon-falls, the mackerel crowded seas,
> Fish, flesh, or fowl, commend all summer long
> Whatever is begotten, born, and dies.
> Caught in that sensual music all neglect
> Monuments of unaging intellect. (lines 1–8)

The opening stanza is in a sense evocative of McCarthy in general, insofar as it focuses and places a premium on the tactile, visual, and sensual, and especially on the transitory nature of the physical world. The references to youth, passion, animal life, the seasons, and finally twice to death, recall many of the descriptions of nature found in McCarthy's earlier novels, especially the Comanche dream sequence in the first chapter of *All the Pretty Horses* (1992, 5) and the concluding paragraph of the same novel. But Yeats finishes the stanza on a specific and pointed thematic note, one that is cautionary and even polemical. Lost in the world of sense, all ignore the "monuments of unaging intellect," the great works of art that transcend time, decay, and death. Art becomes the one endeavor that mitigates the physical processes that bring all to ruin, yet art is the very thing that the world in its frenzy of the physical tends to ignore. The reference to time and decay continues in the next stanza:

> An aged man is but a paltry thing,
> A tattered coat upon a stick, unless
> Soul clap its hands and sing, and louder sing
> For every tatter in its mortal dress. (lines 9–12)

Yeats's reference to the "aged man" and the "tattered coat upon a stick" has an obvious analog in McCarthy's *No Country for Old Men*, specifically in Sheriff Bell and Uncle Ellis. McCarthy works deliberately to emphasize their age and in Bell's case his preoccupation with a fading life and its ultimate meaning in a violent world. In this stanza Yeats heightens the contrast between a world of physicality devoid of art and the "monuments" of "magnificence" that suggest permanence. The world of the sensual is diminished by the reference to age that through repetition is elevated to the level of motif and even symbol. A work of art is "unaging," a monument that lives through the millennia; thus the persona's ultimate quest to sail the seas to the "holy city of Byzantium."

The poem continues as the persona undergoes transition from a characterization of the world to a plaintive call to the mysterious forces that embody the creation of art:

> O sages standing in God's holy fire
> As in the gold mosaic of a wall,
> Come from the holy fire, perne in a gyre,
> And be the singing-masters of my soul.
> Consume my heart away; sick with desire
> And fastened to a dying animal
> It knows not what it is; and gather me
> Into the artifice of eternity. (lines 17–24)

Here Yeats quite deliberately associates art with transcendence, directly in the image of "sages" in "God's holy fire." Byzantium is evoked as simultaneously a realm of high art and permanence and the seat of the Eastern Church. Yeats merges the early images of Christian mythology with the act of artistic creation, and a rich complex of images is conflated into an integrated system of dual meaning. Fire, here associated with God and holiness, is simultaneously an image of purification and regeneration; it will purify his heart and prepare it to be an instrument of creation. Soul as the origin of art should be interpreted in a particular manner, since from it he hopes that a grand work of art will return that will in a very literal sense gather him "into the artifice of eternity."

The persona's desire for transcendence through artistic creation continues in the last stanza:

> Once out of nature I shall never take
> My bodily form from any natural thing,
> But such a form as Grecian goldsmiths make
> Of hammered gold and gold enameling
> To keep a drowsy Emperor awake;
> Or set upon a golden bough to sing
> To lords and ladies of Byzantium
> Of what is past, or passing, or to come. (lines 25–32)

Here art and the artist are elevated beyond the physical, given an almost religious significance. The idea of Byzantium as the holy city remains, together with the artifice of the "Grecian goldsmiths," and the sometimes violent act of creation culminates in permanence. The last line is again evocative of the final line in *All the Pretty Horses*. "Of what is past, or passing, or to come" recalls "Past and paled into the darkening land, the world to come" (*Pretty Horses*, 302), not only in the final phrasing but in the overall sense of time passing, orchestrated through an evocative beauty in language and a sense of the immaterial penetrating and informing the physical world.

Yeats is preoccupied with the mysterious relationship between art and nature, specifically with the role of representation, ritual, and transcendence. *No Country for Old Men* deals with these same issues through a circuitous path of indirection understandable only when considering his other works and the obvious and, I would argue, deliberate shift in style. In other works McCarthy displays overtly and without reserve the artifice of language. For many of us that artistry, his mastery of beauty in language, is the only compensating factor for the bleak and uncompromising world he forces us to confront. In *No Country for Old Men* he alters that style, but he also abandons the previous worlds, many of which are characterized by utter degradation and depravity. For all of the novel's Quentin Tarantino–style violence and bloodletting, a dominant strand of the novel is the interspersed narrative of Bell, and although it involves a tortured reflection on circumstances less than pleasant, it is infused with regular and constant references to the human capacity for commitment and love, specifically in marriage. In that context still, the world of the novel is precisely that world of artless sensuality evoked in the first stanza of the Yeats poem. One passage will serve to demonstrate:

Wells stood on the bridge with the wind off the river tousling his thin and sandy hair. He turned and leaned against the fence and raised the small cheap camera he carried and took a picture of nothing in particular and lowered the camera again. He was standing where Moss had stood four nights ago. He studied the blood on the walk. Where it trailed off to nothing he stopped and stood with his arms folded and his chin in his hand. He didnt bother to take a picture. There was no one watching. He looked downriver at the slow green water. He walked a dozen steps and came back. He stepped into the roadway and crossed to the other side. A truck passed. (*No Country*, 166–67)

In some sense, this passage retains elements of McCarthy's signature style, especially in the preoccupation with visual imagery and objective reality and perception, as well as in the overt rejection of subordinate clauses for strings of independent conjunctions linked with the conjunction "and." In another sense, however, he moves away from his previous style as he avoids the sometimes risky rhetorical flourishes that have been so central to his artistry. What characterizes other passages more typical of McCarthy is both their symbolic and iconographic content and their evocative power. When he succeeds, as he so often does, he succeeds beautifully, and our attention is drawn to the artistry of language, its arrangement and lexical complexity. These passages involve descriptions of the world certainly, but they are also interpretive and artistically rendered and demand attention as creations in and of themselves. The above passage from *No Country for Old Men* is almost Hemingwayesque in its simplicity and vivid focus on physical objects in the context of the living world. The "wind off the river tousling his thin and sandy hair" and the simple statement "A truck passed" are terse, laconic, tight, and effortless, suggesting the classical aesthetic dictum *ars et celera artum*, which translates as "the art is to conceal the art." In the past, this has never been McCarthy's practice, insofar as his art in very deliberate ways reveals itself as art, and in doing so calls attention to a created world fashioned by a dark artificer that we never come fully to know. In *No Country for Old Men* the attempt is to root the reader in a world of sense and raw beauty that is void of artifice and system, a cold world of violence and disorder that Bell must struggle somehow to understand. In short, we are required to reside for a time in the artless world of Yeats's "no country for old men." However, in the novel writ large a structural contrast seems to emerge in the narrative of the primary plot from which the above passage is drawn, dominated by Chigurh, and in the interior world of Bell's consciousness, which appears in italics. The latter is the artless realm "that is no country for old men." The former echoes McCarthy's earlier aesthetic as well as the ideal realm of art and artifice orchestrated by Yeats. Bell's interspersed reflections are quite striking when considered in the context of McCarthy's previous works. In one sense, it is here that McCarthy is at his most Faulknerian. For all of the comparisons that some have made between McCarthy and Faulkner, in previous works McCarthy has almost universally avoided entering the interior consciousness of character. His narrators preside over the events as disembodied and oblique observers, mystical interpreters of a violent and mysterious world. In the Bell sections, McCarthy enters the mind of a character as he has rarely done before, following his intimate thoughts and his pointed concerns, fears, and insecurities. The contrast that emerges is one of style and theme, as Bell's contemplations in prose, especially at the conclusion, are infused not only with a more self-conscious artistry, but with an overt tonality of hope that is either absent or appears only obliquely in previous works. This hope emerges from Bell's reliance on and reverence for the redemptive power of human relationships and from his vague acknowledgement of mystical transcendence. Degradation is vividly and artlessly rendered in Chigurh's world of violence and death. Hope appears in Bell's interior reflections, which culminate in a dreamlike reverie infused with imagery similar to that found in Yeats's "Sailing to Byzantium."

Bell's hopeful vision is born of pain and internal conflict, as he struggles with the reality of his own weakness and his need for love and unity in marriage. His first reference to his wife evokes this issue of marriage and love as sanctuary, as a place where one finds repose in an insular domestic space removed from a world of violence. He says succinctly, "*My wife wont read the papers no more. She's probably right. She generally is*" (*No Country*, 40). Then in a later passage he deepens his contemplation of the redemptive power of their relationship. Referring to his wife Loretta, he says, "*She's a better person than me, which I will admit to anybody that cares to listen. Not that that's sayin a whole lot. She's a better person than anybody I know. Period. . . . I don't recall that I ever give the Lord all that much cause to smile on me. But he did*" (91). And later: "*Then she come around behind my chair and put her arms around my neck and bit me on the ear. She's a very young woman in a lot of ways. If I didn't have her I don't know what I would have. Well, yes I do. You wouldn't need a box to put it in, neither*" (305).

It may not appear so on the surface, especially considering McCarthy's earlier work, but these passages and other of Bell's interior monologues are self-consciously artistic, in a studied and specifically American sense. Mark Twain and the local color tradition come immediately to mind, not just in the use of dialect but in the artful and witty turn of phrase, the folk wisdom, and the pointed impact of the language of reflection. They are also Faulknerian in the manner in which McCarthy carefully articulates a singular consciousness, linking language, dialect, and personality in the form of an extended interior monologue. One might imagine that in the film version, sections would appear in the form of voice-over narrative, and would necessarily be so thinly employed that they would lose their affective power. But what is notable is that amid this artistic rendering of consciousness, essentially within the framework of art, we begin to see articulated a hopeful vision. Bell does not shrink from the brutal realities of the world but in the midst of it he considers himself lucky, and that fortune he attributes to a love that is undeserved and a commitment that is foundational. He is unequivocal in his humble assessment of his own value as an independent being, but he finds value in himself and in his experience because another human being has done so. He attributes his own sense of self to the devotion of his wife, who he freely admits is better and implicitly stronger than himself. He finds hope also in a vague apprehension of religious comfort, if not certitude. This realization occurs in an intimate conversation with his uncle, after he has revealed his great secret. Through Bell, McCarthy yet again takes up the God question:

> Bell watched him. The old man stubbed out his cigarette in the lid. Bell tried to think about his life. Then he tried not to. You aint turned infidel have you Uncle Ellis?
> No. No. Nothin like that.
> Do you think God knows what's happenin?
> I expect he does.
> You think he can stop it?
> No. I don't. (*No Country*, 269)

In *Melville's Quarrel with God*, Lawrence Thompson (1966) explores the spiritual and theological tensions and conflicts that inform the work of Herman Melville, especially from *Mardi* through *Billy Budd*. These conflicts revolve around the issue of evil or the problem of pain. Throughout his work, McCarthy can be seen as a writer engaged in that same quarrel, as he grapples with configurations of evil that transcend time, place, and materiality. At times in McCarthy's hands, this conflict seems like open warfare. But amid the violence of *No Country for Old Men*, it seems from the previous passage that McCarthy makes peace with God, not by embracing any particular orthodoxy or system per se, but by considering seriously and sympathetically a philosophical position that distinguishes God from the created world, thus limiting his capacity to orchestrate the details of its operation. As the novel unfolds and we move again into interior monologue, artistically rendered, separate from the prosaic and artless world of violence and bloodletting, we witness a progression that echoes obliquely a kind of telos, one that again connotes hope, possibility, and transcendence, taking place in a dream-vision of his father:

> *It was like we was both back in older times and I was on horseback goin through the mountains of a night. Goin through this pass in the mountains. It was cold and there*

was snow on the ground and he rode past me and kept on goin. Never said nothing. He just rode on past and he had this blanket wrapped around him and he had his head down and when he rode past I seen he was carryin fire in a horn the way people used to do and I could see the horn from the light inside of it. About the color of the moon. And in the dream I knew that he was goin on ahead and that he was fixin to make a fire somewhere out there in all that dark and all that cold and I knew that whenever I got there he would be there. And then I woke up. (No Country, 309)

The image of his long-dead father carrying a beacon concludes the novel on a note of illumination in darkness. Again, hope is evoked in the notion of human and even familial connection and in accepting the limitations of rationality by embracing an epistemology that permits the answers to the essential questions to reveal themselves only vaguely in the evocative images, motifs, symbols, and archetypes that are the substance of art. In Bell's final dream, we see him returning to Yeats's image of eternal fire. However, this is not the fire of destruction but purification, creation, and light. At Bell's fire, his father will, in Yeats's words, "gather him into the artifice of eternity." In this sense, in *No Country for Old Men* McCarthy juxtaposes two worlds: the external and objective world of sense, of artless violence, disorder, and bloodshed, where passion vents itself in pain; and the interior world of Bell's consciousness, which is a realm infused with the same, but one that seeks and finds a stability and permanence in human love, spiritual transcendence, and a mild and mitigated acceptance. To convey the latter world McCarthy again resorts to an overt artifice, to image, to symbol, and to the language of indirection. The novel by no means reflects the stylistic and structural complexity of the previous works. But I speculate at least that neither does it represent a diminution of his artistic powers or a lamentable artistic compromise. The title clarifies his purpose. It is perhaps yet another experiment in language and the novel form, one that explores the particular role of art in portraying with integrity the complex realities of human beings living and struggling in the world.

REFERENCES

McCarthy, Cormac. 1992. *All the Pretty Horses*. New York: Random House.
———. 2005. *No Country for Old Men*. New York: Vintage.
Thompson, Lawrence R. 1966. *Melville's Quarrel with God*. Princeton, NJ: Princeton University Press.
Yeats, William Butler. 1983. "Sailing to Byzantium." In *The Collected Poems of W. B. Yeats*, ed. Richard J. Finnerman, 193–94. New York: Collier Books.

3

✛

For Whom Bell Tolls: Cormac McCarthy's Sheriff Bell as Spiritual Hero

David Cremean

But heroes often fail . . .

—Gordon Lightfoot, "If You Could Read My Mind"

Perhaps the central question posed by the many reviews of Cormac McCarthy's novel *No Country for Old Men* (2005) is how to interpret the novel's "old man," Sheriff Ed Tom Bell.[1] Numerous reviewers have assumed, on slight evidence, that Bell's conservative views represent McCarthy's own. This fundamental error in McCarthy criticism is so widespread that readers of the novel and viewers of the film alike routinely filter their responses through this presumption. However, a close reading of the novel, aided by logic, biocritical study, and, in particular, Joseph Campbell's analysis (1972) of the mythic hero, establishes that Bell is, or at least becomes, far more than a provincial conservative.

As McCarthy's fellow writer of the dark underbelly of America, Joyce Carol Oates, speculates in her error-riddled "The Treasure of Comanche County" (2005), "It's possible that Cormac McCarthy, described in a recent interview as a 'southern conservative,' intends Bell's social-conservative predilections to speak for his own."[2] Perhaps the most strident review equating Bell's views with McCarthy's own is "It's a Man's, Man's World" by William Deresiewicz (2005) in the progressive periodical the *Nation*.[3] Most egregiously, Deresiewicz fails in his application of biocriticism. He apparently read McCarthy's then-recent *Vanity Fair* interview, wherein Richard Woodward calls the novelist a "quiet 72-year-old southern conservative" (2005, 100). Perhaps Deresiewicz also read Woodward's 1992 interview with McCarthy in the *New York Times Magazine*, wherein Woodward brands him "a radical conservative," although that phrase seems to concern McCarthy's aesthetics, not his politics (30).[4] Deresiewicz also labels McCarthy "a conservative" sans the vital "southern" qualifier employed by Woodward that could fit a number of "conservative" types from the South, ranging from Wendell Berry to Walker Percy. He then conveniently omits that Woodward also mentions McCarthy's having known drug dealers, some of whom he says are or were "lovely, gracious people" (2005, 103), far from the hard-core conservative attitude that informs Deresiewicz's reading. Mike Gibson points out that McCarthy's second ex-wife, Annie DeLisle, "suggests" the following: "'That her former husband's singularly authentic literary bent has more to do with a centuries-old theological construct, with the notion that God, in His grace, can justly bestow life, and therefore adoration, on even the most imperfect creatures. . . . 'He always said, "Just because something isn't pleasant doesn't mean it doesn't exist." He felt for those who were less blessed and that the world the rest of us would ignore, he would delve into it, see where it came from'" (Gibson 2002, 33–34). Such ideas are far closer to theological liberalism than to conservative Christian thinking; they are conservative only in the sense that they date back centuries.

Deresiewicz stresses that the novelist's "father was a prominent Knoxville attorney" (2005, 40), apparently to establish some ideological lineage in the McCarthy family but unfortunately unaware that Cormac's relationship with his father was strained to the point of being adversarial at times. He further neglects to consider McCarthy's three marriages or that he rarely saw his first son, hardly indicators of conservative family values (Woodward 2005, 104). Most important, Deresiewicz ignores elements of McCarthy's writings that suggest their author's conservatism is much more thoughtful than stereotypical conservatism allows for. Among them are the negative attitude toward the Tennessee Valley Authority (for whom McCarthy's father practiced law) in *The Orchard Keeper* (1993b); the antinuclear sensibility of the end of *The Crossing* (1994) and similar overtones in *Cities of the Plain* (1999); the generous sympathies for the lowly, the deviant, and the working class throughout his canon.

These oversights notwithstanding, Deresiewicz ascribes McCarthy's putative conservatism to Sheriff Bell and *No Country for Old Men*: "As the novel nears its end . . . Bell's very doubts about the value of his life's work become the excuse for an affirmation of timeworn verities: the endurance of truth, the existence of God, the nihilism of unbelief, the goodness of the old ways. *The sheriff is clearly McCarthy's mouthpiece here. . . .* McCarthy the conservative has conscripted McCarthy the artist for service in the culture wars" (2005, 40; emphasis mine). Judicious use of biocriticism is a historically and logically defensible though not universally accepted approach to literature—I am employing it in this essay—particularly when applied as one among various contextual and interpretive tools. Sadly, Deresiewicz's use of it here is based on nothing: he merely assumes that his claim is apodictic. As he himself implies above, McCarthy has never previously used a specific character as his "mouthpiece." Yet, following Dersiewicz's logic, one could just as easily argue that Judge Holden or for that matter Anton Chigurh is McCarthy's "voice,"[5] since much of what they say and do arguably dovetails nicely with the attitudes and actions of radical conservatives. It is even debatable whether McCarthy has used even his third person narrative voices in a hortatory way. Dersiewicz, however, has followed the radical conservative practice of over-literalizing and, most ironically, of recruiting his literalist straw man McCarthy for his own "service in the culture wars."

McCarthy and Bell do share at least one trait: both have been known in conversation to make sweeping generalizations. In his *Vanity Fair* interview with Woodward, for instance, McCarthy offers several such statements akin to many of Bell's: that semicolon use constitutes "idiocy" (2005, 103); the claim that "if you can't know where a man is going to be when he says he's going to be there, how can you trust him about anything else?" (100); the observation that "if you're in the drug business, you know when you get up that morning that there's some chance somebody's going to get killed" (103); the statement that "most people don't ever see anyone die. It used to be if you grew up in a family you saw everybody die. They died in their bed at home with everyone gathered around. Death is the major issue in the world. For you, for me, for all of us. It just is" (103–4). Other examples of this trait surface in his earlier *New York Times Book Review* interview with Woodward, who offers this perspective: "McCarthy would much rather orate than confide" (1992, 28). The same essay offers other examples of McCarthy's penchant for homespun pronouncements: "Teaching writing is a hustle" (30) and "There's no such thing as a life without bloodshed" (36). In the end, one may wonder if McCarthy isn't engaging in some self-deprecating humor via Bell's ruminations, since as Woodward notes in his first interview, McCarthy "speaks with and amused, ironic manner" (30).

Bell's utterances often seem akin to the hackneyed phrases and facile judgments regularly spewing from Flannery O'Connor characters, traits she uses to ironic effect. Despite the sympathy with which McCarthy portrays Bell, his knack for homiletic utterances suggests that the sheriff can, and possibly should, be viewed as unreliable in his judgments. In almost all of his italicized monologues and in many of his remarks within the narrative passages of chapters 2–7, Bell proves disinclined to doubt his assumptions, though his readers should. This disinclination is born of his belief that *"people anymore you talk about right and wrong they're liable to smile at you. But I never had a lot of doubts about things like that. In my thoughts about things like that. I hope I never do"* (No Country, 158–59). The beliefs he expresses throughout the early parts of the novel fail to sound like ones he has made his own, wrestled with, or gained through experience, but rather like ones he has merely bitten into, hook, line, and sinker. Bell's anecdote about abortion attests to his dogmatism. Discussing a woman he overheard defending the practice, he narrates the following:

> *She kept on, kept on.* [Something Bell, ironically, tends to do himself, including here.] *Finally told me, said: I dont like the way this country is headed. I want my granddaughter to be able to have an abortion. And I said well mam I dont think you got any worries about the way the country is headed. The way I see it goin I dont have much doubt but what she'll be able to have an abortion. I'm goin to say that not only will she be able to have an abortion, she'll be able to have you put to sleep. Which pretty much ended the conversation.* (196–97)

Bell is clearly guilty of a non sequitur in his confusion of categories, falsely equating abortion with active euthanasia. Nevertheless, Bell later realizes the inadequacy of his ideals, as developed below. Unlike O'Connor's "startling figures," which include characters such as Hulga in "Good Country People" or Hazel Motes in *Wise Blood*, who are usually abandoned while still in shock or killed off, Bell's outlook changes as he recognizes his shortcomings.

Perhaps nothing mitigates against reading Bell as McCarthy's mouthpiece as much as considering him in terms of Joseph Campbell's conception of the mythical hero developed in his classic *The Hero with a Thousand Faces* (1972), in particular since McCarthy is one of modern America's most mythically inclined writers. Ed Tom Bell and Llewelyn Moss incarnate the opposite sides of Campbell's heroic character. Bell, who consistently fails to keep up with a deteriorating situation, survives into old age and learns lessons to bring back from his several failed quests (just what these lessons are, as well as their very nature, can, of course, be debated). Moss is the romantic young Turk who impetuously strives to act heroically but dies in the process.[6] He is consequently unable to return with any boons and only incompletely fill the hero's role that Campbell describes. He thus belongs to Campbell's subcategory of "physical hero" rather than to that of his "spiritual hero." Such distinctions are of course common motifs in and across numerous classical myths.

What Bell in particular has encountered in his past, and now encounters and (non-)faces throughout the present of his narrative, tests his beliefs and tests them profoundly. He enters Campbell's hero stage of trials once he has answered the call to action that begins with Anton Chigurh's murder of a deputy from another county and calls even more loudly with the discovery of the drug-trade murders on isolated land. At once curiously but realistically—and still well within Campbell's framework—during the course of the story, Bell both accepts and rejects his call, as he previously did during World War II. Llewelyn Moss consistently answers his call, yet Moss ends up dead and unable to fulfill the last part of the spiritual hero's journey—returning with a message. Meanwhile Bell's failure to answer his call(s) fully ensures his survival and ironically enables his return with what Campbell terms "the lesson he [the hero] has learned of life renewed" (1972, 20).

Upon first considering Bell's story in mythic terms, I concluded that by novel's end Bell was merely at Campbell's initial threshold stage. Rereadings convinced me otherwise: by narrative's end he is also at the end of the hero's journey, in possession of that wisdom the hero brings back to his or her corner of the world. Bell in fact arrives at the threshold of his inner quest when he discovers the *narcotraficantes'* "colossal goatfuck" (*No Country*, 141). As Campbell argues, "Folk mythologies populate with deceitful and dangerous presences every desert place outside the normal traffic of the village. . . . A dangerous one-legged, one-armed, one-sided figure—the half-man—invisible if viewed from the off-side" (1972, 78). Isolated Terrell County, west Texas, where most of the novel is set, and the mysterious and menacing Anton Chigurh, who is indeed one-sided morally and essentially invisible, in a metaphorical sense fits Campbell's description perfectly. He eventually fits it perfectly in a literal sense as well. Moss badly wounds Chigurh's right leg in their running gunfight outside the hotel in Eagle Pass (*No Country*, 114, 119–20). Finally, Chigurh appears after an automobile accident, and he lurches off the novel's pages with a broken left arm, "limping slightly" (260–62).

However, passing this threshold and entering into his inner quest does not enable Bell to enter a world of heroic action, a call that in fact he refuses; rather, that is Moss's journey. Bell's siege perilous is instead the journey into his own psyche, where he confronts himself past and present, eventually resolved into his heavily archetypal and highly mystical dream of journeying together with his long-dead father, carrier of the "fire in a horn" that lights the horn "about the color of the moon," suggesting the horned moon associated with the Virgin Mary and with various other mythical archetypes (*No Country*, 309).[7]

The lesson(s) any hero learns will be subjective, as all lessons must initially be. Therefore Bell must enter his own unconscious, enter it as honestly as possible by recognizing his own failures, such as his youthful abandonment of his fellow troops during the war in Europe. In short, he must enter a critical phase of the hero's journey, the phase of his trials. As

Northrop Frye attests, this phase is "the labyrinth or maze, the image of lost direction, often with a monster at its heart" (2000, 150). In Bell's case the labyrinth is at once the external maze created by Chigurh and the Mexican drug lords and their American co-conspirators, as well as the internal one created by his past experiences in World War II, his abandonment of a pursuit when shot at (*No Country*, 38–40), and his unwillingness to face Chigurh. As Campbell envisions the spiritual hero, his "passage . . . may be overground, incidentally; fundamentally it is inward" (1972, 29).

Despite his self-doubt Bell is no mere coward, and in the past he undertook at least one physical trial, albeit one that became a "doomed enterprise" (*Crossing*, 129) much like Billy Parham's effort to save the she-wolf. In the World War II encounter Bell fought German soldiers for hours in the dark before finally fleeing. Bell did not hide his misgivings about his flight, since he confessed it to a superior officer. But his worldview is mostly adopted from others, along with his penchant for speaking the homiletic clichés of his region. Bell's religious "faith" is an even lighter, apparently ritual-free version of his wife's light American version of Christianity. As such, his convictions fail him as he works his way through the dual labyrinths of interior and exterior hero-journey. One of Bell's shortcomings is a naïveté about, or at least a disconnection from, the meaning of the history of his region. Though he mentions its bloody past, he nevertheless believes it cannot compare to what he is witnessing now. McCarthy himself of course knows better, as *Blood Meridian* (1992) and the Border Trilogy more than amply attest. Bell's worldview becomes adequate only after contemporaries like the denizens of the drug industry, Chigurh, and Moss force him to answer his hero's calling, enter his labyrinth, and he intuits the truth.[8]

Bell's spiritual sterility and his difficulty in coming to terms with death are metaphorically inflected by his childless marriage. He and his wife, Loretta, had a daughter, but she died young, and he refuses to discuss it early in the novel's time-frame (*No Country*, 90). Bell apparently has never faced her death or grappled with its implications for his simplistic worldview. Until faced with the summons to his journey, the threshold, the labyrinth, Bell is but a member of those whom Campbell identifies as "the multitude of men and women [who] choose the less adventurous way of the comparatively unconscious civic and tribal routines" (1972, 23). Or, as Bob Dylan (1989) has written, "People don't live or die, / People just float." After struggling with the implications of the events narrated by the novel, however, Bell reveals that he is anything but a static character: *"I'm bein asked to stand for something that I dont have the same belief in it I once did. Asked to believe in something I might not hold with the way I once did. . . . I failed at it even when I did. Now I've seen it held to the light. . . . I've been forced to look at it again and I've been forced to look at myself. . . . I never had them sorts of doubts before"* (*No Country*, 296). Bell's experience has taught him these lessons. Existentially, his beliefs did not stand up to reality, and he knows it at novel's end.

McCarthy, both in his first interview with Woodward and in *The Crossing*, has commented on the "one book" idea of all literature, something of a parallel to Campbell's "monomyth" (and in various other guises argued for by literary giants ranging from Percy Bysshe Shelley to T. S. Eliot). His own novels certainly include all sorts of unifying elements such as Moss's link to Jimmy Blevins in *All the Pretty Horses* when Moss tells Carla Jean that he obtained his illegal gun "at the gettin place" (*No Country*, 21) or the ubiquitous refrain "They rode on," most famously used throughout *Blood Meridian* (1992a) but a real presence as early as *Suttree* with "He rowed on" (1992b, 11), and as recently as *The Road* (2006), with its frequent variations on the motif "They went on." These and numerous other unifying motifs resound throughout McCarthy's writings, pulling and holding his fictional world together.[9]

The ending of *No Country* proves no exception to this practice. Bell's focus has shifted back to what the first chapter of the novel intimated: that he has become a changed man and, as in the final stage of Campbell's hero-quest, is bearing a message back to the rest of his world. His final homily, arguably the only completely profound one he utters, at once bears and is born of this message. It occurs at the end of chapter 8, also the number of the missing floor in the drug kingpin's office building, as remarked upon by Carson Wells (*No Country*, 142). "*I'm not the man of an older time they say I am*," Bell admits. "*I wish I was. I'm a man of this time*" (279). In Bell's first monologue in chapter 1, he bears the changes that his hero's journey has wrought in him. He has progressively grown uncertain, all but abandoned his truisms, his proclamations, his certainties, and seemingly found consolation in uncertainty itself: "*It* [the sum of the events of the story to follow] *has done brought me to a place in my life I would not of thought I'd come to*" (4); "*I dont know a damn thing*" (213); "*And this* [the drugs and violence of the border region] *aint goin away. And that's about the only thing I do know*" (216–17); "*I dont know nothin. I wish I did. Or I think I wish it*" (299).

Unlike Moss, who in wife Carla Jean's words "never has" quit anything (*No Country*, 127), Bell quits the job to which he realizes he is unequal, having reached knowingly and honestly back into history as shown when he returns for the final time to the site of the eight murders. His narration concerning that visit reveals he has learned that "*this country has got a strange kind of history and a damned bloody one too. About anywhere you care to look. . . . I dont make excuses for the way I think. Not no more*" (284–85). Bell has examined his old certitudes and found them lacking, recognized them to be at heart but mere excuses. He is now unconcerned with what others think, has moved beyond thinking and acting the way he was expected to. In fact, in chapter 8 Bell ultimately reaches back beyond history into prehistory, back into archetypal aspects of the unconscious and represented by the eternal elements of fire and stone, stretches his arms and soul into the mystery and the mystical. As Campbell describes it, "The modern hero-deed must be that of questing to bring to light again the lost Atlantis of the co-ordinated soul. . . . The problem is nothing if not that of rendering the modern world spiritually significant—or rather . . . nothing if not that of making it possible for men and women to come to full human maturity through the conditions of contemporary life" (1972, 388). By novel's end, Bell has reached this point, this still center. Some of the relatively little we know about McCarthy resonates with this idea as well. Summarizing a letter McCarthy sent him, Garry Wallace states, "He ended with the thought that our inability to see spiritual truth is the greatest mystery" (1992, 138).

Consequently, it is in his final spiritual move into the mystical that Bell reconfigures his "conservatism," and it is here that we may find traces of McCarthy's own. For Bell has indeed fulfilled Campbell's notion of the hero: "The man or woman who has been able to battle past his personal and local historical limitations to the generally valid, normally human forms. . . . The hero has died as a modern man; but as eternal man— perfected, unspecific, universal man—he has been reborn" (1972, 20). In the ending of *No Country for Old Men*, as in the epilogue to *Blood Meridian*, what matters are the timeless elements like stone and fire and all that they symbolically imply; the hero triumphant, defeated, or filled with failure, or some state partaking of all three; the long-lived handiwork of humanity; the mystical apprehension of God where truth has its origin, its very being, and endures. Even the violence that thunders throughout McCarthy's canon is a timeless element, probably the trait for which he, like director Sam Peckinpah, is most famous. As René Girard notes, "Violence is the heart and secret soul of the transcendent and the sacred" (1993, 31)—perhaps in part because, as he later declares, *"violence operates without reason"* (46).

NOTES

1. I envision this chapter, extensively revised here from its original publication in the *Cormac McCarthy Journal*, as the first installment of a "trinity" of articles, each examining in some fashions the novel's three major characters: Bell, Chigurh, and Moss.

2. Oates's errors are egregious. The abundance of factual errors in this article is particularly disconcerting given the fact that Oates's reviews are frequently cited

as significant aspects of her formidable literary reputation. First, her title itself contains one. Roger D. Hodge observes in a footnote, "For some reason, Joyce Carol Oates believes that Bell is the sheriff of Comanche County, which is more than 300 miles to the northeast [of Bell's actual Terrell County]. This error explains the otherwise inexplicable title of her *New York Review* essay, 'The Treasure of Comanche County'" (2005, 69). Oates claims that Llewelyn Moss "takes some Mexican brown heroin" (2005, para. 31) with him when in fact he does no such thing, but only tastes it on his fingertip while at the mass murder site. She also maintains, incredibly, that "McCarthy has eliminated all quotation marks from his prose so that his characters' speech isn't distinct from the narrative voice" (para. 6), when in fact his characters' speech is colloquial and easily distinguished from the non-colloquial third-person narrative voices in *all* of McCarthy's works. And her errors ride on.

3. A resident of the West myself (I live in the Black Hills of far-western South Dakota), I think it is essential to point out that the essays by Oates and Deresiewicz unfortunately indicate that much (but I hasten to add, not all) of the eastern literary establishment continues to misunderstand the American West.

4. The full quotation reads, "Rightful heir to the Southern Gothic tradition, McCarthy is a radical conservative who still believes that the novel can, in his words, 'encompass all the various disciplines and interests of humanity'" (Woodward 1992, 30). In fact, much of what little we know of McCarthy's life and even more of his fiction indicates a libertarian, even anarchistic, tendency toward matters political and governmental. He was, after all, friends with the professed anarchist Edward Abbey, himself a curious mix of his time's conservatism and liberalism while far more than just that mix (Woodward 1992, 30). Moreover, he told David Kushner he has never voted, though the fact that he said "poets shouldn't vote" sounds like a humorous allusion to Plato's notorious (and likely humorous, since he himself was one) comments in *The Republic* about slaying all poets (Kushner 2007–2008, 46).

5. Or, for that matter, an equivalent argument might be that Llewelyn Moss's wife, Carla Jean, is McCarthy's mouthpiece, since she bears his initials: C. J. M. (Charles Joseph McCarthy).

6. As for the temptation lurking behind Moss's act of absconding with the drug money, much could be said. For the purpose of this article, however, it is sufficient to note that the actual actions and pursuits of heroes are frequently morally and ethically dubious at best. Moss's own reverberates with acts of many classical heroes and heroines, ranging from Pandora to Jason to Eve to King David. Moss particularly inflects such flaws in his "betrayal" of Carla Jean, reminiscent in a general sense of Jason's betrayal of Medea.

7. Fire is a frequent symbol consistently freighted with meaning in most if not all of McCarthy's writing, and the connection here to the ending of *The Road* is particularly potent. An inversion of sorts also brings the ending of *The Road* to mind: much as the boy prays to his dead father in *The Road*, late in *No Country* Bell, earlier unwilling to speak about his long-dead daughter (90), mentions speaking with his only child (her early death in all likelihood one reason for his opposition to abortion): *"She would be thirty now. . . . I listen to her. . . . It dont get mixed up with my own ignorance or my own meanness. I listen to what she says and what she says makes*

good sense. I wish she'd say more of it. I can use all the help I can get" (285). The comments he makes regarding his own negative traits and need for help are two other
major pieces of evidence about Bell's growth into self-knowledge. The daughter
archetypally represents Bell's own Teiresian "feminine side," in Jungian terms his
anima, his own inner, mystical voice.

8. The principle force necessitating Bell's changes is Chigurh (*No Country*, 4),
whom Bell terms, in my view unreliably, "some new kind of person" (3). Ironically enough, Chigurh is likely a Frankenstein's monster sort of creature made
by the United States, Bell's own country in another sense of the word, strongly
suggesting that the title of the novel may be seen correctly as multiply suggestive.
Possessor of a seemingly unplaceable ethnic surname (though it seems likely Mc-
Carthy intends a sort of inside reference to the northeastern New Mexico town
of Anton Chico), "kindly dark complected" (291) with "dark hair" (112) yet blue-
eyed ("blue as lapis," 56), Chigurh is "faintly exotic" (112) and at once "looked
like anybody" and "didnt look like anybody" (292). Consonant with his physical
appearance but even more important, as Bell surmises after finding the FBI cannot (or more likely will not) match Chigurh's fingerprints, "He's a ghost" (248).
This terminology suggests further playfulness on McCarthy's part, since "ghost"
suggests "spook" in the latter's slang term sense of "spy." The times, Chigurh's
formidable skills, and the familiarity with him evidenced by those in the drug
world like Wells and the mysterious businessman to whom Chigurh returns the
money (250) all indicate Chigurh likely came out of Special Forces (like Wells,
who identifies himself to Moss as having been a lieutenant colonel in them in Viet
Nam, 156), the CIA, the FBI itself, or some combination thereof and may well be
being protected.

9. The McCarthy critic who pioneered this territory is Edwin T. Arnold, particularly in his important essay "The Mosaic of Cormac McCarthy's Fiction" (2002).
In admiration for his work on McCarthy that began long before McCarthy's reputation had risen, I would like to dedicate this article to him.

REFERENCES

Arnold, Edwin T. 2002. "The Mosaic of McCarthy's Fiction." In *Sacred Violence*,
    2nd ed., vol. 1, ed. Wade Hall and Rick Wallach, 1–8. El Paso: Texas Western
    University Press.
Campbell, Joseph. 1972. *The Hero with a Thousand Faces*. Bollingen Series 17. Princ-
    eton: Princeton University Press.
Deresiewicz, William. 2005. "It's a Man's, Man's World." Review of *No Country for
    Old Men*. *Nation*, September 12, 38–41.
Dylan, Bob. 1989. "Man in the Long Black Coat." *Oh Mercy*. Sony.
Frye, Northrop. 2000. "Archetypal Criticism: Theory of Myths." In *Anatomy of Criti-
    cism: Four Essays*, 129–239. Princeton and Oxford: Princeton University Press.
Gibson, Mike. 2002. "Knoxville Gave McCarthy the Raw Material of His Art. And
    He Gave It Back." In *Sacred Violence: Volume 1, Cormac McCarthy's Appalachian*

Work, ed. Wade Hall and Rick Wallach, 23–34. El Paso: Texas Western University Press.

Girard, René. 1993. *Violence and the Sacred*. Trans. Patrick Gregory. Baltimore: Johns Hopkins University Press.

Hodge, Roger D. 2006. "Blood and Time: Cormac McCarthy and the Twilight of the West." Review of *No Country for Old Men*. *Harper's*, February, 65–72.

Kushner, David. 2007–2008. "Cormac McCarthy's Apocalypse." *Rolling Stone*, December 27–January 10, 43, 46, 48, 52–53.

McCarthy, Cormac. 1992a. *Blood Meridian, or, The Evening Redness in the West*. New York: Vintage.

———. 1992b. *Suttree*. New York: Vintage.

———. 1993a. *All the Pretty Horses*. New York: Alfred A. Knopf.

———. 1993b. *The Orchard Keeper*. New York: Vintage

———. 1994. *The Crossing*. New York: Alfred A. Knopf.

———. 1999. *Cities of the Plain*. New York: Vintage.

———. 2005. *No Country for Old Men*. New York: Alfred A. Knopf.

———. 2006. *The Road*. New York: Alfred A. Knopf.

Oates, Joyce Carol. 2005. "The Treasure of Comanche County." Review of *No Country for Old Men*. *New York Review of Books*, October 20. http://www.nybooks.com/articles/18359 (October 4, 2005).

Wallace, Garry. 1992. "Meeting McCarthy." *Southern Quarterly* 30, no. 4: 134–39.

Woodward, Richard B. 1992. "Cormac McCarthy's Venomous Fiction." *New York Times Magazine*, April 19, sec. 6, 28+.

———. 2005. "Cormac Country." *Vanity Fair*, August, 98+.

4

No Allegory
for Casual Readers

John Vanderheide

THEORETICAL OVERVIEW

*N*o *Country for Old Men* (2005) may strike the casual reader of Cormac McCarthy as indicative of a substantially different direction for the writer. A hardboiled detective fiction set in a world largely expunged of McCarthy's signature descriptions of nature, and written alternately in terse third-person narration and rambling first-person testimonials—the novel's novelty appears a function not only of its ostensible genre, but also its setting and schizophrenic style. *No Country* seems to stick out of McCarthy's oeuvre as something rather odd, but as many seasoned readers of McCarthy have already realized, the novel's apparent oddness dissipates upon closer rereading, and its structural and thematic resonance with its predecessors becomes unmistakably manifest. Indeed, one could understand *No Country* as an oblique interpretation of what might be called the aesthetic totality of McCarthy's project—an allegorical refashioning of the one or selfsame tale that, as the Caborcan pensioner of *The Crossing* (1994) would say, all of the novels tell.

The mention of allegory is not unmotivated. The aesthetic and ideational consistency of McCarthy's entire output follows from a rigorously developed, yet discretely deployed allegorical outlook. But—one might well ask—if McCarthy's novels are allegories, what are they allegories *of*? The disrepute that has dogged the allegorical for centuries follows mostly from the mistaken notion that allegory mechanically forces narrative to represent a single concept or single idea. Few nowadays would agree that Shakespeare wrote *Hamlet* as an allegory of indecision, or that the melancholy prince is simply a personification of velleity. But if allegory does not deploy narrative merely to treat a singular concept, then what does it deploy narrative to treat? In his masterpiece on the subject, Angus Fletcher concludes that allegories "are the natural mirrors of ideology" (1964, 368). For Fletcher, then, allegory deploys narrative to treat not a concept, but an ideology, an entire worldview or vision of the absolute. An ideology, of course, is not merely a dispassionate description of the world as it is imagined to be. It always contains both ontological *and* ethical dimensions. An ideology states: because the world is like *that*, one should behave like *this*. Allegory's infamous didacticism would then follow the ethical contours of the ideology it reflects. Of course, Fletcher is quick to point out that allegory never presents a single ideology in isolation. Rather, allegory narrates the collision and conflict between incompatible ideologies. As Fletcher writes, "The war between absolutes [is] the ground plan of all allegories" (1964, 224). If an allegory conveys ethical prescriptions, these prescriptions follow from the testing and evaluation of competing ideologies in a given narrative setting.[1]

As in any conflict, the allegorical war between absolutes comes down to a question of power. What, then, is the specific power of an ideology, and how would one determine the victor in a conflict between opposing ones? If an ideology is comprised of both ontological and ethical notions, then its power must be understood as twofold—at once a function of how well it can make sense of things (i.e., how well it can organize available information into a satisfactory construction of the world at large), but also how empowering it proves to its potential subjects. As an ideologist, the allegorist presumes that the happiness and fulfillment of a human being is a byproduct of the power he or she enjoys. As Fletcher would say, "The search for pure power is at the heart of all allegorical quests" (1964, 338). In the allegorical war between absolutes, the victorious ideology is therefore the one that endows its subjects with the most power. Given the classic examples of allegory including Spenser's *The Faerie Queene* (1970) and Bunyan's *Pilgrim's Progress* (1996), it should be apparent that allegory more often than not differentiates between "spiritual" and "material" forms of power. In Spenser's Elizabethan allegory, these two forms unite (properly in Anglicanism, improperly in Catholicism). In Bunyan's more plebeian allegorical vision, the two types of power reciprocally exclude one another. The burden of Bunyan's task involves constructing the spiritual power granted to the successful pilgrim as infinitely greater and therefore infinitely more desirable than its counterpart. The material world must therefore be given up if one hopes for access to the world of spirit.

As Bunyan's radically Protestant allegorism gives way to the allegorical forms of romanticism, transcendentalism, and modernism, the ideologies tested and championed become less identifiably Christian and much more radically subjective and ambiguous in their constructions of the world and their accounts of "spiritual" and "material" power. Thus, while the allegorical fictions of McCarthy's immediate forebears— Hawthorne and Melville in the nineteenth century and such high modernists as Yeats and Joyce in the twentieth—continue to narrate the war between absolutes, the principals of this war have become increasingly difficult to discern. Certainly the works of such allegorists express deep concern with the organization of immanent social life under the capitalist mode of production. Nevertheless, the respective ideological visions these works mirror still include, however open or indirect, some kind of construction of transcendence—Joyce's "monad," for example, in which literary form itself becomes the transcendent principle.

The same seems true of the absolutes that McCarthy's allegorical narratives set into opposition, analyze, and evaluate. If McCarthy's novels consistently critique the capitalist mode of production (and I think they do), it is because capitalism cannot but divert human beings from the more "spiritual" forms of power available to them—in particular, the poetic power to consolidate or federate themselves into an affirmative and self-empowering collective that is no longer consumed in a self-destructive psychomachia. The narrative logic of the novels indicates that a predominantly passive or reflective mode of existence predicates the concretization of such higher potentialities, whereas capitalism forces "actionism" upon its subjects. As such, capitalist production becomes readable as a vehicle of an occluded metaphysical evil—a nihilism deriving from the idea of sovereign power and functioning quite literally to bring nothingness about. In the ideological warfare that McCarthy's novels narrate, the possibility of victory over such nihilism, the possibility of access to the higher forms of power available to humanity, springs from an act of renunciation, in particular a rejection of the temptation to battle the nihilism directly. For in acceding to this temptation, one is immediately constituted as a subject of the nihilism one claims to be fighting. In what follows, I thus hope to show how all of the narrative action of *No Country for Old Men* serves to illuminate the preconditions, consequences, and virtue of such an act of renunciation, an act upon which one's very humanity depends.

THE PROOF TEXT OF BELL'S PROGRESS

The theme of renunciation in *No Country for Old Men* declares itself plainly in the novel's title. McCarthy lifted the titular phrase from the first line of William Butler Yeats's poem "Sailing to Byzantium" (1990), but why does McCarthy do this? Is the phrase torn from its context to suit some alien thematic purpose or does its citation indicate some more significant connection between the two works? Many theorists of allegory have observed how allegorists present their own narratives as retellings of antecedent works that have some kind of cultural authority. As Edwin Honig suggests, there is a "twice-told" aspect to the allegorical tale, and this aspect "indicates that some venerated or proverbial antecedent (old) story has become a pattern for another (the new) story" (1966, 12). In relation to the new work, the old thus stands as what Deborah Madsen would call the new work's "proof-text" (1996, 6), and it is part of the function of the new work to renew the intelligibility and the authority of its antecedent. Does "Sailing to Byzantium" thus represent the allegorical proof-text of McCarthy's novel? It could be, if the central narrative of the novel patterns itself after the implicit narrative of the poem.

The story that Yeats's modernist masterpiece tells is that of an anonymous old man—the poem's speaker—who declares that he has undertaken a journey from the transient world of nature and history to the permanent, if not eternal, realm of art. In some sense, the man has already begun his journey, since the demonstrative pronoun he uses to refer to the immanent "country" he is renouncing is the distal "that" rather than the proximal "this"—"*That* is no country for old men" (line 1, emphasis mine). If the old man has not yet reached his transcendent destination, he seems in some sense to have already departed from his point of origin. The poem thus locates him somewhere between the two worlds, and between two events, the death that awaits him in one world and the artificial immortality that awaits him in the other.

The quest narrative undergirding Yeats's poem can be understood to represent an example of what Angus Fletcher would call an allegorical "progress." For Fletcher, allegorical narratives resolve themselves into two fundamental formal patterns, which he calls "progress" and "battle" (1964, 151). Fletcher describes the progress as a kind of "questing journey" in which the hero leaves one home to find "another better [one]" (151). In some instances of the form, the new "home" sought after is qualitatively different from the one left behind. As Bunyan's famous allegory would attest, the allegorical progress very often narrates an anagogical movement out of nature and history into the "world to come." Yeats's poem certainly presents itself as a species of this sort of progress "upward." If "Sailing to Byzantium" and *Pilgrim's Progress* diverge in terms of doctrinal content—the way in which they respectively conceive of the world of transcendence and the means to attain it—they nevertheless resonate in a certain formal respect. In both works the pilgrims seek to overcome the powerlessness imposed upon them in the temporal world and to gain access to the empowerment awaiting them in eternity. Thus, we can say that the point of origin in an allegorical progress is a state of impotence, the destination a state of empowerment.

It is clear enough that McCarthy associates the Yeatsian title of *No Country for Old Men* predominantly with one character—Ed Tom Bell, the sheriff whose decision to quit law enforcement constitutes the novel's central narrative strand. With this association, the novel thus instructs us to read Sheriff Bell as a type of allegorical pilgrim and to read his narrative as a type of allegorical progress.

The novel presents Bell's story in two ways—in the third-person narration of the chapters and in Bell's first-person testimonials that preface each chapter. In presenting Bell's narrative in this schizophrenic fashion, the novel disrupts its proper timeline. For the most part, his first-person testimonials are further ahead in the timeline of Bell's narrative than the events narrated in the chapters proper. Those events therefore represent the past of the one who speaks directly in the chapter prefaces. In the chapters, Bell is a participant in the unfolding events, pursuing both Moss and Chigurh. In the prefaces, Bell has already resigned and is looking back on those events, seeking to make sense of how things turned out. Straightening out the timeline, the reader is thus able to construct the beginning, middle, and end of Bell's narrative within the novel. It begins with Bell's investigations into the murders of two of Chigurh's victims (Lamar's deputy and Bill Wyrick), and the aftermath of the soured drug deal discovered in the desert. It continues with Bell as a participant in the ensuing events, until he decides to quit. The narrative that follows from this point (tersely spoken, as it were, in a single paragraph in chapter 11) consists of Bell reflecting on the previous events and, more broadly, on his life up to that point.

Now one may ask how this reconstructed narrative constitutes an allegorical progress. Bunyan's famous allegory narrates every aspect of the progress, from the point of origin (Christian Salvation's old home in the City of Destruction) to the destination (Christian's new home in the Celestial City). In "Sailing to Byzantium," Yeats presents only an indeterminate section of his pilgrim's progress, locating him somewhere between the immanent point of origin (the country he rejects) and the transcendent destination he seeks (figured as the holy city). In McCarthy's novel, we have yet another, although still eminently modernist, strategy at work. The bulk of Bell's narrative takes place *before* the beginning of his progress. In other words, that part of Bell's narrative recounted in the third person focuses on the coming-to-be of his spiritual pilgrimage, the preconditions for his setting out on such a journey. The journey itself therefore begins roughly with Bell's act of quitting, the renunciation of his pursuit of Chigurh. This act transforms Bell's narrative into an allegorical progress.

What the novel relates of his progress is therefore its coming-to-be and its beginning. The ultimate success or failure of the pilgrim in reaching his new home is something the novel leaves untold. With regard to this openness or indeterminacy of the progress, the novel's genetic relationship to the high modernists is clear. (*Ulysses*, for example, ends precisely where the progresses of both Leopold Bloom and Stephen Dedalus begin, figuratively back in "Ithaca.") No longer viewing history as the unfolding of a providential plan, and no longer certain of the relationship between immanence and transcendence, modernist allegorists eschew narrating the endpoint of the progress. What matters is the analysis of the conditions of beginning, and of the act of beginning itself.

Reading Bunyan and Yeats, I previously suggested that the allegorical progress narrates the transformation of impotence into empowerment. The protagonist's desire to become a pilgrim in the first place thus emerges out of a certain experience of powerlessness. The speaker of Yeats's poem departs his old home because there all that matters is youth and sensuality, and he is no longer young and presumably no longer sexually potent. The old man's leave-taking is indeed painful; for despite his bodily decrepitude, his heart is still "sick with desire" (line 21). The experience of impotence or powerlessness is precisely a consequence of the disjunction between his desire and his capacity to act on it. The progress itself can only begin with the renunciation of the aggravating desire that he can no longer satisfy.

Granted, the inciting incident at the root of Bell's own leave-taking "aint of a sexual nature" (*No Country*, 273). Nevertheless, it likewise boils down to a matter of impotence, as Bell himself continually suggests. Ostensibly it is Bell's indirect encounter with the elusive and deadly Anton Chigurh that elicits in him a sense of his own powerlessness. As he confesses, "*I aim to quit and a good part of it is just knowin that I wont be called on to hunt this man*" (282). Elsewhere Bell reformulates this reason, reflecting that "*you realize that you have come upon somethin that you may very well not be equal to and I think that this is one of them things*" (299). The third-person narrative amplifies and endorses Bell's interpretation in the terse description of his last day on the job: "He walked down the steps and out the back door and got in his truck and sat there. He couldnt name the feeling. It was sadness but it was something else besides. And the something else besides was what had him sitting there instead of starting the truck. He'd felt like this before but not in a long time and when he said that, then he knew what it was. It was defeat. It was being beaten. More bitter to him than death" (306).

Several factors contribute to Bell's feeling of defeat. Firstly there is his sense of being overmatched. At the same time, Bell thinks that the criminals he is pursuing must likewise feel that he poses no threat to them.

As he speculates, *"The worst of it is knowin that probably the only reason I'm even still alive is that they have no respect for me"* (*No Country*, 217). If Bell really had the capacity to interfere or stop them, they would have taken action against him (as they did against the federal judge Bell mentions in the same breath). This is not to say that Bell does not wish he could bring them to justice. Again, the bitterness that the feeling of defeat leaves Bell surely reflects the coexistence of relative powerlessness and a furious, unsatisfied desire.

In an insightful essay on the novel, Robert Jarrett observes that "if he is to 'put things right' . . . Bell must display a fascistic power that rivals Chigurh's" (2005, 93). For Jarrett, Bell's retirement "from the role of the detective/police hero" (92) is to be understood not only as a "prudential affirmation of his own life" (93), but also as a refusal to "fall into fascism" (92). The difficulty of this refusal is briefly illustrated in Bell's late encounter with the Mexican incarcerated in Huntsville. As Bell recounts, *"I just wanted him to know that I done the best I could for him and that I was sorry because I didnt think he done it"* (*No Country*, 297). Rather than expressing his gratitude, however, the convict goads Bell with a series of insults. Confirming how easily the convict played him, Bell states, *"Well. These people can read you pretty good. If I had of smacked him in the mouth that guard would not of said word one. And he knew that. He knew that"* (297). Tempting the sheriff (who indeed seems tempted) to explode into fascistic or sadistic violence, the convict functions as agent of the ideology against which not only Bell, but the novel itself and McCarthy's aesthetic project in general, struggles. Formally speaking, this ideology seeks to divert Bell from undertaking his allegorical progress by drawing him (and reshaping his narrative) into an allegorical battle.

THE TEMPTATION OF BATTLE

Fletcher suggests the primary effects of the battle form are "symmetry and balance," the "stasis [of] conflict caught at a given moment in time" (1964, 159). As he elaborates, "The back and forth of battle, when translated to a mental conflict or an ideological warfare, becomes the symmetrical presentation of first the argument on one side, then the argument on another. The debaters of the debate are presented in an equality, so that each side gets its fair share of the action" (159).

In *No Country for Old Men*, the battle form appears to shape the narrative in two distinct ways. First, the novel presents an overarching battle between two incompatible ideologies, whose primary agents and theoreticians are Bell and Chigurh, respectively. As Bell's confrontation with the convict attests, however, the novel also portrays a battle internal to the nihilistic ideology that Bell opposes. This ideology is nihilistic not because it does battle with other ideological formations, but precisely because it sets its *own* subjects against one another. The self-canceling nihilism Chigurh embodies strives relentlessly to convert being into nothingness by means of any kind of violence.

For Fletcher, the battle form is intimately linked to the idea of temptation. Ultimately Bell resists the temptation to recognize himself as a subject of Chigurh's ideology. Moss, regrettably, does not. Moss's narrative assumes the shape of an allegorical battle the moment he accedes to the temptation of taking the satchel full of drug money. Recalling C. S. Lewis's assertion that "temptation is the natural theme of allegory," Fletcher notes that the feeling of being tempted can arise only in the immanence of conflicting ideological imperatives, one of which prescribes the attainment of the tempting object, the other which forbids it (1964, 36). When this collision of imperatives takes place in a subject, the emotive result is ambivalence, by which Fletcher means "a mixture of diametrically opposed feelings" (224). Temptation is thus a symptom of a psychomachia, an internal battle between opposing ideologies that has rendered the subject fractured and incoherent. The scene in which Moss discovers the money portrays him in precisely such a state of self-division: "Moss absolutely knew what was in the case and he was scared in a way that he didnt even understand" (*No Country*, 17). "You live to be a hundred, he said, and there wont be another day like this one. As soon as he said it he was sorry" (20).

From this scene on, the novel shows Moss as unwilling and incapable of resolving his internal conflict. But if the original scene of temptation depicts Moss at a genuine ideological crossroads, the subsequent moments of self-conflict appear somehow qualitatively different. The internal battle no longer indicates a struggle against nihilism, but a mode of nihilism that uses its ideological opposite to realize its own ends. How else can one understand the grimly ironic reversals of Moss's disastrous act of sympathy? His return to the desert to deliver water to the wounded Mexican driver leads to his identification by Chigurh, introducing him as a principal in the external conflict between the hit man and his erstwhile employers. As Jarrett has noted, Moss's action is "largely inexplicable on the terms of the realistic narrative" (2005, 77). It might even appear as an awkwardly executed contrivance on the part of the author to initiate Chigurh's pursuit of Moss. However, the narrative itself forecloses this reading when it presents for comparison the consequences of Moss's later sympathetic treatment of the teen hitchhiker. Moss treats the girl with decorous kindness; he resists her sexual advances, engages her intellectually, and gives her a good deal of money to fund her travels. Unfortunately this kindness, which the girl clearly finds attractive, serves only to draw her into the conflict wherein she very quickly loses her life.

Moss's generosity with the stolen money is not restricted to his dona-
tion to the girl. Throughout the narrative he spends it prodigally. In a
representative scene, he tears five hundred-dollar bills in two, attempting
to persuade a cabbie to wait for him while he goes to retrieve the satchel
from the riverbank by the border bridge. What seems to compel Moss to
keep the money despite all the trouble it has caused is precisely the power
it confers on him. Carla Jean's complaint that the money is a "false god"
(*No Country*, 182) thus misses the mark. For Moss, the money is desirable
not in itself, but as a means of empowerment.

This empowerment is not only material. The power of the money seems
additionally amplified rather than diminished by the fact that it is dirty,
and that Moss knows with "dead certainty" that "someone was going
to come looking for [it]" (*No Country*, 19). In possession of something
desired by "several someones" (19), Moss's gain means their loss, his
empowerment their impotence. Taking the money, Moss instantaneously
becomes a principal in the battle for its possession. Not only does he
know this, but he also seems to take pleasure in it—as his indirect boasting to both Carla Jean and the teen hitcher would indicate. His decision
thus entails his immediate conversion into a subject of the same ideology
as those who hunt him.

Recalling Rick Wallach's analysis of *Blood Meridian* in his essay "From
Beowulf to *Blood Meridian*: Cormac McCarthy's Demystification of the
Martial Code," one could grasp the ideology to which Moss becomes
subjected as a kind of martial code. Framing his analysis through René
Girard's studies of violence and mimetic desire, Wallach observes that
the martial code "*appears* to reconstitute through a doubling effect [that
Girard] ascribes to mimetic desire" (1998, 114). The moment an individual
mimetically desires the same object as another, each becomes the double
and therefore rival of the other. With desire canalized to take as its object
something that cannot be equally shared, every relationship becomes
structured as antagonistic and every interaction presents the possibility of
violence. There is no way out for the subject of such a structured system.
Any given victory over one rival necessarily leads to a confrontation with
another. Hence, as Wallach suggests, "everything is ultimately sanctified
by and sacrificed to the code"; it "consumes imperatives of nationhood,
blood relations, friendship" (1998, 113). As in *Blood Meridian* (1985), so
it is in *No Country for Old Men*. The roughly 130 years that has elapsed
between the mid-nineteenth-century setting of *Blood Meridian* and the late
twentieth century of Ronald Reagan has changed nothing. The system of
relationships that Moss enters into with his decision to take the money
has the same structure as the one into which the kid stumbles when he
signs with Captain White's filibusters or, subsequently, John Glanton's
gang of contract scalphunters.

Subjects sacrifice everything to the code for the sake of the power that the code offers them in recompense. If Chigurh has the same advantage over Moss as *Blood Meridian*'s Judge Holden has over the kid, it is because like Holden, Chigurh has reflected upon and come to understand the inner workings of the nihilism to which he is subject, including the precise form of power that it offers—*sovereign power*. Michel Foucault has described sovereign power as a twofold, or dissymmetrical, power to decide life and death. As Foucault writes, "The sovereign exercised his right of life only by exercising his right to kill, or by refraining from killing; he evidenced his power over life only through the death he was capable of requiring. The right which was formulated as the "power of life and death" was in reality the right to *take* life or *let* live" (1990, 136). Chigurh's identification as an instrument of sovereign power is clear enough from his ritual coin tosses. It is not by accident that the novel only narrates this ritual twice, to opposite outcomes. Each instance illustrates one of the two aspects of Chigurh's assumed sovereignty. Respecting the gas station proprietor's lucky call, Chigurh reaffirms his right to let the man live, while in Carla Jean's case, he demonstrates his right to take life. Of course, Chigurh also articulates the duality of his sovereign power in his conversation with Moss, promising to let Carla Jean live if Moss brings him the money. "You bring me the money and I'll let her walk. Otherwise she's accountable. The same as you. I dont know if you care about that. But that's the best deal you're going to get. I wont tell you you can save yourself because you cant" (*No Country*, 184). Chigurh goads Moss in a manner corresponding to the Mexican prisoner's treatment of Bell. Unlike Bell, though, Moss takes the bait and makes a counter-threat: "I'm goin to bring you somethin all right. . . . I've decided to make you a special project of mine. You aint goin to have to look for me at all" (185). With this threat, Moss articulates his right to take life, and therefore demonstrates his assumption of sovereign power. He has already demonstrated this assumption when, in ambushing Chigurh in the motel room, he let him live. If this act appears as problematic and unrealistic as the kid's refusal to kill Holden when he has the chance in *Blood Meridian*, it is because it has not been properly framed through the twofold concept of sovereign power. Like the kid, Moss unwisely manifests his sovereignty by exercising his right to refrain from killing. If Chigurh allows himself to manifest this right to let live, he does so only before those who, like the gas station proprietor, do not pose a threat to him as a rival and a double.

INTO THE TRANSCENDENT REACHES

When Foucault reads the history of sovereignty and its theorization, he observes that the sovereign's power extends only over the living. "In the passage from this world to the other," he thus writes, "death was the manner in which a terrestrial sovereignty was relieved by another, singularly more powerful sovereignty" (1990, 138). Limited to a strictly immanent context, the power of the terrestrial sovereign—understood as the right to kill or refrain from killing—is a power exercised by the living over the living. The terrestrial sovereign cannot lay claim on the dead, yet this is precisely what Chigurh does. The sovereign Chigurh attempts to embody is not the terrestrial but the absolute sovereign. As he tells Carla Jean, "Even a nonbeliever might find it useful to model himself after God. Very useful, in fact" (*No Country*, 256). This comment follows upon Chigurh's strange explanation of the reason for his visitation. In coming to kill her, he is fulfilling a promise he made to Moss.

> You give your word to my husband to kill me?
> Yes.
> He's dead. My husband is dead.
> Yes. But I'm not.
> You dont owe nothin to dead people.
> Chigurh cocked his head slightly. No? he said.
> How can you?
> How can you not?
> They're dead.
> Yes. But my word is not dead. Nothing can change that. (255)

The God after which Chigurh models himself approximates the God of orthodox Jewish, Christian, and Islamic theology. He emulates a God who binds himself to His own will and who therefore cannot do, or want anything other, than what he has willed, a supreme arbiter who subsequently rewards or punishes His subjects—alive or dead—according to what they have done or what they can no longer undo. Chigurh's mimesis of absolute sovereign power demonstrates how this power is predicated upon the powerlessness to reverse or negate anything that one has once willed: "I have only one way to live. It I allow for special cases" (*No Country*, 259). Regardless of Moss's death, Chigurh must fulfill his promise to him. Hence Chigurh declares himself to be "at the mercy of the dead" (255).

Upon closer examination, however, this declaration is an inversion of Chigurh's real desire. In his search for absolute sovereign power, Chigurh wishes to have even the dead at his mercy. As the fulfillment of a promise, the act of killing Carla Jean is symbolic. It is an act undertaken for the sake of a third party, an act that is supposed to be witnessed. That the intended witness in this case is dead does not matter. If Chigurh has his way, not even death can secure Moss from further harm. Death only makes Moss all the more powerless to stop what Chigurh forces him to witness. Chigurh's actions suggest a presumption on his part that while the dead may have passed from the sphere of terrestrial reality, they have not passed away from reality altogether and that in some way terrestrial events continue to affect them. Exceeding the bounds of immanence, the nihilism at the heart of the ideology Chigurh personifies spreads into the transcendent reaches of reality. The telos of this ideology therefore involves the annihilation of the dead as much as the living, the annihilation of humanity past, present, and future.[2]

As much as Bell personifies an ideology opposed to Chigurh's nihilism, he nevertheless seems to share many of the same convictions. Most importantly, he displays a remarkably similar attitude toward the dead. The novel first indicates this in the conversation Bell has with his deputy as they survey the scene in the desert. When Wendell makes a disparaging remark about the appearance of the corpses, Bell suggests that "there probably aint no luck in [cussin the dead]" (*No Country*, 73). When Wendell suggests that they were "just a bunch of Mexican drugrunners," Bell responds, "They were. They aint now" (73). When Wendell asks for clarification as to what Bell is saying, Bell responds, "I'm just sayin that whatever they were the only thing they are now is dead" (73). For Bell, the transformation of the "Mexican drugrunners" into "the dead" does not seem to entail the erasure of their being. They continue to possess some kind of reality.

Moreover, Bell also appears to agree with Chigurh that the dead continue to be affected by events in the land of the living. This attitude is of course most poignantly revealed in Bell's description of his ongoing relationship with his dead daughter:

> I talk to my daughter. She would be thirty now. That's all right. I dont care how that sounds. I like talkin to her. Call it superstition or whatever you want. I know that over the years I have give her the heart I always wanted for myself and that's all right. That's why I listen to her. I know I'll always get the best from her. It dont get mixed up with my own ignorance or my own meanness. I know how that sounds and I guess I'd have to say that I dont care. . . . I listen to what she says and what she says makes good sense. I wish she'd say more of it. I can use all the help I can get. (285)

With this strange confession, Bell sets forth not only the obligation the living have to the dead, but also the task demanded of the living to fulfill this obligation. Giving his daughter the heart he always wanted for himself, Bell constructs the task of the living as the completing or perfecting of the dead, of restoring to the dead the potentialities from which death has separated them. Had Bell's daughter lived, she would have been thirty. Death deprived her of the chance to realize in time the potentialities of her being. By virtue of the relationship he establishes with her, Bell gives her back the chance, breathing potentiality back into her being simply by his mindful remembrance. By asserting that she responds with good sense and useful advice, Bell constructs his act of talking to her as the establishment of a circuit between the living and the dead, thus empowering them both.

The goals of the ideologies McCarthy's allegorical narrative sets into opposition could not therefore be more contrary. While Chigurh's nihilism seeks absolutely to consume the being of the living and the dead, Bell's fustian ideology functions to consolidate humanity past, present, and future into a self-empowering collective. Bell counters Chigurh's promise to exercise absolute sovereign power with a promise of his own. It is a promise of the kind Bell saw expressed in the stone trough of the French stonemason whom he admired so much. *"So I think about him settin there with his hammer and his chisel, maybe just an hour or two after supper, I dont know. And I have to say that the only thing I can think is that there was some sort of promise in his heart. And I dont have no intentions of carvin a stone water trough. But I would like to be able to make that kind of promise. I think that's what I would like most of all"* (*No Country*, 308). It may well be that McCarthy inserts an element of parody into his narrative by effectively juxtaposing the eternal golden bird of "Byzantium" with the rough hewn trough in wartime France. Nevertheless, the power that Bell searches for is ultimately poetic. It is a power to make an artifact of inherently social value, like a stone water trough, or like an allegory that presents the manner in which nihilism can be fought, in which a different kind of narrative can begin.

NOTES

1. Historically speaking, many prominent theorists of allegory have thus located the genre's origins in the conflict between antiquity and Christianity. In *Allegory and Violence*, for example, Gordon Teskey argues that the specific historical conditions in which allegory first appears "were brought about by the convulsive effect of a major ideological change: the transition from paganism to Christianity, from a culture of the numen to a culture of the sign. Allegory was imaginatively possible only after a violent purging of the classical gods from the world" (1996, 34).

2. That this nihilism does not restrict itself to humanity but also uses humanity to destroy other forms of existence is clear when we consider other McCarthy novels. As Mr. Johnson ruminates in *Cities of the Plain* (1998), "It had always seemed to me that something can live and die but that the kind of thing that they were was always there. I didnt know you could poison that. I aint heard a wolf howl in thirty odd years. I dont know where youd go to hear one. There may not be any such a place" (126).

REFERENCES

Bunyan, John. 1996. *The Pilgrim's Progress*. Ed. Tom Griffith. Hertfordshire: Wordsworth Editions Limited.

Fletcher, Angus. 1964. *Allegory: The Theory of a Symbolic Mode*. Ithaca, NY: Cornell University Press.

Foucault, Michel. 1990. *The History of Sexuality: An Introduction*. Trans. Robert Hurley. New York: Vintage.

Honig, Edwin. 1966. *Dark Conceit: The Making of Allegory*. New York: Oxford University Press.

Jarrett, Robert. 2005. "Genre, Voice and Ethos: McCarthy's Perverse Thriller." *Cormac McCarthy Journal* 5, no. 1 (Spring): 74–96.

Madsen, Deborah. 1996. *Allegory in America: From Puritanism to Postmodernism*. Houndmills, Basingstoke, Hampshire: Macmillan Press.

McCarthy, Cormac. 1985. *Blood Meridian, or, The Evening Redness in the West*. New York: Vintage.

———. 1994. *The Crossing*. New York: Alfred A. Knopf.

———. 1998. *Cities of the Plain*. New York: Alfred A. Knopf.

———. 2005. *No Country for Old Men*. New York: Alfred A. Knopf.

Spenser, Edmund. 1970. *The Faerie Queene*. In *Poetical Works*, ed. J. C. Smith and E. de Selincourt. Oxford: Oxford University Press.

Teskey, Gordon. 1996. *Allegory and Violence*. Ithaca, NY: Cornell University Press.

Wallach, Rick. 1998. "From *Beowulf* to *Blood Meridian*: Cormac McCarthy's Demystification of the Martial Code." *Southern Quarterly* 36, no. 4 (Summer): 113–20.

Yeats, William Butler. 1990. "Sailing to Byzantium." In *Collected Poems*, ed. Augustine Martin, 199–200. London: Arena Books.

5

✛

Oedipus Rests: Mimesis and Allegory in *No Country for Old Men*

John Cant

This is a goddamned homicidal lunatic, Ed Tom.
Yeah. I don't think he's a lunatic though.
Well what would you call him?
I don't know.

—Cormac McCarthy, *No Country for Old Men*

"Never trust the artist. Trust the tale." D. H. Lawrence's dictum appeared in his *Studies in Classic American Literature*, now something of a classic itself. His advice has been considered sage, even by those of us who have come to trust neither artist nor tale nor indeed language itself. Our opportunities to mistrust McCarthy have been severely limited by his studied avoidance of utterance outside his published works. However I suggest that his two published interviews contain remarks which are exceptions to Lawrence's rule.[1]

The first of these contained McCarthy's much quoted acknowledgement "books are made out of other books" and that he considered this to be "an ugly fact" (Woodward 1992, 36). The eclecticism of McCarthy's writing, the novels in particular, has been remarked upon and analyzed at length elsewhere; his intertextual sources have been noted as extraordinarily varied, but little attention seems to have been paid to his use of the word *ugly*. One of those sources is T. S. Eliot, whose use of text and imagery from the past, the "fragments . . . shored against my ruin" (1982,

79), seems to be accomplished lovingly, the ugliness lying in the modernity against which Eliot rails. I suggest that McCarthy's angst is that of a writer who feels the need to establish his own voice within a tradition that intimidates as much as it inspires. Flannery O'Connor writes, "The presence alone of Faulkner in our midst makes a great difference in what the writer can and cannot permit himself to do. Nobody wants his mule and wagon stalled on the same track the Dixie Limited is roaring down" (1999, 45).

Bakhtin wrote of the writer's struggle to go beyond the literary tradition, what he called "the voice of the fathers," and this seems an even more appropriate context in which to consider McCarthy's work as a whole. The Southern cultural tradition in which McCarthy spent most of his formative years placed considerable emphasis on paternal authority. As Robert Jarrett notes in his book on McCarthy for Twayne's U.S. authors, "The weak, dead or dying fathers of McCarthy's fiction point towards an imaginative repudiation of the central importance of patriarchal father and family in Southern culture and the South's heroic myth of its history figured in the revered patriarch—Robert E. Lee or Colonel Sartoris—of the Confederate Lost Cause" (1997, 23).

Both classical and Christian traditions were influential in creating that tradition; Christian founding mythology is associated with the garden, and George Guillemin has interpreted McCarthy's works (prior to *No Country for Old Men*) in terms of pastoral and ecopastoral melancholy. The myth of Oedipus forms part of the classical foundation and in his *Oedipus Philosopher* (1993), Jean-Joseph Goux interprets Oedipus's solving of the riddle of the Sphinx as the casting down by patriarchy of the old order of the Goddess; Oedipus, the first philosopher, institutes the symbolic order. With patriarchy's granting of subjectivity and agency to the male, conflict between father and son becomes one of the continuing characteristics of the patriarchal paradigm. Oedipal conflict is very strongly apparent in McCarthy's work; however, this aspect has received comparatively little attention. Occasional articles have considered it, but on the whole critical attention has lain elsewhere. John Wesley Rattner grows up indifferent to the fate of his absent father, killed in self-defense by Marion Sylder, the boy's paternal surrogate; Culla Holme abandons his new-born son in the forest in a tale that bears many parallels with the Oedipus myth itself; Lester Ballard's father hangs himself, leaving his young son bereft of emotional and material patrimony; Cornelius Suttree rejects his father's bourgeois values, lives the life of the prodigal son, and is estranged from his own son; the kid's father lies in drunken stupor, his neglect driving his son into the Western wilderness where he encounters "a parricide hanged at a crossroads"(*Blood Meridian* [1990], 5) and the ultimate devouring father in the person of the judge; John Grady Cole's flight into Mexico is motivated in part by the emotional detachment of his dying father—he competes with his paternal surrogate, Don Hector, for the love of the daughter rather than the mother but the outcome is similarly destructive; and Billy Parham flees his father's authority, feels responsible for his death, and spends his life trying to live up to the impossible ideal that the father represented. *The Crossing* (1995) contains hints that Boyd was the true rebel of the family but this aspect of the story is not given emphasis; only in *Cities of the Plain* (1998) does the Oedipal strain of McCarthy's work begin to lose intensity, but even here John Grady's surrogate father, the rancher Mac MacDonald, fails to protect the headstrong boy from himself. In *The Gardener's Son* (1996) the Oedipal theme is represented even more strongly than in the novels, and it reaches a peak in *The Stonemason* (1994c). Even "A Drowning Incident" (1960), one of the McCarthy short stories published in the University of Tennessee magazine (the *Phoenix*), features a small boy finding in the local creek the rotting corpses of puppies, born to the family dog and drowned by his father; he fishes one of them out, takes it home, places it beside his baby sister in her cot, and waits for the father to return. Personal circumstances may well motivate such an insistent theme, but McCarthy is such an accomplished and self-aware writer, so obviously well versed in the various theories that inform analysis of literary texts that it seems inconceivable that he should have structured his work in this consistent manner without having some specifically literary purpose.

Thus the "ugliness" that McCarthy remarks with respect to the intertextuality that he knows to be both unavoidable and a rich source of imagery, narrative, and language, can indeed be interpreted as a product of the rage of the rebellious writer, seeking to usurp the place of those literary forebears, to kill the father and take his place, to still the voice of authority as John Grady stills that of Eduardo in their fight to the death in the alley in Cuidad Juarez. This interpretation is supported by two further aspects of McCarthy's work: (1) in "quoting" the works of the past, he frequently inverts or transforms their meanings or values,[2] and (2) in the confident ambition and intellectual scope of his works, he takes upon himself the task of challenging canonical writers and contemplating the great questions of human existence, a task that has ceased to be seen as lying within the compass of most contemporary novelists.[3] While news of the death of the grand narratives will certainly have reached El Paso, McCarthy continues to demonstrate his rejection of this notion of the diminution of literature's purpose.

What distinguishes *No Country for Old Men* (2005) from the rest of McCarthy's oeuvre is the extent to which the Oedipal theme is in abeyance. The Oedipal fire seems to have died down at last and the lessening of intensity that characterized *Cities of the Plain* has been carried to what may prove to be a conclusion. The principal structural means by which this development is made possible has two aspects. First and crucially, Sheriff Bell is no Oedipus, no wayward rebellious son fleeing paternal authority and desperate to make his own way in the world. On the contrary, Bell is himself the father in this text and an aging father at that. In addition he has the father's voice and the narrative's italicized sections are in that voice. He speaks to us directly and in so doing reveals the other structural means of conveying the fading of the Oedipal theme. Bell speaks from the heart; he examines his own life, beliefs, and values, measuring them against his experience of the world. In other words he conveys that new thing in McCarthy—the revelation of the inner man, of character, person- ality, and belief. In previous texts only Suttree has come close to being revealed from within in this way;[4] indeed given the allegorical nature of so much of McCarthy's writing, the inner lives of most of his characters are not revealed at all since they exist as types,[5] the power of their stories lying in the intensity of the narrative, the dynamism of the action, the convincing rendering of dialogue, and the vivid use of language—lyrical, majestic, and colloquial by turns. To this can be added the power of the allegorical meanings themselves[6] and the multitude of other theories and ideas that McCarthy weaves into his works, works united by the concep- tion of narrative as the "category of categories" (McCarthy, 1995, 155) conveyed in the words of the ex-priest in the church at Huisiachepic in *The Crossing*, "Rightly heard all tales are one" (143).

What Bell expresses are the thoughts and emotions of an aging man, a father whose only child is dead: *"Me and my wife has been married thirty-one years. No children. We lost a girl but I wont talk about that"* (*No Country*, 66). He knows a father's grief, none greater than that due to the loss of a child. The poignancy of this loss is subtly accentuated a full 215 pages later: *"I could stand back off and smile about such thoughts as them but I still have em. I don't make excuses for the way I think. Not no more. I talk to my daughter. She would be thirty now. That's all right. I don't care how that sounds. I like talking to her. Call it superstition or whatever you want. I know over the years I have give her the heart I always wanted for myself and that's all right. That's why I listen to her. I know I'll always get the best from her"* (283–84). Nothing could be further from the Oedipal rage of Suttree, the kid, Blevins, or Boyd Parham. Of course the two passages here quoted contradict each other. Close reading of Bell's monologues reveals that this is a pattern that runs throughout the novel. Many of his early pronouncements, often express- ing the confident simplicities of the "good old boy" of Southwestern tradition, are contradicted by later passages revealing that Bell's simple faith has not stood the test of bitter experience. Like so many of McCar- thy's protagonists, Bell finds that the world deals harshly with the myths that his culture has provided as his guide through life. His impotence in the face of the drug wars, funded, as he rightly remarks, *"with our own money"* (298), forces him to decide to quit his life's work as sheriff, but his meditation on this event concerns his life as a whole. He has reflected on his "cowardice"[7] in deserting his comrades in action in World War II, his guilt at being forced to accept a decoration for this and for allowing this mark of "heroism" to count in his favor when running for sheriff in the first place. He has complained that the country has gone from being a place where folks could live in peace to being a place of violence and insecurity, but later acknowledges that *"this country has a strange kind of history and a damned bloody one too"* (279). He knows that *"there's peace officers along this border getting rich off of narcotics"* and that this *"is just a damned abomination"* (212). He has discovered that Wells, somehow involved in the slaughter that has overwhelmed his world, was "a ex-army colonel . . . Regular army. Twenty-four years service" (191).[8]

He notes that the drug traders had found it prudent to assassinate a federal judge. But his act of acceptance of his own "failure" expresses the wisdom of resignation rather than the folly of despair:

> Part of it was I always thought I could at least someway put things right and I guess I just don't feel that way no more. I don't know what I do feel like. I feel like them old people I was talkin about. Which aint goin to get better neither. I'm bein asked to stand for something that I don't have the same belief in I once did. Asked to believe in something I might not hold with the way I once did. That's the problem. I failed at it even when I did. Now I've seen it held to the light. Seen any number of believers fall away. I've been forced to look at it again and I've been forced to look at myself. For better or for worse I do not know. I don't know that I would even advise you to throw in with me, and I never had them sorts of doubts before. If I'm wiser in the ways of the world it come at a price. Pretty good price too. When I told her I was quittin she at first didn't take me to mean it literally but I told her I did so mean it. I told her I hoped the people of this county would have better sense than to even vote for me. I told her it didn't feel right takin their money. She said well you don't mean that and I told her I meant it ever word. . . . And she smiled and she said: You aim to quit while you're ahead? And I said no mam I just aim to quit. I aint ahead by a damn sight. I never will be. (*No Country*, 291)

Bell's speech expands on Billy Parham's conclusion at the end of *Cities of the Plain*: "In everything that he'd ever thought about the world and about his life in it he'd been wrong" (266). Bell will survive because he has the consolation of his love for his wife, a love that he perceives to be returned; there is no Oedipal contest in relation to the faithful Loretta. The fading of the Oedipal structuring of McCarthy's texts is signified very powerfully in Bell's recollection of his father: *"My daddy always told me just to do the best you knew how and to tell the truth. He said there was nothing to set a man's mind at ease like wakin up in the morning and not havin to decide who you were.*

And if you done something wrong just stand up and say you done it and say
you're sorry and get on with it. Don't haul stuff around with you. I guess all that
sounds pretty simple today. Even to me" (*No Country*, 245). Bell understands
the limitations of his father's notions. He acknowledges that he rebelled
somewhat himself: "*I might have strayed from all of that some as a younger*
man." The crucial point is that now he sees things differently: "*but when*
I got back on that road I pretty much decided not to quit it again and I didn't"
(245). The contrast with Suttree's protestations could not be more vivid:
"In my father's last letter he said that the world is run by those willing to
take the responsibility for the running of it. If it is life that you feel you
are missing I can tell you where to find it. In the law courts, in business,
in government. There is nothing occurring in the streets. Nothing but a
dumbshow composed of the helpless and the impotent. *From all old seamy*
throats of elders, musty books, I've salvaged not a word" (*Suttree* [1989], 13–14;
emphasis mine).

This contrast is rendered conclusively in Bell's dream, recounted on
the book's final page and symbolizing the passing of the Oedipal turn in
McCarthy's works:

> It was like we was both back in older times and I was on horseback goin through the
> mountains of a night. Goin through this pass in the mountains. It was cold and there
> was snow on the ground and he rode past me and kept on goin. Never said nothing.
> He just rode on past and he had this blanket wrapped around him and he had his head
> down and when he rode past I seen he was carryin fire in a horn the way people used
> to do and I could see the horn from the light inside of it. About the color of the moon.
> And in the dream I knew that he was goin on ahead and that he was fixin to make a
> fire somewhere out there in all that dark and all that cold and I knew that whenever
> I got there he would be there. And then I woke up. (*No Country*, 304)

The phallic symbolism of the horn of fire stands in this case for life, con-
tinuity, and civilization. Thus the novel closes with an image that is in
contrast to its other phallic signifier, the ubiquitous gun, instrument of
equally ubiquitous death.

What can this dying away of such a consistent theme mean for us
in reading McCarthy's work? It is reasonable to suppose that it simply
reflects the fact that he is himself now a man approaching old age. In
biblical terms, always significant for McCarthy,[9] he has passed his allot-
ted three-score years and ten. But the sense of McCarthy as a critic of his
culture and his times remains as strong as ever. If my interpretation is
correct, then we can assume that he has begun to feel that he no longer
has to strive to usurp the voice of the literary fathers and that his own
voice can now be heard clearly, even if he remains aware of his debt to
"other books."

Evidence of this hard-won confidence in matching his own voice with those of the past lies in the genre and style of *No Country for Old Men*. No attempt is made to disguise the novel's generic forebears: it is clearly related to the "hard-boiled" school of Chandler, Hammett, and, more latterly, Ellroy. Its fierce pace and the tight, minimalist style of the action sequences make it a compelling read. I completed it in two sessions, only interrupted by the need for sleep, and many other readers have made similar claims. Although he seems to have largely abandoned the complex, highly wrought, and often lyrical prose of his previous novels, in this latest work McCarthy continues to match form and content in a manner that produces a highly polished result, and like all highly polished things, its glistening surface is raised on an adamantine base and those that feature Chigurh have the spare precision of the killer himself:

> The headlights picked up some kind of large bird sitting on the aluminium bridgerail up ahead and Chigurh pushed the button to let the window down. Cool air coming in off the lake. He took the pistol from beside the box and cocked and levelled it out the window, resting the barrel on the rearview mirror. The pistol had been fitted with a silencer sweated onto the end of the barrel. The silencer was made out of brass mapp-gas burners fitted into a hairspray can and the whole thing stuffed with fibreglass roofing insulation and painted flat black. He fired just as the bird spread its wings. (*No Country*, 96–97)

It is significant that Chigurh does not know what kind of bird this is; the contrast with Bell is acute.

No Country for Old Men is not composed entirely of action sequences, of chase, flight, and death. As already noted, Bell's italicized passages are meditations in his own voice and in the relaxed and laconic idiom of his time and place. The contrast in styles reflects the contrast in the content and meaning of the two aspects of the text. A comparison with Chandler's *The Big Sleep* (1992; originally published in 1939) is appropriate, the whole narrative of which is given in the first person and in the voice of Marlowe. Unlike Bell, Marlowe succeeds in his pursuit of the truth and is able to find and dispatch the criminals who inhabit his world. McCarthy also eschews Chandler's radical misogyny; there is no femme fatale in *No Country for Old Men*, quite the contrary. In other respects, however, the two novels bear direct comparison. The economy of style is similar. Both portray a world of ubiquitous corruption and criminal violence; in each case the roots of this corruption lie in an ill-founded belief that human appetites can be controlled by a legal prohibition that large numbers of people find irrelevant to their own experience,[10] a fact that Bell does not understand.

Finally the "big sleep" is, of course, the sleep of death. McCarthy's intertextuality may be more overt, but he clearly has the confidence to step outside the limitations of the generic form; both these factors reinforce the notion that he no longer feels the "anxiety of influence" (Bloom 1997) to the extent that he once did. This idea is further supported by his choice of title: "No country for old men" has a poetic note that suggests quotation. Even those unfamiliar with its source may well be stimulated to seek it out it, and in the Google age, it is not hard to find.[11] Thus we may conclude that from the outset McCarthy makes his source accessible; his use of it is overt, unabashed—*ugly* has ceased to seem an appropriate word. We may compare it with a previous "quotation" from Yeats, insinuated into the thoughts of Ather Ownby in *The Orchard Keeper* (1994a): "If I was a younger man, he told himself, I would move to them mountains. I would find me a clearwater branch and build me a log house with a fireplace. And my bees would make black mountain honey. And I wouldn't care for no man" (55).

Although recognized by literary scholars, the relation to Yeats's "The Lake Isle of Innisfree" (1978a) is oblique to say the least:

> I will arise and go now, and go to Innisfree,
> And a small cabin build there, of clay and wattles made:
> Nine bean-rows will I have there, a hive for the honey-bee,
> And live alone in the bee-loud glade. (lines 1–4)

As I initially suggested, McCarthy's second Woodward interview also contains a remark that, in my view, escapes Lawrence's dictum. In discussing the themes of his latest work, McCarthy points up the centrality of the fact of death: "Death is a major issue in the world. For you, for me, for all of us. It just is. To not be able to talk about it is very odd" (Woodward 2005, 104). It can come as no surprise to learn that a man into his eighth decade should feel the need to contemplate mortality. We may presume that Sheriff Bell, himself well on in years (he was a young man in World War II), is similarly aware; indeed given the circumstance of his profession as they are presented in the text he could not fail to be acutely so, even if he were a young man in his prime. It is reasonable to presume that this has been responsible in no small part for his period of reflection and his decision to pass judgment upon the manner in which he has lived up to his ideals. But all McCarthy's works have featured death to a greater or lesser extent. In *Suttree* in particular Suttree himself is obsessed by the image of his stillborn twin sibling; life and death battle it out for him; life wins, but it is a close run thing as he almost succumbs to typhoid. Of course it is easy to see that *No Country for Old Men* features a great many deaths, most of them violent and not a few due to the relentless and unstoppable efforts of

Chigurh. I will return to his significance later, but first I want to consider other aspects of the text's representation of mortality.

In fact death is mentioned very frequently throughout and in many different circumstances. The first words, spoken by Bell, are "*I sent one boy to the gas chamber at Huntsville.*" The young man had murdered a girlfriend, "*had been planning to kill somebody for as long a he could remember. Said if they turned him out he would do it again*" (*No Country*, 1). Moss tells Carla Jean, "If I don't come back tell Mother I love her"; she rejects the joke: "Your mother's dead Llewelyn" (22). Moss's decision to take the money is clearly the result of a death wish. As he returns bringing water to the wounded drug dealer (already dead of course), compounding his initial suicidal action, he feels himself "a trespasser. Among the dead. Don't get weird on me, he said. You ain't one of em. Not yet" (24). He remarks that he is "too dumb to live" (25). As the killers search for Moss in the darkness, he asserts, "Now you're goin to die" (27). And shortly afterward, "You need to be put out of your misery. Be the best thing for everybody" (26). Like Bell, Moss has experienced death in war: "Waiting. He'd had this feeling before. In another country. He never thought he have it again" (28). When Carla Jean asks after the truck, Moss answers, "Gone the way of all flesh. Nothin's forever" (47). Bell speaks of attending an execution and opines that "*the ones that really ought to be on death row will never make it*" (58). I have already noted that Bell's daughter is dead; how or why we do not know. As he meditates on his family history, he states that "*the dead have more claims on you than what you might want to admit to or even what you might know about and them claims can be very strong indeed.*"[12] He goes on to relate a newspaper story about "*this couple in California they would rent out rooms to old people and then kill em and bury em in the yard and cash their social security checks. They'd torture em first, I don't know why*" (120). Carla Jean's mother has cancer; by the end of the book she is dead: "Her funeral was on a cold and windy day in March" (249). Bell relates his wartime trauma: "*I lost a whole squad of men. . . . They died and I got a medal*" (191). He considers the social aspect of death as old men must: "*I've lost a lot of friends over these last few years. Not all of em older than me neither. One of the things you realise about getting older is that not everbody is goin to get older with you*" (212). Moss tells his hitchhiker that he is wearing his wild boar's tusk for "a dead somebody" (221). In warning his young companion he is actually describing his own death-haunted behavior: "Most people'll run from their own mother to get to hug death by the neck. They cant wait to see him" (230). Bell's conversation with Ellis is punctuated by references to death. The man who shot Ellis "died in prison" (203). Harold was killed in the war, "dyin in a ditch somewhere. . . . Seventeen year old" (264). Uncle Mac "was shot down on his own porch in Hudspeth County" (265). "This country will kill you in a heartbeat and still people love it"

(267). And all this excludes the slaughter carried out by Chigurh and the drug gangs: *No Country for Old Men* is indeed a death-haunted text.

George Guillemin identifies McCarthy's texts as essentially melancholic. He quotes Tim Poland, compellingly in my opinion, to the effect that the site of the novels moves from the South to the West because "rather than a landscape [the South] that exists as a setting for human action and is imprinted with human qualities, the landscape in much western writing functions more like a character in itself and imprints on the human characters its own qualities" (Guillemin 2004, 37).[13] The desert landscape may be thought to have imprinted itself on Bell and Moss both, but with differing results. The desert's indifference to human life is challenged by Moss with fatal results: for the reflective Bell the consequence is "defeat. It was being beaten. More bitter to him than death" (*No Country*, 301). If McCarthy has shaken off the melancholy associated with the task of challenging the literary fathers he continues to express the twin griefs resulting from his vision of human insignificance in an indifferent universe and the consequences of his culture's overreaching gnosis. As ever he counters this melancholy by expressing it in vital and compelling literary form.

The ironic paradox of this vitality has been apparent in much of McCarthy's fiction. Much of what he has written is allegorical in character. Figures such as Judge Holden and the "grim triune" of *Outer Dark* are diminished by attempts to read them mimetically, so we turn our attention at last to Chigurh. He is indomitable, all-seeing, and entirely without humor or sexuality. He kills without emotion, men and women alike. Drug runners, other hit men, policemen, motel desk clerks, corporate executives, someone who insults him in a bar, motorists encountered by chance—all are one to him. The only way to survive an encounter with him is by the toss of a coin—in other words, by chance. He (mis)understands his use of language to be absolute: "I don't have some way to put it. That's the way it is" (*No Country*, 52). His eyes are "at once glistening and totally opaque. Like wet stones" (53), no "windows of the soul" are these. He is impervious to temperature: "It was cold out on the barrial and he had no jacket but he didn't seem to notice" (56). His weapon of choice is the "humane killer" used to slaughter animals; to him humans, birds, and animals are equals. Hurt in a shootout, he treats his own wounds: "Other than a little light sweat on his forehead there was little evidence that his labors had cost him anything at all" (160). When Wells tells him, "You're not outside of death," he speaks more than he knows. Chigurh replies truthfully, "It doesn't mean to me what it means to you" (173). He is equally truthful when asserts that he is "completely reliable and completely honest" (248). He is not boasting when he says "I have no enemies. I don't permit such a thing"

(249). As he explains to Carla Jean (Chigurh chooses to meet his victims face to face whenever he can, to engage with them in a discourse of life and death), once he has decided on a victim he cannot change his mind: "My word is not dead. Nothing can change that" (251). "You're asking me to make myself vulnerable and that I can never do. I have only one way to live. It doesn't allow for special cases. A coin toss perhaps. In this case to small purpose. Most people don't believe that there can be such a person. You can see what a problem that must be for them. How to prevail over that which you refuse to acknowledge the existence of. . . . When I came into your life your life was over" (255–56).

Although McCarthy gives Chigurh human form, he denies him human qualities. In other words, Chigurh is not to be read as a human being: he is another of those allegorical figures that McCarthy has woven into previous texts, the judge being first among them.[14] Chigurh's actions and words make his meaning abundantly clear; he is death personified. This explains why it is that Moss does not kill Chigurh when he has him under his gun in the Eagle Pass motel (*No Country*, 108–9). You cannot kill death; even chance and irony fail to accomplish this. Chigurh walks away from the car crash in Midland; it is the drugged boys in the Buick who die. It also explains the constant references to chance and luck in the novel, for who knows when death comes?[15] A single example will suffice, but there are many more. At the Eagle Pass motel by the merest chance (from the nightclerk's own point of view), "The nightclerk got killed. About as bad a piece of luck as you could have I reckon" (131–32).

What then is the category into which we must place *No Country for Old Men*? I suggest that it is a hybrid in at least two ways. First generically: the relation to the hard-boiled crime novel has been commented on above, and by other critics. The cars, automatic weapons, motel rooms, corporate offices, and city locations are the province of the genre developed by Chandler, Hammett, Cain, and Ellroy and given cinematic form as film noir and its derivatives. But the sheriff and his deputies, the hunter Moss, the riders on horseback, and the landscape of desert, plain, and river are, of course, elements of the Western, and the Southwest is the quintessential location of its mythic history. The gangster film and the Western are the two cinematic genres that are specifically and uniquely American and they both have their roots in literature. It can be argued that the gangster genre is the twentieth-century urban equivalent of the Western. McCarthy interweaves both genres in this latest novel. That interweaving provides the form for his other hybridization. He combines the mimetic and the allegorical as he weaves together the musings of the realistically human Bell and his one-dimensional opaque opponent. It is this interweaving that lifts the novel from being a simple but utterly compelling "pulp fiction" read, relying for its success on a racy narrative and a spare, highly polished, minimalistic style and turns it into something more complex and satisfying. Bell is forced to contemplate the approach of the one certain thing in human life. His retrospective on his own life forces him to admit, like all McCarthy's "heroes," that there are no heroes and that the culture that taught him to believe in them, and that he could become one of them, was false. Above all he has to contemplate what the American West has come to and to see the fate, allegorized in the person of Chigurh, of the place that Mrs. Jorgensen, the pioneer wife in John Ford's *The Searchers* (1956), claimed would one day be "a fine good place to be."

NOTES

1. Both interviews were with Richard B. Woodward (1992, 2005).

2. An example: the rushing of the hogs over the bluff in *Outer Dark* (1994b, 216–19) is drawn from the story of the Gadarene swine in the New Testament. In the biblical version Christ destroyed evil spirits by casting them out of their human location and into the pigs. McCarthy depicts the "evil spirits" as remaining in the drovers as they blame Culla for the stampede and seek to lynch him.

3. Consider, for example, the words of the "narrator," met by Billy Parham at the end of *Cities of the Plain*: "Each man is the bard of his own existence. This is how he is joined to the world. For escaping from the world's dream of him this is at once his penalty and his reward" (203). These are not the words of a writer lacking in philosophical ambition.

4. And Ather Ownby, to a very limited extent. See note 14.

5. A fact pointed out by numerous critics.

6. See Guillemin's analysis of various examples in *The Pastoral Vision of Cormac McCarthy* (2004).

7. As he sees it. He is hard on himself as Ellis remarks.

8. We know, but Bell does not, that Wells and Chigurh are acquainted. Both are associated, one way or another, with the Metacumbe Petroleum Company of Houston. McCarthy makes clear the universal nature of the narcotics industry and its interpenetration of all aspects of life. The international drug trade reportedly has the second largest financial turnover in the world—after the oil industry.

9. The significance lies in the language and imagery of the King James Version rather than any religious interpretation.

10. In this respect *No Country for Old Men* refers back to *The Orchard Keeper* (1994a). Marion Sylder's job as a whiskey runner "had gone off the market December fifth 1933" (32). He was able to return to Red Branch and continue his vocation because Knoxville remained "dry."

11. The reference is "That is no country for old men," line 1 of Yeats (1978b, 82).

12. Ownby's memories of his distant and unhappy past are, like Bell's, rendered in italics, in contrast to most of the rest of the text of *The Orchard Keeper*.

13. Guillemin is quoting from Poland (1991, 37).

14. First in significance, not in order of appearance.

15. "Somewhere in the gray wood by the river is the huntsman and in the brooming corn and in the castellated press of cities. His work lies all wheres and his hounds tire not. I have seen them in a dream, slaverous and wild and their eyes crazed with ravening for souls in this world. Fly them" (*Suttree*, 471).

REFERENCES

Bloom, Harold. 1997. *The Anxiety of Influence: A Theory of Poetry*. New York: Oxford University Press.

Chandler, Raymond. 1992. *The Big Sleep*. London: Penguin.

Eliot, T. S. 1982. *The Waste Land*. In *Selected Poems*, 61–86. London: Faber.

Goux, Jean-Joseph. 1993. *Oedipus Philosopher*. Trans. Porter, C. Stanford: Stanford University Press.

Guillemin, George. 2004. *The Pastoral Vision of Cormac McCarthy*. College Station: Texas A&M University Press.

Jarrett, Robert L. 1997. *Cormac McCarthy*. New York: Twayne.

Lawrence, D. H. 1924. *Studies in Classic American Literature*. London: Heinemann.

McCarthy, Cormac. 1960. "A Drowning Incident." *Phoenix*, University of Tennessee Magazine, Knoxville.

———. 1989. *Suttree*. London: Picador.

———. 1990. *Blood Meridian, or, The Evening Redness in the West*. London: Picador.

———. 1993. *All the Pretty Horses*. London: Picador.

———. 1994a. *The Orchard Keeper*. London: Picador.

———. 1994b. *Outer Dark*. London: Picador.

———. 1994c. *The Stonemason*. Hopewell, NJ: Ecco Press.

———. 1995. *The Crossing*. London: Picador.

———. 1996. *The Gardener's Son*. Hopewell, NJ: Ecco Press.

———. 1998. *Cities of the Plain*. London: Picador.

———. 2005. *No Country for Old Men*. Review edition.

O'Connor, Flannery. 1999. "Some Aspects of the Grotesque in Southern Fiction." In *Mystery and Manners*, 36–50. New York: Noonday.

Poland, Tim. 1991. "'A Relative to All That Is': The Eco-Hero in Western American Literature." *Western American Literature* 26, no. 3 (Fall): 195–208.

The Searchers. 1956. Dir. John Ford. C. V. Whitney Pictures.

Woodward, Richard. 1992. "Cormac McCarthy's Venomous Fiction." *New York Times Magazine*, April 19, 28–31.

———. 2005. "Cormac Country." *Vanity Fair*, August, 98+.

Yeats, William B. 1978a. "The Lake Isle of Innisfree." In *The Oxford Book of Twentieth Century English Verse*, ed. Philip Larkin, 75. Oxford: Oxford University Press.

———. 1978b. "Sailing to Byzantium." In *The Oxford Book of Twentieth Century English Verse*, ed. Philip Larkin, 77. Oxford: Oxford University Press.

6

✛

Genre, Voice, and Ethos: McCarthy's Perverse "Thriller"

Robert Jarrett

No Country for Old Men (2005) operates on two distinct levels: first, it mimics the popular thriller while deconstructing the narrative and metaphysical assumptions of the genre. Second, it is a metaphysical novel that interrogates the real, questioning whether a narrative of the contemporary world should be grounded in the natural, in an existential notion of free choice, or in some conception of the historical—history defined primarily as a function of economic forces or perhaps a new providential history written by a worldly will that manipulates these forces.

No Country imitates both the novel of detection and the postmodern gothic crime drama, each with its distinct plot and metaphysical assumptions. If the detection of evil is central to both forms, in the novel of detection—in Thomas Harris's *Silence of the Lambs* (1988), in Patricia Cornwell's novels, and in other forensic thrillers—the awareness of the forensic detective interprets the semiotic clues left by the serial killer. In these novels the confrontation with an ostensibly supernatural evil is progressively psychologized and the serial killer's violence is progressively reduced to a language that expresses his or her psychological trauma. The threat of metaphysical evil is thus naturalized, as in Ann Radcliffe's late eighteenth-century gothic.

The mode of the postmodern crime gothic reaches its exemplary popular form in John Grisham's early trilogy of legal fictions: *The Pelican Brief* (1992), *The Client* (1993), and *The Firm* (1991). The trilogy is based on the formula of young, naïve, unprotected protagonists who unwittingly discover, then confront, an institutionalized evil by fleeing it and thus exposing it in the open. In *The Pelican Brief*, evil takes the form of a violent political conspiracy between agents of the executive branch and its corporate financiers. In *The Client* a youth is trapped between organized crime and a remorseless prosecutor who blackmails his testimony as a means to political prominence. In *The Firm* a young lawyer recognizes that the eminently respectable corporate law firm that hired him is laundering money for organized crime. In the earlier gothic romance, the threat of the demonic functions to expose the insufficiency of innocence, whether sexual or moral, to comprehend the unrestricted will to power of the European past. This power is represented in the aristocratic and the clerical estates whose social power was relatively unrestricted by law. If we may refer again to the gothic of Ann Radcliffe, in the key recognition scene an evil whose source appears to be supernatural is reduced to a villainy that has concealed the natural within the trappings of the supernatural. In his sociological analysis of religion in *The Sacred Canopy*, Peter Berger (1967) notes that in combination with bourgeois capitalism, the Protestant Reformation successfully desacralized the universe, reducing the panoply of saints to the Trinity, exorcizing the demon world, substituting the priesthood of the believer for the intercession of church and church hierarchy, and so on. In similar fashion, the Radcliffean gothic and the classical novel of detection expose evil as a psychological or biological function of the will to power. Grisham's thrillers debunk the "legal fictions" of liberalism: lawyers as ethical forces in society, the law and the courts functioning as forces to inhibit unrestrained accumulation of power in the hands of corporate or crime syndicates. Nevertheless, at the narrative's end, order is symbolically restored, after the open exposure of institutionalized evil to the police. Conan Doyle's Sherlock Holmes mysteries (1938) exhibit this structure in the exposure and arrest of the villain; although specter-like, the arch-villain Moriarty haunts Conan Doyle's mystery, if the stories are considered as a complete narrative. The detective novel that emerges after Conan Doyle domesticates Moriarty by individualizing the villain into a single antagonist, one encircled by the social order, whose crime must be detected and exposed to the view of society. Through the act of detection, society thus controls and contains the disorder that this figure symbolizes, a disorder that has threatened to destabilize the larger social order. Chigurh's ghostly existence at the end of McCarthy's novel must be contrasted to this rule of the detective thriller.

If much of the suspense of the Grisham novel is indebted to the chase in gothic fiction, its psychological impact is predicated upon the horror of the recognition scene. In this scene the banality of the real is reinvigorated—momentarily spiritualized—in the innocent's recognition of the true nature of evil hidden behind the social mask. This moment might be termed a postmodern sublime, one in which a contemporary consumer experiences a momentary shock that, in structure, mimics the Romantic natural sublime. In *No Country for Old Men*, Anton Chigurh is this signifier of metaphysical evil, although the banality and flatness of the world represented in the novel exists to erase his metaphysical function. This narrative erasure leaves readers with only the outline of this metaphysical function.

In similar fashion, the novel's opening scene subjects the metaphysical to a naturalized erasure. When read realistically, the moment that initiates the plot is problematic. Throughout the novel Llewelyn Moss almost instinctively anticipates danger, reacting cannily to the dangers that befall him until his death in the Van Horn motel. So his return with water to the scene of the shoot-out to offer a drink to the dying Mexican is largely inexplicable on the terms of the realistic narrative, as is his refusal to shoot Chigurh in the Laredo motel (*No Country*, 111–13). A common sense reading objects to the absurdity of Moss's belief that a severely wounded man without water could survive the desert heat and evening chill: "I'm fixin to go do something dumbern hell but I'm goin anyways. If I don't come back tell Mother I love her" (24). This one-sentence abstract encapsulates the plot of Moss's segment of the novel. A returned veteran, his intervention into a conflict not his own evokes broad contexts such as the American intervention into Indo-China. But at the novel's beginning, more compelling is the analogy between Moss's charity and that of the kid in McCarthy's *Blood Meridian* (1992), whose problematic "clemency" (299) is extended to David Brown when he draws the arrow from his leg (162–63); to the wounded Shelby by refusing to kill him (207–9); to the "heathen," if readers should credit Judge Holden's accusation; finally to Judge Holden himself, when after the Yuma attack the kid refuses to shoot with Holden in his gun sights (285, 298–99). These passages provide an intertext within the McCarthy oeuvre for Moss's problematic clemency for the drug runner. Yet another that may provide a more compelling context for Moss's return with water to the wounded drug runner faintly evokes the parables of the Good Samaritan and of Lazarus and Dives, reenacted within the contemporary purgatory of the American Southwest.

By this gesture of sympathy, Moss's fate, and that of his wife, is clearly foretold to informed readers of McCarthy's fiction. Readers associating the narrative with the thriller are, however, fooled by a series of false signals: Moss's initial escape in the arroyo, his ability to dress his own wounds, his ability to solicit medical help across the border, his canniness in concealing then recovering the money, his arming himself with a cut-off shotgun. Perversely, the narrative thus allows Moss to be misread as the American action hero. For those who would read the text as popular fiction, the novel's ending occurs at the scene of Moss's death at the motel in Van Horn (*No Country*, 236–42), or with Carla Jean's murder in El Paso (260), or with Sheriff Bell's explanation of his decision not to pursue Chigurh (244–45). The narrative erases its pastiche of popular crime narrative through Chigurh's ghostly disappearance after Carla Jean's murder: "*He's a ghost. But he's out there*," says Bell (248).

Even sophisticated readers can be misled by the generic mimicry of the novel. James Wood, in his review of the novel in the *New Yorker*, concludes that McCarthy's attempt at a literary thriller entraps this work into a "metaphysical cheapness," referring presumably to the murders of Carla Jean, Moss, and the teen hitchhiker when he terms the novel's violence as "senseless" (2005, 93, 92). Wood's repudiation of the novel's violence reads it as incomplete thriller. Or perhaps this critique is an ideological rejection of the narrative plot, dismissing it as the filler that temporally strings together Chigurh's moments of violence. Such a critique resembles Fredric Jameson's reading of *Speed* (1994), the Sandra Bullock vehicle directed by Jon de Bont, a film which Jameson views as the exemplary action film. To Jameson, in this new form of the genre, its violence "must never slow down at its own generic peril" (2003, 715).

Against these readings of violence as the significance of McCarthy's narrative, I would argue for a structural analysis of Chigurh's violence and of its essential relation to the narrative. If Chigurh's violence appears senseless, this is so only because we refract the text's violence through the lens of the thriller. In realistic terms, outside of the aesthetics of the thriller, for the last decade Nuevo Laredo on the southwestern border has been the center of a series of drug wars and drug-related violence—a violence that make a great deal of "sense," at least when analyzed under economic terms as the struggle between rival cartels for market supremacy and as an existential expression of the control of illicit commerce over the "forces" of law and order. In political terms, this violence has undercut the myth of the United States' "control" of its always-permeable southwestern borderlands. After the recent daylight assassination of a journalist in his office in Nuevo Laredo, Chigurh's violence almost appears tame beside a grim social reality. In this respect, Chigurh's violence may be the opposite of the nonsensical, marking the realist-naturalistic imperative driving *No Country for Old Men* as a contemporary analogue to the hyperrealistic depiction of nineteenth-century violence in *Blood Meridian*.

The narrative technique of *No Country for Old Men* works to frustrate, erase, or suspend an ultimate confrontation with metaphysical evil that always seems within the narrative's horizon. Traditionally, this confrontation takes on the form of a plot only after the resolution that contains the violent evil that disrupts the social order. But this is not the logic of McCarthy's narrative, nor does the novel function only to represent the phenomenological pornography of violent moments that Jameson argues is the logic of the American action film (2003, 714).

With two exceptions—the gas station proprietor and Sheriff Bell—the revelation of evil is vouchsafed only to Chigurh's victims only seconds before their murder. In essence, the novel's structure rewrites Flannery O'Connor's "A Good Man Is Hard to Find." In a shock of momentary insight that ironically occurs just before her murder, the grandmother perceives an epiphany of The Misfit's nature, then evokes Christian grace in her maternal embrace of The Misfit, confusing him with her son. It is her attempt to embrace the criminal that provokes her murder. Its focal character murdered, O'Connor's narration then focalizes upon the spectacles of its villain: "The Misfit sprang back as if a snake had bitten him and shot her three times through the chest. Then he put his gun down on the ground and took off his glasses and began to clean them. . . . Without his glasses, The Misfit's eyes were red-rimmed and pale and defenseless-looking" (1955, 29). If O'Connor's text is indeed a matriarchal source of McCarthy's violent myth in *No Country for Old Men*, the latter operates as a textual misfit, an orphan that denies its origins through a reversal of influence. Chigurh insists on shooting his victims in the face, often gazing into the eyes or faces of most of his victims. What he wishes to see is the reversed image of the grandmother's acceptance of The Misfit as her son. Chigurh's desire is for his victims' view of history to be abnegated as they acknowledge that they exist only on his sufferance, this harbinger of a postmodern Death (*No Country*, 6, 7, 104, 122, 260). The exception is the murder of Wells. Because Wells already knows him and rejects him as a "psychopath" (178), Chigurh insists, "You think you wont close your eyes. But you will" (177). The text then insists, several times, that Wells does "close his eyes." Then the instant after death the text focalizes on the retrospective "in-sight" that impossibly emerges to consciousness: "Everything that Wells had ever known or thought or loved drained slowly down the wall behind him. His mother's face, his First Communion, women he had known. The faces of men as they died on their knees before him. The body of a child dead in a roadside ravine in another country. He lay half headless on the bed" (178). In this remarkable reversal of O'Connor's violent myth, McCarthy inscribes his own postmodern form of a natural supernaturalism.

Even in a moment of profane economic exchange between Chigurh and the proprietor of the filling station, Chigurh's self-revelation of his malign essence naturalizes the metaphysical. This scene is enacted within a narrative that is stripped to the bare bones of a dramatic script, one that sketches only the literal gestures, speech, and bare details of the setting, in the manner of a Hopper painting or in the linguistic style of Hemingway's "A Clean, Well-Lighted Place" (1987). After the proprietor's inquisitive small-talk—"Is there somethin wrong?" (*No Country*, 53)—Chigurh reveals to this innocent his essential nature by insisting six times that the proprietor "call" the coin (57–58):

> Call it.
>> I don't know what it is I stand to win.
>> In the blue light the man's face was beaded thinly with sweat. He licked his upper lip. . . .
> You stand to win everything, Chigurh said. Everything. (57)

The proprietor may be one of McCarthy's least aware characters, rivaled perhaps only by the "idiot" in *Blood Meridian*. At this point even the proprietor reads aright the threat Chigurh represents. Within this bathetic southwestern gas station of postmodernity, suddenly aware of the dramatic irony of his situation, the proprietor senses the shift of this mercantile "exchange" into the symbolic, then the metaphysical registers: he "stands," of course, before Chigurh's judgment in order to win his own life, if not his soul. The world of commodity exchange is here momentarily spiritualized by the threat of Chigurh.

Chigurh's function here is to enact a counter-myth of fall of consciousness, beyond the mundane of a consumer capitalism that now rules the Southwest, into an existential, absurdist moment that is defined in the false choice of "calling" the coin. The proprietor had presumed that Chigurh's questions and the exchange of his cash for gas implied a commonality between them. Chigurh interprets the proprietor's small talk as either a threat or as the imposition of a false equality: "What business is it of yours where I'm from, friendo?" (*No Country*, 52). In this sense, both the text's metaphysical levels and its capitalist hyper-reality is placed in a relation of textual exchange by Chigurh. His insistence that the proprietor call the coin transforms it into a divinatory object that can leash or unleash Chigurh's violence: "Well you say. It's just a coin. For instance. Nothing special there. What could that be an instrument of?" (58). McCarthy's coin evokes the coin Ahab nails to the mast and, through it, the metaphysical novel in which the real is momentarily transcended by the metaphysical or the sacred: "He [the proprietor] laid the coin on the counter and looked at it. He put both hands on the counter and just stood leaning there with his head bowed" (58). Chigurh's evil is thus recirculated continually within the novel's representation of the commercialized American Southwest.

In his novels McCarthy has repeatedly employed this motif of sacrifice. It is parodied uncannily near the ending of *Outer Dark* (1993), when the bearded outlaw murders Culla Holme's child in front of him. In denying the identity of his son, Culla sacrifices the child, a sacrifice that ironically evokes the sacred in that Culla "loses" a salvation in his own death. The denial of the child incurs guilt in Culla; hence only his child can play the role of Isaac, the sacrificial innocent, as a substitute for the guilty father. In the murder, Culla is momentarily initiated into the covenant of the grim "triune," thus ensuring the death-in-life of his wandering existence at the novel's end. In *The Crossing* (1994), watching the phenomenal world fade from the mirror of the she-wolf's eyes, Billy Parham experiences the epiphany of the matrix (127).

In Chigurh's murderous dialogues with the gas station proprietor, Wells, and Carla Jean, McCarthy writes an ironic end to the literary history of the American romance. When death is evoked in Hemingway's fiction—in war, in the sacrifice of the bull, in the successful lure and retrieval of the trout—the flow of phenomenal appearances of the real is first fixed, then as the participants (killer, prey, and witness) apperceive the sacrificial death they momentarily access the sacred. Along the lines of René Girard's structural analysis of ritualistic sacrifice and narrative in *Deceit, Desire, and the Novel* (1965), the modern real is thus momentarily transfixed; violent death transformed as sacrifice restores momentarily a trace of the sacred to postmodern narrative, as in witnesses who travel through time to witness the car crash in J. G. Ballard's *Crash* (1973). Thus in the dream vision at the ending of *Cities of the Plain* (1998), the mountain sacrifice of the wanderer perhaps stands at the close of McCarthy's writing project. Here postmodernity's relation to the sacred is reversed, with the Real enclosed within the dream-state of the dying victim. Chigurh's murders in *No Country for Old Men* should be read in the larger context of these ritualistic sacrifices of the innocent.

In his *Ethics* the theologian Dietrich Bonhoeffer describes the metaphysical recognition of evil in literary terms, analyzing Shakespearian villains like Iago and the martyrs of the early church as contrasts in metaphysical absolutes: "Both the villain and the saint have little or nothing to do with systematic ethical studies. They emerge from primeval depths and by their appearance they tear open the infernal or the divine abyss from which they come and enable us to see for a moment into mysteries of which we have never dreamed" (1995, 66–67). Bound by a Real in which evil and good must exist in only relative forms, Bonhoeffer notes that a systematic or normative ethics is unable to recognize or effectively confront such evil: "One who is committed to an ethical programme can only waste his forces on the empty air, and even his martyrdom will not be a source of strength for his cause or a serious threat to the wicked" (67). If Bonhoeffer's analysis of the futile action of the good against the metaphysical rather uncannily predicts his own death as the result of his implication in a futile plot to assassinate Hitler, it provides a convenient gloss to Moss's conversation with Chigurh and accurately outlines for us the ethical dilemma of Sheriff Bell.

Henry James's fiction is constructed around a series of innocents whose perception of the real is suddenly transformed in an epiphanic insight into an evil concealed behind the social, aestheticized mask of civilization. The vision of James's characters is blinded by their personal and cultural innocence, and only on foreign ground can they recognize the Other. This recognition awakens their conscience out of its submersion in mundane social realism or the lure of the aesthetic; James thus fends off the "art for art's sake" mode of Wilde and of a purely aesthetic, decadent art. In the celebrated boat scene of *The Ambassadors* (James 1964), as Chad and Madame de Vionnet float out of an impressionistic canvas to awaken his moral perception, Strether suddenly recognizes the nature of the relation between the two.

Chigurh's encounter with Carla Jean extends into postmodernity James's doctrine of the Miltonic fortunate fall:

Carla: You aim to kill me.
Chigurh: I'm sorry. (*No Country*, 256)

A trailer-park pastiche of the Jamesian heroine, Carla cannot survive for more than a moment this worldly knowledge that Chigurh represents: "Most people don't believe that there can be such a person. You can see what a problem that must be for them. This is the end. You can say that things could have turned out differently. That they could have been some other way. But what does that mean? They are not some other way. They are this way. You're asking that I second say the world. Do you see?" (260). Chigurh revises a central character in McCarthy's works, although this logic of the narrative is hardly available to readers who approach *No Country for Old Men* on its own. In *Blood Meridian* Judge Holden confronts the kid in similar terms at the bar before murdering him in the jakes. In *The Crossing* in front of the captured rebels, Captain Wirtz "walked their enfilade and bent to study each in turn and note in their eyes the workings of death as the assassinations continued behind him" (276). While many reviews associate Sheriff Bell's moralistic monologues with the text's narrative voice, at the moment in the text quoted above it is Chigurh, not Bell, who voices a defense of McCarthy's narrative. Anticipating critiques like Wood's reading (2005) of Carla Jean's murder as senseless, Chigurh and McCarthy point to the reality principle as the law that establishes the limits of this text's emplotment: "You're asking that I second say the world." These critiques would transform the narrative's ending into a "nice" thriller, a romantic Xanadu projecting the imagination's wish to order the world as a projection of its own desire, not to recognize the historical limits of that desire.

This perverse echo of narration uniting Chigurh to McCarthy's narrator is only momentary. In Chigurh's reading of the text, Carla's murder fulfills the "contract" Moss has placed on his wife when he refuses to return the money (*No Country*, 184–85). Evoking Puzo's mob sagas (1969), Chigurh insists that Moss must pay his life as interest on the capital that he has misappropriated. McCarthy's reality principle here is misogynist in the sense that Carla is the metaphysical vigorish that Chigurh exacts from Moss. Carla is thus the price the text's readers must pay for imaginatively identifying with Moss and Carla Jean. In *Outer Dark* Culla extends his own life by paying his son's, but this payment implicitly denies the matriarchal claim of Rinthy, Culla's sister, to name her child. Her claim to have a "say" in what happens to her child is denied, with a patriarchal identity (in the form of Culla's denial of the child) substituting for her maternal claim.

With his life at stake, Sheriff Bell abdicates a "final" confrontation with Chigurh, marking the novel's final violation of the generic code of the thriller. Sheriff Bell too "buys" his life from Chigurh by refusing to contest the latter's claim to rule over this postmodern Southwest. Occupying the nominal position of hero within the text, with his abdication Bell thus renders the novel senseless as a thriller, since no force remains to oppose Chigurh effectively. Bell thus transforms from hero to witness. A conclusion that would restore the social is available within this text only as the naturalized, geographic symbol of Warner's Well. This wilderness pastoral outside Bell's house can be accessed only by horseback: "Put it up, she said. It's nice just to be here" (*No Country*, 302). This symbolic paradise in the text is locked inside this fleet moment. Retired, Bell soon will be barred from access to the wilderness paradise. Bell says to his wife, "You hate it. . . . Leavin here" (301).

Completely banal outside the text's moments of violence, Chigurh positions postmodernity between metaphysics and the existential. Evoked by Bell's discussion of Vietnam with Moss's father, the imperial-political context of the novel can be read in the light of Reinhold Niebuhr's application of original sin to his reading of American foreign policy from pre–World War II to the Cold War and to his critique of the "boundless social optimism" he identifies as the tragic weakness of modern liberal democracy (1944, 16). In *The Children of Light and the Children of Darkness*, Niebuhr employs a modernized notion of original sin: "The children of darkness are evil because they know no law beyond the self. They are wise, though evil, because they understand the power of self-interest. The children of light are . . . usually foolish because they do not know the power of self-will. They underestimate the peril of anarchy in both the national and the international community" (10–11).

It is no accident that Bell's two counterparts within the novel, Chigurh and Moss, had both fought in Vietnam (Chigurh, apparently, in the Special Forces). Bell's conversation with his uncle allows him to confess what we already know—that he is no hero, that his ethical bearings were originally lost in World War II, the last "good" war, not in the American apocalypse of the Vietnam era. Moss's and Carla Jean's error is to believe this myth of original American innocence. As we have seen, *No Country for Old Men* begins with Moss's naïve belief that he can take the money yet return with water to restore his innocence. Referring to the Cold War, Niebuhr warns that in warring against an external enemy, America was blind to its own original sin, the "power of self-interest among themselves" (1944, 11). The novel encapsulates the paradoxes of the foreign policy of an American empire vacillating between the paranoid self-interest of Chigurh and Bell's democratic idealism. Moss's father tells Bell, *"People will tell you it was Vietnam brought this country to its knees. But I never believed that. It was already in bad shape. . . . We didn't have nothing to give to em to take over there"* (*No Country*, 293).

On the one hand voicing nostalgia for the naïve evil of the young of the pre–World War II era prior to the triumph of commodity capitalism—an evil of *"Chewin gum. Copyin homework"* (*No Country*, 196)—Bell is aware nonetheless of Chigurh's argument that the country's providential history must be abandoned for a focus on the phenomenal significance of the present: "You see the problem. To separate the act from the thing. As if the parts of some moment in history might be interchangeable with the parts of some other moment" (57). Bell has become sheriff as a result of this error, in an attempt to exchange his present service for his abandonment of his comrades in World War II. Chigurh's triumph over Moss and Bell purges the sheriff of this idealistic view of himself and of American exceptionalism, a view that has enabled him to enact a role in society based on bad faith: *"Part of it was I always thought I could at least some way put things right and I guess I just don't feel that way no more. I don't know what I do feel like. . . . I'm bein asked to stand for something that I don't have the same belief in it I once did. . . . I've been forced to look at it agin and I've been forced to look at myself'* (296).

If he is to "put things right," to rewrite the novel as a thriller, Bell must display a fascistic power that rivals Chigurh's. The novel's final betrayal of the genre of thriller lies in its proper association of Chigurh, not Bell, with the Western postmodern antihero of Clint Eastwood and his imitators. If, in his over-veneration of a moral past, Bell functions as a mouthpiece of southern conservatism, the narrative contains this ideology, locating its apocalypse or ascesis in a Puritanical fascism, in which law is replaced by a narrow morality imposed by force upon the social order. To this fall into fascism or to an absurdist sacrificial death, Bell prefers cowardice, retirement from the battlefield both in World War II and against Chigurh. Referring to his war experiences, he confesses to his uncle, "I didn't know you could steal your own life. And I didn't know that it would bring you no more benefit than about anything else you might steal" (*No Country*, 278). Bell speaks here for most of the McCarthy witnesses who survive their encounters with the world.

Bonhoeffer provides an existential reading of this abdication, Bell's choice that will determine the novel's final form. In a chapter entitled "History and the Good," Bonhoeffer rejects a definition of the ethical "transposed into the vacuum of the purely private and the purely ideal." This would be "an abstraction from life . . . which forcibly detaches man from the historicity of his existence" (1995, 212). Bonhoeffer instead insists upon an existential and situational ethics that he associates with the term *deputyship*: "The obligation assumes the form of deputyship and of correspondence with reality; freedom displays itself in the self-examination of life and of action and in the venture of a concrete decision" (221). Aware that his death is likely to result from a solitary engagement with Chigurh in the motel parking lot or from the impending Nazi night-time attack on the farmhouse, Sheriff Bell enacts this role of deputyship in "correspondence with reality" and chooses life over abstract principle. Of course, his call for backup against Chigurh follows police procedure, but through it Sheriff Bell retires from the role of the detective/police hero.

This retirement would appear a failure, and Bell interprets it in these terms. To Bonhoeffer, however, the responsible man "has no principle at his disposal which possesses absolute validity and which he has to put into effect fanatically, overcoming all the resistance which is offered to it by reality, but he sees in the given situation what is necessary and what is 'right' for him to grasp and to do" (1995, 224).

Bell's prudential affirmation of his own life in the face of the contingency of the real rewrites John Grady Cole's heroic foolishness in his decision to face Eduardo at the close of *Cities of the Plain*. A rather close parallel to Moss is Sheriff Baker in John Carlos Blake's *Red Grass River* (1998), a text identified by some readers as influenced by McCarthy's work. At the close of the novel, to win his "war" against the outlaw John Ashley, Sheriff Bob Baker murders the Ashley gang on the river bridge after their surrender. While this murder upholds an abstract social order, it is at the cost of Sheriff Baker's descent to a moral level below the outlaw John Ashley. Baker's own fascistic will to power and his repudiation of the law is stronger than that of the outlaws; hence his problematic victory. Deploying the Pauline critique of the "old law" of sin, Bonhoeffer (1995) defines existential and ethical freedom as the result of the free acceptance, then rejection, of the guilt that is incurred by the impossibility of judging the self against the idealism of an abstract law. While Bell's guilt persists throughout, his freedom in the wilderness at the novel's end can be read in these existential terms. Bell's retirement instead acknowledges Chigurh's reality principle in an acceptance, however grudging, of his own limitations. This recognition, of course, delimits the possibility of the heroic and defines the narrative's generic form: *"When you encounter certain things in the world, the evidence for certain things, you realize that you have come upon something that you may very well not be equal to. . . . When you've said that it's real and not just in your head, I'm not all that sure what it is you have said"* (*No Country*, 299).

This echo of the Pauline definition of faith—the evidence of things hoped for—ironically concludes the novel, in Bell's acceptance of the mundane present of postmodernity despite his recognition of Chigurh as symbol of a postmodern American apocalypse. It is this vision that Bell, his wife, and we alone live to witness at the conclusion of *No Country for Old Men*.

REFERENCES

Ballard, J. G. 1973. *Crash*. New York: Farrar, Straus and Giroux.

Berger, Peter. 1967. *The Sacred Canopy: Elements of a Sociological Theory of Religion*. Garden City, NY: Doubleday.

Blake, James Carlos. 1998. *Red Grass River: A Legend*. New York: Avon.

Bonhoeffer, Dietrich. 1995. *Ethics*. Ed. Eberhard Bethge. Trans. Neville Horton Smith. New York: Touchstone.

Conan Doyle, Sir Arthur. 1938. *The Complete Sherlock Holmes*. New York: Garden City Publishing.

Girard, René. 1965. *Deceit, Desire, and the Novel*. Baltimore: Johns Hopkins University Press.

Grisham, John. 1991. *The Firm*. New York: Doubleday.

———. 1992. *The Pelican Brief*. New York: Doubleday.

———. 1993. *The Client*. New York: Doubleday.

Harris, Thomas. 1988. *The Silence of the Lambs*. New York: St. Martin's Press.

Hemingway, Ernest. 1987. "A Clean, Well-Lighted Place." In *The Complete Short Stories of Ernest Hemingway*, 288–91. New York: Charles Scribner's Sons.

James, Henry. 1964. *The Ambassadors*. Ed. S.P.Rosenbaum. New York: W.W. Norton.

Jameson, Fredric. 2003. "The End of Temporality." *Critical Inquiry* 29 (Summer): 695–718.

McCarthy, Cormac. 1992. *Blood Meridian, or, The Evening Redness in the West*. New York: Vintage Books.

———. 1993. *Outer Dark*. Repr. New York: Vintage.

———. 1994. *The Crossing*. New York: Alfred A. Knopf.

———. 1998. *Cities of the Plain*. London: Vintage.

———. 2005. *No Country for Old Men*. New York: Alfred A. Knopf.

Niebuhr, Reinhold. 1944. *The Children of Light and the Children of Darkness*. New York: Charles Scribner's Sons.

O'Connor, Flannery. 1955. *"A Good Man Is Hard to Find" and Other Stories*. New York: Harcourt Brace.

Puzo, Mario. 1969. *The Godfather*. New York: Putnam.

Speed. 1994. Dir. Jan de Bont. Twentieth Century Fox.

Wood, James. 2005. "Red Planet: The Sanguinary Sublime of Cormac McCarthy." A review of *No Country for Old Men*. *New Yorker*, July 25, 88–93.

7

+

Borderline Evil:
The Dark Side of Byzantium
in *No Country for Old Men,*
Novel and Film

Jim Welsh

Let's begin with a comparison between a distinctive novel and an equally distinctive, award-winning film, engaged as if involved in a thrilling and dangerous dance, involving artfully executed and then artfully imitated steps and measures. First and foremost, of course, Cormac McCarthy's *No Country for Old Men* (2005) is a Western, set on a border, a frontier, a no-man's land of death and destruction. But this novel, which takes its title from the first line of the William Butler Yeats poem "Sailing to Byzantium" (1960b) is more than simply a Western, for it stretches genre boundaries as well as chronology, and it is also a symbolic narrative, an allegory of salvation, or even, perhaps, a moral allegory for post–September 11, Neocon America. As a Western, it of course follows certain conventions expected of the genre (such as sinister, malevolent hired guns, some of whom kill partly for sadistic pleasure, like Jack Palance's assassin, Wilson, in *Shane* [1953]), but genre expectations are also thwarted in this narrative. One may be reminded of the "classic" political Western, *High Noon* (1952), with Sheriff Ed Tom Bell in McCarthy's novel resembling Marshal Kane in Fred Zinnemann's film. Both men are about to retire and not so confident in their abilities as they once were. "An aged man is but a paltry thing," as Yeats wrote in his second stanza; Sheriff Ed Tom feels overmatched and "unable to put things right" (*No Country,* 296). However, in McCarthy's novel the second hand of the iconic and cinematic clock never quite reaches high noon. There is no

ultimate showdown between the professional lawman and the professional assassin, and one wonders if this is by accident or by design. The
sheriff is cautious: "The crime you see now," he says, "it's hard even to
take its measure." Not that he's afraid of it: "I always knew that you had
to be willin to die to even do this job," he explains, but "I wont push my
chips forward" to confront "a true and living prophet of destruction"
(*No Country*, 6). And who could "understand" this killer's logic? Sheriff
Bell is tracking a killer, but there will be no clear, dramatic confrontation,
perhaps because Sheriff Bell knows that he can't cheat Death or kill the
Devil, that the deck may be stacked against him. If not the Devil, then
maybe a ghost, as Bell himself suggests? So who said he was chasing an
abstraction?

Certainly the novel is a Western, even though its 1980s setting has been
updated way beyond Frederick Jackson Turner's "disappearing frontier,"
which reached its terminus in 1896. Perhaps this story, set in the 1980s, is
more properly a "post-Western," but it is also an allegory, and the killer,
the "ghost," Anton Chigurh, seems too spooky, too otherworldly to be
"real." Considering what happens to him in the story, Chigurh ought to
be dead, but at the end, after being broadsided in an auto accident, he
limps away to continue his never exactly specified mission. The man and
his motives are utterly mysterious. Chigurh would seem to be the very
personification of the Antichrist, that slouching "rough beast" of Yeats's
1919 poem "The Second Coming" (Yeats 1960c). He is a force and a presence that goes well beyond the banality of an ordinary paid assassin or
bounty hunter. Like Death itself, he is larger than life, not merely a stereo-
type, but an allegorical abstraction. Even if the novel's title is borrowed
from "Sailing to Byzantium," Rick Wallach of the Cormac McCarthy Society would stress the Yeats influence further, to a later Yeats (1960a) poem,
"Byzantium" (written in 1930), that mentions "an image, man or shade, /
Shade more than man, more image than a shade," a shade from "Hades'
bobbin bound in mummy-cloth," a "superhuman figure" the poet calls
"death-in-life and life-in-death" (lines 9–16).

Time magazine critic Richard Corliss noted that *No Country for Old
Men*, in the running for Best Picture of 2008 was, along with *There Will
Be Blood* (2007), one of "two ultra-violent dramas much loved by critics
but too weird to be crowd-pleasers" (2008, 68). Well and truly said, but
perhaps the word *respected* rather than *loved* would better describe the
critical response. To check the weirdness reaction, one only has to consult
the blogosphere, where weirdness thrives in thickets of wild opinion. But
this is a film that will challenge critics and philosophers as well as other
puzzled viewers. For Royal Brown, reviewing the film for *Cineaste*, for
example, the novel and the film "go out and meet something akin to pure
nihilism" (2008, 9). Brown believes that the Coen brothers manage to find,

"on every level, the consummate cinematic means for communicating not only that which cannot be understood but also the fact that the word 'understand' has no relevance in this climate" (9).

Dennis Rothermel, who chairs the philosophy department at California State University at Chico, would probably argue to the contrary, however, about the Chigurh "shade," who is to be taken seriously as something more than an allegorical figure: "Chigurh we have to understand as a man, not merely as a symbol or cipher," Rothermel asserts. "Albeit shuddering to contemplate, his self-understanding as willfully arbitrary inquisitioner and executioner is within the spectrum of possibility for human nature. That possibility may well be as rare as his stoic sense of purpose in treating his leg wound after being shot by Llewelyn" (Rothermel, pers. comm.). More important is Chigurh's explicit questioning, as put to Carson Wells, "If the rule that you followed led you to this of what use was the rule?" (*No Country*, 175). The "rule," of course, "is a strategy, a profession, a road, a pathway, a philosophy of life, or just life. It is up to Ed Tom to come to that confrontation independent of actually meeting Chigurh. He does come close to it in his visit with Ellis and with those two culminating dreams" articulated by Sheriff Bell at the end of the film (Rothermel, pers. comm.).

Depending on what one concludes about the humanity of Chigurh, this would seem to suggest that the characters are coded symbolically in the novel, but they are also coded in more conventional ways, onomastically (with sweet irony in the case of the villain), for example, and by Western types as well, though it is difficult to locate a "hero" with confidence here, since Llewelyn Moss (who seems to be the protagonist most of the way through the story) is at best a good/bad man (though not quite a professional, like Shane, but certainly unlike his nemesis, Anton Chigurh, who is simply a killing machine) who wanders astray in the wilderness when he gives in to temptation and steals money that he finds on a drug-strewn battleground. His mistake is not only taking the money, but believing he has the survival skills to get away with it. Or, to quote Joel Coen from a bonus DVD feature on the making of the film, "It's about a good guy, a bad guy, and a guy in between. Moss is the guy in between" ("The Making of *No Country*," 2008). Ultimately, Moss is being tracked down by several professional killers. Sheriff Bell is also in pursuit, but he is apparently unable (or perhaps unwilling?) either to intercept or to save Moss. This is a very serviceable genre story for the Coen brothers to transform into an Oscar-worthy motion picture, and a playground of archetypes (from the mythical Celtic to the Bible) and stereotypes raised above the level of cliché and taken beyond the realm of allegory.

This chapter intends to explore those archetypes and stereotypes as well as the intertextual possibilities involved in what the Motion Picture

Academy judged the best film of 2007 as well as the best film adaptation from another medium. The Coen brothers' adaptation raises the old questions of fidelity and intertextuality in interesting and even unexpected ways. Michael Wood remarked in the *London Review of Books* that "the movie manages to be very different from Cormac McCarthy's novel through an extravagant literal fidelity to a great deal of it" (2008, 17). By and large, the film is faithful to the *text* of the original novel by Cormac McCarthy, but fidelity of nuance (potentially involving symbolic meaning) is quite another matter, and the story is told in two voices. The first-person "narration" of Bell is balanced against third-person objective, and Bell's comments are not simply narrative, since Bell is as much chorus as narrator. The final product in the film involves a richly layered intertextuality, building interestingly upon the intertextual borrowings found in the McCarthy source, overlapped with intertexual motifs from earlier Coen brothers features, especially *Fargo* (1996) but also *Raising Arizona* (1987), and, arguably, from the fiction of Flannery O'Connor as well. One doesn't necessarily have to argue that the film may be "better" than the book, but it is most certainly and demonstrably *different* and satisfying in ways that go well beyond the original. The challenge, therefore, is to sort out the steps and measures of the complex intertextual dance that is the film.

On the textual evidence of *No Country for Old Men*, one wonders if Cormac McCarthy is sufficiently old-fashioned to be considered a modernist writer as well as the minimalist writer he appears to be, laconic in the best Western sense, a writer of sparsely toughened prose. Christopher Sharrett claims McCarthy's ambition and language may be typical of what he calls "high modernism" (2008, 11), whereas officials of the Cormac McCarthy Society might suggest the term "late Modernist," which, given its often self-subverting ethos, seems a more accurate description. If so, one might argue that the Coens' film adaptation of this novel is, by contrast, postmodern, as Steven Carter suggested in his essay "'Flare to White': *Fargo* and the Postmodern Turn," is the case with an earlier Coen film to which *No Country for Old Men* bears a clear stylistic resemblance, *Fargo*. Carter commented perceptively about the disjunction and consequent humor in this earlier Coen brothers feature that has nothing to do with North Dakota, but belongs in language and spirit in the frozen north of Minnesota. One might argue that the film adaptation of *No Country* takes a very similar "postmodern turn." *Fargo*, Carter claims, is *not* a crime film, strictly speaking, though it "is about crime. The brilliance of the film, rather, lies in its ability to critique a certain contemporary, or postmodern, response to the crime of murder" (1999, 239). Very like, in other words, what seems to be happening in *No Country for Old Men*, especially in Sheriff Bell's case. Though the later film is not ultimately humorous (though Christopher Sharrett [2008], who reviewed it for *Cineaste*, would probably argue to the contrary, an argument that could be further supported by the "comic" mayhem of both *Fargo* and the more recently zany *Burn after Reading* [2008]), traces of the Coen comic sensibility linger, leaving an aftertaste of vile, even repulsive, cynicism. For the DVD bonus feature, Tommy Lee Jones also remarks about the film's comedic possibilities, though adding that the film is not conventionally "funny" ("The Making of" 2008).

In general, the Coens can't help being wry. They playfully name their characters (Evelle Snopes in *Raising Arizona*, for example, or Wash Hogwallop in *O Brother, Where Art Thou?* [2000]) and they certainly have ventured into allegorical territory: *Barton Fink* (1991), for example, might be described as an allegory about success in Hollywood, or, how to get a head in Hollywood. Surely *No Country for Old Men* could be "read" as an allegory concerning the murderous anxieties consequent upon terrorism and Neocon America, threatened abroad because of its preemptive war with Iraq and at home as well (presumably) by radical Islamists, to say nothing of the conservative hobgoblin fear of an alien invasion from south of the border. The murderous wasteland witnessed in *No Country for Old Men* brings these anxieties to mind. The devastation spread before Moss at the beginning of the film would also fit the murderous wastelands of Iraq or Afghanistan. And as John Vanderheide demonstrates elsewhere in this anthology, the story also makes sense as a more conventional religious allegory of temptation and salvation tied to Moss's mistaken judgment (to take the money) and to the "progress" of Sheriff Bell, at least in the novel.

The same could be argued with regard to character. In a paper given before the Popular Culture Association in San Francisco, Mark Hoffer (2008) interestingly compared *No Country for Old Men* with an even earlier Coen brothers film, *Raising Arizona* (1987), in terms of both background (the anxieties of a foreign war seeping into the culture of the American homeland as the anxieties of the Vietnam war had done decades before) and characters. Though the characters of the later film had of course been adapted from those created by Cormac McCarthy, Hoffer suggested clear parallels between *No Country* and *Raising Arizona*, such as H. I. "Hi" McDunnough with Llewelyn Moss and Evelle Snopes with Anton Chigurh. Hoffer's title drew a reasonable existential comparison: "Raising Dystopia: *No Country for Old Men* and the Nightmare of Neocon America." Certainly, the "dystopia" is there in *No Country for Old Men*, but not the "wild, surreal, and hilarious" humor of *Raising Arizona* (Connors and Craddock 1999, 729).

Rick Wallach saw an even richer intertextual terrain in comparing the filmmakers and the novelist, working from *Blood Meridian* (1985) to *No Country for Old Men*, the Judge Holden/Anton Chigurh analogy, and then moving into Coen territory: "The Coens have a long history of arch-villains (the corrupt PI/killer in *Blood Simple*, the bounty hunter in *Raising Arizona*, the lunatic next door in *Barton Fink*, Eddie Dane in *Miller's Crossing*, John Goodman *redux* as the Klansman/Cyclops in *O Brother, Where Art Thou?*— you could even (at a stretch) include old man Lebowski in *The Big Lebowski*") (Wallach, pers. comm.). In McCarthy, Wallach continued,

> the idea starts slow—Legwater in *The Orchard Keeper* isn't much to work with but Lester Ballard in *Child of God* surely is; the trio of killer-cannibals in *Outer Dark* and (perhaps at another stretch) the ghostly anti-self in *Suttree*. By the time you get west it's a much better defined theme: the judge [in *Blood Meridian*], the police captain in *All the Pretty Horses* (and come to think of it, isn't Ed Tom a logical extension of the world-weary but decent judge at the end of *All the Pretty Horses*?), the murderous Indian in *The Crossing* and the pimp Eduardo in *Cities of the Plain*. You could say that Eduardo is a stripped-down McCarthy villain on the way to the ultimately stripped-down Chigurh—at least, they are if you use Holden as the fully realized figure in [McCarthy's] *oeuvre*.

Judge Holden is a precursor of Chigurh and other later McCarthy characters, though the one character is not simply a mere reflection of the other.

For my immediate purposes in the Coen brothers context, however, the most striking comparison is with *Fargo*. The characters of *No Country for Old Men* can be sorted out into roughly the same categories as the characters of the earlier film. Likable but puzzled law officers driven by a reluctant sense of duty (both are a bit off-center and unexpected: the pregnant Marge in *Fargo*, the soon-to-be retired Sheriff Bell in *No Country for Old Men*, both of them preoccupied with an indeterminate future); their friends and loved ones, who share their protected, privileged, "normal," familial "comfort zone"; and the threatening, "un-normal" criminals, murderers, misfits, and psychopaths who populate the chaotic and unpredictable and scary outside world at large. The frozen, moonscape wasteland of Minnesota and North Dakota in the first film is mirrored by the desert moonscape wasteland of the Texas border country in the second, and in both settings, Evil exists in the wilderness, waiting to break through into the "normal" world. Characters at these two extremes share little (if any) mutual understanding. The law-abiding characters do seem to understand the dangers of the unpredictable world that threatens to draw them into its nightmare territory.

Each world is governed by its own codes of ethics or mayhem. Characters in the "Comfort Zone" tend to believe in righteous behavior, in a world as it *ought* to be, recalling the religious convictions of the self-righteous and generally deluded characters found in the gothic fiction of Flannery O'Connor (such as the self-righteous Mrs. Turpin in the story

"Revelation")—characters who believe themselves to be better than others (or Others) and therefore "saved," but whose moral vision may be blinkered, characters who may be forced to encounter terrible moments of epiphany and self-redemption through self-understanding. Such moments occur when the "outer world" invades the "inner world" (usually with disturbing consequences), the world of what I have defined as the Comfort Zone of the "good" and righteous, more ordinary characters. The problem is that such characters are also banal, and they are not at all protected by their banality.

But such questions of intertextual borrowing get increasingly dodgy. Moreover, it seems to be more apparent in the Coen brothers' treatment than in McCarthy's source novel, which seems more consciously bound to the realistic and less inclined toward the metaphorical and metaphysical, for the presumed influence of O'Connor would push the characters toward symbolic and the allegorical dimensions, and it may be pushing the envelope way too far to suggest that the film adaptation is somehow transformed into an allegory of salvation and that Anton Chigurh may be a heaven-sent agent to demonstrate the Truth of Evil to myopic mortals. Consider, for example, the structural function of Chigurh in *No Country for Old Men* in comparison to the parallel figure of The Misfit in Flannery O'Connor's story "A Good Man Is Hard to Find" (1983). Both clearly are "misfits," both are psychopaths, both are structural agents of change, disturbing the Ordinary and destroying the very illusion of Ordinariness (the perception of ordinary, "normal" decency, for example). In both instances their disturbances bring about revelation and discovery (in the Aristotelian sense, impinging upon self-awareness), and therefore opening the door to grace and salvation. In O'Connor's story The Misfit says, after murdering the archetypical and apparently "normal" grandmother, "She would have been a good woman . . . if it had been somebody there to shoot her every minute of her life" (1983, 22). Without intending to wrench Cormac McCarthy's meaning into moral allegory, at least with regard to the film adaptation such a "reading" may seem plausible and even helpful in making sense of the film. Arguably, Sheriff Bell has a new insight into himself and the nature of the world at the end of the story.

Is Anton Chigurh a figure of Fatality? He is defined by his tendency to settle questions of life and death by flipping a coin. In his *Cineaste* review of the film, Christopher Sharrett, who considered the film greatly overrated, compared Chigurh to Two-Face, the cartoon villain from the Batman comics, "who also uses a flipped coin (go through the history of crime fiction to find this gimmick) to decide what horror will befall his victims" (2008, 12). So, is the coin flip merely a pulp cliché, or is it something more involved? Is human behavior governed by fate or simply by luck? The equivalent of the flip of a coin, maybe? Louis Petrich, a friend who teaches at St. John's College, Annapolis, asked me if I had read Pascal's coin-flip metaphor as a formula to "prove" the existence of God. Heads, he exists; tails, he doesn't. If so, how the coin falls makes all the difference in the world. So the question to be asked is how well read was Cormac McCarthy? Did he arguably have such "thoughts"? Could one perversely suppose that a coin flip might be used to "prove" the opposite, the existence of the Devil? Potentially something far more significant than comic books or pulp-fiction clichés may be at issue here. Or maybe the Coen brothers and Cormac McCarthy are thinking in entirely different ways?

Cormac McCarthy's novel certainly involves a journey, but not necessarily one of redemption, as might be expected of Christian allegory: Moss, a Texas Everyman, goes into the wilderness on a hunting expedition but loses his way and ultimately his moral bearings when he stumbles into temptation. Moss experiences at first hand a battleground littered with corpses and the consequences of a drug deal gone horribly wrong. He is tempted to steal when he finds a briefcase, containing over $2 million in drug funds. He is seduced by the money and attempts to make off with it, only to be tracked, relentlessly, by an avenging angel of death, or is Chigurh simply an arbiter of justice? The novel turns this allegorical journey into a realistic story about a Vietnam veteran who foolishly but confidently thinks he can outsmart those who will inevitably come tracking him to recover the money. Unfortunately, Moss cannot understand that the odds are seriously against him. As the story progresses, his chances for survival diminish, but this realization comes by way of dramatic irony. Eventually, Moss will lose the money and the woman he loves, as well as his own life. Besides being an allegory of greed, this is an allegory of survival, but could it also be an allegory of grace and salvation?

I would argue that there are alternate meanings attached to the characters of Anton Chigurh, whose character I prefer to "read" allegorically, although such a psychopath certainly could exist in the known world. Sheriff Bell carries allegorical significance as well. Chigurh is a more complex character in the novel. As played by Javier Bardem in the film, he is horrifically unpredictable, his behavior governed by a code that has its own cryptic logic, making him an apparently unbending agent of a fatality that itself seems irrational. Exchanges involving Chigurh in the novel are missing from the film, for example, as when Chigurh returns the cash to one of the cartel chiefs. Rick Wallach believes this plot change constitutes "an unfortunate oversight because, given the information from the film, it looks like Chigurh is simply after the money. In the novel, he's after something else that has to do with his own eccentric moral code," and that (arguably) "makes him more interesting, or at any rate, more enigmatic." Wallach supposes that "the Coens figured that his comments to Carla Jean before he shoots her filled in nicely for that issue, and yet . . ." (pers. comm.). And yet, indeed.

At the end of the day, as they might say in the West (or at least on the *West Wing*), *No Country for Old Men* is still an updated Western, though reflecting more the West of *Junior Bonner* (1972) or *Hud* (1963), also influenced by Tony Richardson's *The Border* (1982) and John Sayles's *Lone Star* (1996). This is the "frustrated frontier" of the late twentieth century, a dystopic West where Evil has a postmodern spin, where men are still men and villains are still killers, but also a West where White Hats are mingled with a cockeyed, out-of-place killer sporting a bizarre Prince Valliant haircut. Such displacements of archetypal iconography are vintage Cormac McCarthy, to be sure, but also Cormac McCarthy reedited and popularized, recreated in a more agreeable and even cartoonish way, not exactly simplified, but changed so subtly that perhaps most viewers may not even notice. "The whole art of Kafka consists in forcing the reader to reread," Albert Camus observed in his *Notebooks* (qtd. in Dirda 2008, 12), and the same might be said of Cormac McCarthy at his most grotesque.

So, what is one to make, finally, of Sheriff Ed Tom Bell? We leave him in the novel carrying on like a banal and tiresome old geezer, rendered helpless by circumstances beyond his control. He complains that the world is being taken over by barbarians with green hair and bones through their noses. As he becomes tiresome in his complaints, he seems akin to one of Flannery O'Connor's caricatures. The perception in the film is rather different, however. He suffers disappointment and bitter resignation, but the stance seems more dignified, perhaps because Sheriff Bell does less complaining and is more laconic, or perhaps because he is played with considerable dignity by Tommy Lee Jones.

Suppose that McCarthy, like Yeats before him in the poem from which the novel takes its title, is yearning to establish a sense of transcendence, using Sheriff Bell as his surrogate (and, yes, I realize that one should be wary about confusing the artist with his creation; this is not to suggest that Bell is a spokesman or even a sounding board for the novelist). Sheriff Bell has attempted to serve the people of his jurisdiction through his efforts to keep the peace and maintain law and order, but he sees the social order and the legal system crumbling around him, his faith and confidence shaken. Is the novel's conclusion a sort of palinode, then? And, if so, is that same nuance preserved through Tommy Lee Jones's performance at the end of the film?

The level of perception attached to the choric commentary of Sheriff Bell is clearly different in the novel as compared to the film. In the novel one finds the outrage of a man puzzled by existence, angered by seeming incoherence, frustrated by what seems to be illogical and unmotivated cruelty, by a world that has changed around him, making him feel misplaced, inadequate and even out of control. In the novel Sheriff Bell is mainly an observer, whereas the film threatens to draw him into the cycle of violence and leads, arguably, to a different level of moral understanding. By circumstance or design, Bell ultimately avoids the centers of violence in this story as he appears to investigate them, but always belatedly. This perhaps bespeaks a judicious restraint reflecting the wisdom of a man who has already witnessed too much human folly and destruction. In the film, his wisdom is appropriately and admirably laconic. For viewers, Bell is the existential link to the world of the film, a narrator we would like to consider reliable and trustworthy, if not avuncular. But is his main function to narrate? For the reader Bell seems merely confused and incoherent and far too talkative, at times even befuddled. In other words, the film transforms Bell into a more trustworthy figure than the apparently confused old fellow McCarthy created.

That is not the impression Tommy Lee Jones leaves us with. The film leaves viewers with a different sense of closure, but not much in the way of satisfaction. If this part of Texas is "no country for old men," can there be much hope or comfort for Sheriff Bell? Nearly everybody else who has seen the Devil has perished (except the two young bicyclists, who in the novel have to be pressured to tell the truth by Bell and in the film are corrupted with the money Chigurh forces on them, despite their innocent concern for his injuries and their willingness to help him without recompense), and the Devil is still on the loose. All that viewers can conclude is that the story has found an apparent ending. The Coen brothers appear to be laughing at the grotesque folly they have recorded, and that is not, I think, true to the spirit of the novel.

At issue here is the basic difference between literature and film. According to Andrew Sarris, "Movies deal with surfaces; they don't deal with essences" (Macklin 2000, 324). The Coens have shown the surface of *No Country for Old Men* brilliantly, but at the expense of the narrative's literary essence, which is complex and potentially allegorical. Both narratives, literary and cinematic, make sense on the realistic level, which is much enhanced by the realistic medium of film. As Sarris told interviewer Tony Macklin, cinema "is more a medium of incantation than of information; it's more a medium of emotion than intellect" (Macklin 2000, 323).

I should like to conclude, then, with a reflection upon the notion of "adaptability," and what might be called the "fidelity fallacy" (comparable to what critics two generations ago called the "intentional fallacy"). "Good fences make good neighbors," Robert Frost once proclaimed in one of his most quotable poetic lines, seeming to contain a nugget of folk wisdom, which makes the line pleasantly memorable. Nuance, however, makes the line more difficult, just as nuance makes *life* more difficult, though maybe not for certain politicians recently. The critically minded might ask, did the poet really *mean* what he seemed to say? Do "good fences" *really* "make good neighbors"? Was Robert Frost really innocent of irony?

These questions lead to what I believe may be the core question of adaptability: do good readers make good viewers? Or, for film audiences, is reading the ultimate "spoiler"? Consider, for example, *The Kite Runner* (2007), adapted to cinema from the popular 2003 novel by Khaled Hosseini, which may seem at first blush to be a perfectly agreeable movie, even an inspiring one, apparently about fathers and sons, friendship and brotherhood, guilt and redemption, Communism and monarchy, the Taliban and—forgive a slight "spoiler" here—sodomy, in late twentieth-century Afghanistan. The film was in many ways literally "true" to the novel upon which it was based and seems therefore to be a very "faithful" adaptation. The novel is "about" a sensitive and artistic Pashtun boy named Amir, who aspires to be a teller of stories, and ultimately becomes a novelist in America. Amir's uneducated friend Hassan, hearing one of Amir's fantastic stories about a man whose tears turn into pearls, a man who ruins his life by seeking reasons to weep and become wealthy, points out an obvious failure of plot logic, a lesson that the film's adapting screenwriter might better have taken to heart. In fact, the problem with this film adaptation has more to do with motivation than simply with plot.

At any rate, the reader of the novel will have a much better understanding of what motivates the characters, whose behavior may seem enigmatic or even peculiar when presented out of context on the screen. If so, the informed viewer may be forgiven for falling back on that hoariest of clichés, "The book was better!" committing what many cinema studies experts might consider the "fidelity fallacy." But who among us would not forgive the general reader, innocent of cinema studies theory, for having actually read the novel, or for having thought independently about what it might "mean," and for drawing such a conclusion about the virtues of the source novel?

Of course, this line of reasoning about fidelity—*The book was better!*—does not always hold true. Though one might not agree that it applies with *The Kite Runner*, there are other examples one might consider, such as the far better known *No Country for Old Men*, involving the 2007 postmodern treatment of Cormac McCarthy's late modernist novel, adapted by the impudently postmodern Coen brothers. Again, the film is in many ways "faithful" to the novel, but not entirely, and the differences make *all* the difference. The more laconic voice-over narration in the film (severely limited by comparison with the novel) of Sherriff Ed Tom Bell, played by Tommy Lee Jones, who has seemed to some to be the "moral center" of the film, is nuanced differently in the film, making the character more sympathetic and tolerable, one might well argue. One might also be drawn to the conclusion that in this instance the novel is *not* necessarily "better" than the film, though it is at the same time demonstrably different and interestingly intertextual. And perhaps that sort of difference is what marks a superior adaptation. *No Country for Old Men* resembles no other Western ever made. It is unique, and that may explain why it was both a critical and a commercial success, earning over $72 million, putting it in a league with *Fargo*, the next most successful Coen brothers film, but one which only earned $24 million in 1996. Most (though not all) of the details of the McCarthy adaptation are consistent with the novel; much of Sheriff Bell's voice-over narrative survives; the surface is apparently (and agreeably) smooth. And for most viewers, that will probably seem sufficient. The film follows its own conventions, seamlessly.

NOTE

These comments resulted from conversations started at one Popular Culture conference in Albuquerque, New Mexico, in March of 2008 in a panel organized by Lynnea Chapman King and continued at another Popular Culture conference in San Francisco in April, as well as through continuing correspondence. I owe a tremendous debt to voluminous correspondences involving Lynnea Chapman King; Rick Wallach, secretary-treasurer of the Cormac McCarthy Society; and Dennis Rothermel, chair of the philosophy department at California State University at Chico. Outside that circle, I also owe a debt of gratitude to Louis Petrich of St. John's College, Annapolis, for sharing his thoughts on Pascal with me.

REFERENCES

Barton Fink. 1991. Dir. Joel Coen and Ethan Coen. Circle Films.
The Big Lebowski. 1998. Dir. Joel Coen and Ethan Coen. Polygram, Working Title.
Blood Simple. 1984. Dir. Joel Coen and Ethan Coen. River Road Productions, Circle Releasing.
The Border. 1982. Dir. Tony Richardson. Efer Productions.
Brown, Royal. 2008. "No Exit in Texas." *Cineaste* 33, no. 3 (Summer): 9–10.
Burn after Reading. 2008. Dir. Ethan Coen and Joel Coen. Mike Zoss Productions.
Carter, Stephen. 1999. "'Flare to White': *Fargo* and the Postmodern Turn." *Literature/Film Quarterly* 27, no. 4: 238–44.
Connors, Martin, and Jim Craddock, eds. 1999. *Videohound's Golden Movie Retriever 1999*. Detroit: Visible Ink.
Corliss, Richard. 2008. "The Big Picture." *Time*, January 14, 68.
Dirda, Michael. 2008. "The 'True Glory' and 'Overwhelming Pressure' of Being Albert Camus." *Washington Post Book World*, May 11, 12.
Fargo. 1996. Dir. Joel Coen and Ethan Coen. PolyGram Filmed Entertainment.

Frost, Robert. 1964. "Mending Wall." In *Complete Poems of Robert Frost*, 47–48. New York: Holt, Rinehart and Winston.

High Noon. 1952. Dir. Fred Zimmerman. Stanley Kramer Productions.

Hoffer, Mark. 2008. "Raising Dystopia: *No Country for Old Men* and the Nightmare of Neocon America." Paper presented at the Popular Culture Association, San Francisco, April.

Hosseini, Khaled. 2003. *The Kite Runner*. New York: Riverhead Books

Hud. 1963. Dir. Martin Ritt. Paramount Pictures.

Junior Bonner. 1972. Dir. Sam Peckinpah. American Broadcasting Company.

The Kite Runner. 2007. Dir. Marc Forster. DreamWorks SKG.

Lone Star. 1996. Dir. John Sayles. Columbia Pictures.

Macklin, Tony. 2000. "The Critic." Interview with Andrew Sarris. In *Voices from the Set: The* Film Heritage *Interviews*, ed. Tony Macklin and Nick Pici 318–27. Lanham, MD: Scarecrow Press.

"The Making of *No Country for Old Men*." 2008. *No Country for Old Men*, special features. DVD. Dir. Ethan Coen and Joel Coen. Buena Vista Home Entertainment, Inc., and Paramount Vantage.

McCarthy, Cormac. 1985. *Blood Meridian, or, The Evening Redness in the West*. New York: Random House.

———. 2005. *No Country for Old Men: A Novel*. New York: Vintage International.

Miller's Crossing. 1990. Dir. Joel Coen and Ethan Coen. Twentieth Century-Fox.

No Country for Old Men. 2007. Dir. Ethan Coen and Joel Coen. Miramax Films.

O Brother, Where Art Thou? 2000. Dir. Joel Coen and Ethan Coen. Touchstone Pictures.

O'Connor, Flannery. 1983. *"A Good Man Is Hard to Find" and Other Stories*. Orlando, FL: Harcourt/Harvest Books.

Raising Arizona. 1987. Dir. Joel Coen and Ethan Coen. Circle Films.

Shane. 1953. Dir. George Stevens. Paramount Pictures.

Sharrett, Christopher. 2008. "Comic Dread in the Modern Frontier." *Cineaste* 33, no. 3 (Summer): 11–13.

There Will Be Blood. 2007. Dir. Paul Thomas Anderson. Ghoulardi Film Company.

Wood, Michael. 2008. "At the Movies." *London Review of Books*, February 21, 17.

Yeats, William Butler. 1960a. "Byzantium." In *The Collected Poems of W. B. Yeats*, 243–44. New York: Macmillan.

———. 1960b. "Sailing to Byzantium." In *The Collected Poems of W. B. Yeats*, 191–92. New York: Macmillan.

———. 1960c. "The Second Coming." In *The Collected Poems of W. B. Yeats*, 184–85. New York: Macmillan.

8

✝

"Of what is past, or passing, or to come": Characters as Relics in *No Country for Old Men*

Pat Tyrer and Pat Nickell

In Cormac McCarthy's novel (2005) and the Coen brothers' film (2007) *No Country for Old Men*, the three central characters, Ed Tom Bell, Llewelyn Moss, and Anton Chigurh, seem to be remnants of the Old West. Each man represents a watered-down version of a familiar Western character: the local lawman who maintains order and dispenses justice; the opportunistic, but basically solid citizen who succumbs to temptation; and the outlaw who lives by his gun. However, in both novel and film these contemporary western characters have faded into shadows of their original forms. Gone are the recognizable characters who rode across hundreds of movie screens coast to coast. Instead of the clear delineation between the "good guy" and the "bad guy," *No Country for Old Men* presents its audience with characters who imperfectly represent both and adds a third, one who is neither good nor evil but who accurately represents a modern citizen, a person who wants his share of the American dream and is willing to sacrifice his principles to get it. Moss, a young man, wants to retire in financial ease, and the audience, while divided over what he ought to do with all that money, wants Moss to survive. Poverty is no country for old men any more than violence is.

In William Butler Yeats's poem, "Sailing to Byzantium" (n.d.), the first line of which serves as the title of McCarthy's novel, the "aged man" has rejected the natural world from which he believes himself to be alienated. Like the aged man of the poem, Ed Tom Bell is coming to the end of his journey, yet he yearns for the past. He recognizes that "an aged man is but a paltry thing, / a tattered coat upon a stick" (lines 9–10). However, Bell also imagines himself as part of an ancient tradition. He is delighted by the story of the West and deliberate in his actions. In a voice-over at the beginning of the film, he establishes his legacy by explaining, "My grandfather was a lawman, my father too." Bell identifies with the old timers: "some of the old-time sheriffs never even wore a gun. . . . I always liked to hear about the old timers; never missed a chance to do so; you can't help but compare yourself against the old timers." The voice-over ends with Bell's clear declaration that he does not consider himself a part of his current world, instead seeing himself aligned with the "old timers" and his memory of how things used to be. Bell's voice-over commentary demonstrates his incomprehension of this new type of outlaw:

> There's this boy I sent to the 'lectric chair there at Huntsville a while back. My arrest and my testimony. He killed a fourteen-year-old girl. The papers said it was a crime of passion, but he told me there wasn't any passion to it. . . . He told me he'd been planning to kill somebody for about as long as he could remember. Said that if they turned him out he'd do it again. Said he knew he's goin' to hell. Be there in about 15 minutes. I don't know what to make of that, I surely don't; the crime you see now it's hard to even take its measure.

The series of scenes of Bell lamenting the past begins with the sheriff wistfully wondering how the previous generation of sheriffs would "have operated in these times." He acknowledges wryly, "I always knew you had to be willing to die to even do this job." This comment recalls lines from any number of Westerns, such as Gary Cooper's Marshal Will Kane from *High Noon* (1952) when he declares, "In the end, you end up dying all alone on a dirty street. And for what? For nothing" (Dillon 1993, 84). However, Ed Tom Bell is not eager for such an end, as he continues, "But, I don't want to push my chips forward and go out and meet something I don't understand. A man would have to put his soul at hazard. He'd have to say, 'OK, I'll be part of this world.'" Bell tells stories occasionally to illustrate that he does not understand modern violence and brutality, and he suggests that it is much worse, in his eyes, than it once was. For when he tells his deputy the tale of the gang who killed the elderly for their Social Security checks, he adds, "They tortured them for awhile [before killing them]; don't know why. Maybe the television set was broke." Bell sees himself, however, as a part of the problem, as he explains to his Uncle Ellis during a visit to see his dad's retired deputy who was himself crippled in a gunfight. Bell is at a loss to understand these new criminal elements. He tells Ellis he "feels overmatched" by them.

William Handley, in writing about the relationship of history to narrative, questions whether "we can ever read the past or its relation to the present except as, or through, plots, stories, narratives, or poetic constructs" (2002, 44). Because he has constructed his own view of both the past and his relationship to the present, Ed Tom Bell regrets his inability to effect change. Ellis tells him the story of his Uncle Mac, a Texas Ranger, and how he was "shot down on his own porch there in Hudspeth County." He assures Ed Tom, "What you got ain't nothin new. This country is hard on people. Hard and crazy. Got the devil in it, yet folks never seem to hold it to account." When Ed Tom admits that he's discouraged Ellis cautions him, "You can't stop what's comin. Ain't all waitin' on you." He accuses Ed Tom of "vanity" and reminds him that the Texas borderlands have always had a history of violence. Yet this yearning for the past that he believes existed is not Bell's only ironic flaw; he also is a lawman who abhors violence.

Bell further admits his own alienation from the present with his laconic lament and headshake: "signs and wonders, signs and wonders." He sees the modern age as full of omens and incredible events, and his reference to the television set as possibly on the fritz suggests that he understands, subconsciously at least, that this new breed of criminal simply sees its own handiwork as entertainment, a sort of violent reality show. Bell's remark also carries a biblical subtext, prophetic of the end of the world. Clearly, it is the end of Ed Tom's world.

Bell's inability to comprehend the nature of the new violence, as well as his fear of it, makes him reluctant to pursue Chigurh. When at the Moss trailer, the deputy asks if they need to go in once they see the door lock has been removed. The sheriff replies, "Gun up and out." The deputy asks, "What about yours?" Bell answers, "I'm hidin' behind you." His deputy wonders aloud if Moss has any idea of the viciousness of the man who seeks him, and Bell responds, "I don't know. He ought to. He's seen the same things I've seen and it certainly impressed me." When Sheriff Giddens calls the mysterious killer we know is Chigurh "a God damned homicidal lunatic," Bell responds that he thinks he's a "ghost." Giddens however, disagrees: "He's real, all right. . . . He shoots the desk clerk one day, and walks right back in the next and shoots a retired army colonel. . . . Strolls right back into a crime scene. Who would do such a thing? How do you defend against it?" Although Ed Tom clearly feels that there really is no defense against such incomprehensible violence, he nevertheless returns to the motel where Moss was killed and where he suspects Chigurh may have gone to retrieve the money. As he enters the room, his shadow hands seem poised above his holster as if he were bracing for a gunfight in an ironic vignette from a traditional Western. Uncertain whether Chigurh is hiding in the bathroom he hesitates as he opens the bathroom door to find only an empty room. He sits wearily on the motel bed looking defeated, yet relieved that he has not encountered his mysterious adversary. This is the closest Bell comes to acting heroically. As a pursuer, he arrives moments too late and remains spotless and "impressed" through the film.

References to traditional Westerns and to the history of this region arise periodically in the film, perhaps an homage to the dead, maybe a small inside joke for the fans of the Western, another dying breed. The Coens insert modest tableaus such as the shot of pointy boot toes turned toward heaven, the "bad guy" dressed in black, or at least very dark clothing, plus requisite shots of hats, horses, and guns. Juxtaposed against these iconic images are symbols of modern crime: automatic weapons, pickup trucks, drugs, flashing lights, telephones, and motel rooms. In an inversion of a Western cliché, Llewelyn Moss frequently runs from his pursuers. His pickup is disabled early—he never has a horse and seems to take cabs wherever he needs to go. In Western movies, traditionally the stars are all but bullet-proof, and even when nicked or grazed, shake off the pain and fight heroically. Moss has no heroic moments, and spends much of the film wounded, weakened, or disabled.

Moss is only a dim reflection of the solid citizen as traditionally represented in Westerns, willing to step in to cover the sheriff's back, protect the town, and ensure the safety of his wife and family. Upon first seeing him on the screen, his "cowboy" identity is quickly established by his clothing and demeanor. Larry McMurtry argues that "historically, perhaps even mythologically, the inseparability of cowboys and boots would seem to be clearly established: a part, if only a tiny part, of the national consciousness" (1987, 125). Cowboy boots may be the last accessible symbol of a way of life that has come and gone. As Moss lies on the ground, sighting pronghorn, he supports the gun on one of his boots and says, "You hold still," yet this command holds no authority as he misses the shot and only wounds the deer when his bullet glances off a nearby rock. As Lee Clark Mitchell argues in *Making the Man in Fiction and Film,*

> The familiar materials of the western genre's beginning—a lone man packing a gun, astride a horse, hat pulled close to his eyes, emerging as if by magic out of a landscape from which he seems ineluctably a part—are brought together as a set of problems recurring in an endless combination: the problem of progress, envisioned as a passing of frontiers; the problem of honor, defined in a context of social expediency; the problem of law or justice, enacted in a conflict of vengeance and social control; the problem of violence, in acknowledging its value yet honoring occasions when it can be controlled; and subsuming all, the problem of what it means to be a man, as aging victim of progress, embodiment of honor, champion of justice in an unjust world. (1996, 3)

Alone against the vast landscape, Moss initially appears to be a rugged individualist and capable hunter, yet none of this is true. First he misses his shot; then, once Moss stumbles upon the massacred drug dealers, any sense of this character's inherent honor is quickly dispelled. Moss assesses the situation and proceeds to hunt down the "last man standing," and quickly locates the drug money and the dead drug dealer. The honorable cowboy in the white hat vanishes as the modern opportunist emerges. Jason Mitchell suggests that the idealized cowboy is similar to the classic mythological hero and "serves for Americans the same purpose as Hercules did for the Greeks and Beowulf for the Anglo-Saxons." He is "the exemplar of the American" (2000, 293). Yet even the idealized image of this cowboy shadowed against the western sky belies Moss's true nature which is not, as Joseph Rosa writes, "the heroic image of the lone crusader who fights evil in order that good may prevail—a paragon of virtue, beyond reproach" (1969, v). Moss is neither heroic nor "good." In fact, his only "good deed," returning with water for the dying drug runner, is the act that predicates his eventual demise.

As a villain, Chigurh is unlike any previous Western movie villain. He is nearly inscrutable, both to the other characters in the film as well as to the audience. Early in the film, Chigurh is delivered to the local jail by an unnamed deputy, who leaves Chigurh sitting handcuffed on a bench while he telephones the sheriff explaining the arrest and the confiscation of Chigurh's unusual equipment: "Sheriff, he had some sort of thing on him like one of them oxygen tanks for emphysema or somethin'. And a hose from it run down his sleeve. Well, you got me sir; you can see it when you get in." Unfortunately, the deputy is unaware of the threat he has left behind him. Chigurh calmly and deliberately slips the handcuffs under his legs, then walks up behind the deputy and strangles him with his handcuffs as soon as he puts down the telephone. Falling to the floor, he pulls the deputy down and chokes him to death in a torturous scene that plays for nearly thirty seconds of screen time. Chigurh's face reflects his concentrated, impassive effort with a chilling lack of emotion. Equally disturbing is the method Chigurh chooses for executing his other victims: a pneumatic bolt pistol used for killing cattle, which he regains after murdering the deputy and shortly uses to kill dispassionately a second victim whose car he needs. Few movie villains compare to the taciturnity and heartlessness of this mechanized killer. He leaves no witnesses to his actual crimes, although an early survivor is rewarded by having called a coin toss correctly because in Chigurh's sense of justice, good fortune has prevailed. Later Moss's wife, Carla Jean, refuses to call the coin toss, and presumably dies, as the fulfillment of a promise that Chigurh had made with her now-dead husband:

Chigurh: So this is what I'll offer. You bring me the money and I'll let her go. Otherwise, she's accountable. The same as you. That's the best deal you're going to get. I won't tell you that you can save yourself because you can't.

Moss: Yeah I'm gonna bring you somethin' all right. I've decided to make you a special project of mine. You ain't gonna have to look for me at all.

Chigurh offers Carla Jean a chance when he confronts her in her own bedroom, coldly explaining to her that her husband had a chance to save her and failed to take it. Carla Jean, facing her own certain death, resists the implication: "It's not like that; you don't understand." She slowly accepts her fate, instinctively recognizing the evil that her husband completely ignored and that the gas station owner Chigurh had menaced earlier could not comprehend. Carla Jean admits to Chigurh, "I knowed you was crazy when I saw you sitting there. I knowed exactly what was in store for me." This offering of a chance at survival in the form of a coin toss is characteristic of Chigurh's psychotic personality. As rival hit man Carson Wells points out to Moss, "He has principles that transcend drugs or money or anything else. He not like you. He's not even like me." Wells does his best to try to warn the naïve Moss that he, too, is overmatched. Ironically Wells does not believe he himself is overmatched, and yet he is one of Chigurh's easiest victims, practically walking into Chigurh's arms after having warned Moss of the danger from Chigurh. Chigurh's icy demeanor is made apparent when he calmly speaks to Moss on the telephone as Wells' spreading blood threatens his stiletto-toed alligator boots. Chigurh simply raises his glossy feet to rest on the bed, safe from the encroaching gore.

Chigurh bears little resemblance to traditional bad guys, and in fact, wears no Western apparel. He appears archetypal in his menace rather than an expression of the region in which he operates. His character personifies fear itself, that danger that cannot be denied. Chigurh is the undefinable "what's coming."

No gray moral areas exist in the formula Western, but in the hands of the Coen brothers the moral view seems to be gray and indistinct, revealed not in the characters but in the situations. Traditionally, in Westerns, each character type is clearly identifiable. The hero is saintly or at least honorable in his intentions; the villain has no redeeming qualities, and even the fence sitters eventually choose good over evil. There is no moral confusion and certainly no moral self-deception. Such clarity is not evident in *No Country for Old Men:* Sheriff Bell knows he has trod too close to evil to have remained pure, Llewelyn Moss regards his act of mercy as one of his "stupid" actions. Bell's soliloquy at the end of the film appears colored by his own subconscious recognition that the myth of a heroic West has been exposed as a dream.

As a villain, Chigurh is chilling as the representation of evil with a per-verted sense of justice, logic, and opportunity. As Chigurh literally "fol-lows the money," he does so by checking a telephone bill pushed through a nonexistent mail slot, but mostly with the aid of a transponder hidden in the stolen $2 million. He is cold, calculating, and certain that those with whom he comes into contact deserve whatever fate he inflicts upon them. Sean Weitner, associate editor of *Flak Magazine*, a digital e-zine of art and media, writes of Chigurh, "Whenever he meets someone, he doesn't look for reasons to kill him; he looks for reasons to let him live, and rarely finds any, which is bad news for the other guy if Chigurh thinks he can make a clean getaway. . . . Chigurh's attitude toward those who come up with their own rules to justify whatever way of living they choose while simultaneously trying to integrate that into the larger context of a society based on shared ethics. . . [is] opposed to Chigurh's utter indifference to both society and other people" (2007, para. 5). Todd McCarthy, writing in *Variety*, describes Chigurh as someone who deals fairly with anyone who crosses his path; he explains to his soon-to-be victim that "if everything you've done in your life has led you to him . . . your time might just have come" (2007, para. 6). Chigurh's sense of fair play is best demonstrated when he stops to buy gas and a snack at an out-of-the-way convenience store and gas station. The proprietor's attempts at small talk lead to a terrifying few moments as the killer twists what should have been a momentary exchange of pleasantries into an increasingly hostile and derisive conversation, during which he slaps a quarter onto the counter and demands that the proprietor call heads or tails. Clearly confused by the entire incident, the proprietor at first refuses, saying he didn't put up anything, only to be assured by Chigurh, "Yes you did. You been putting it up your whole life. You just didn't know it." Chigurh warns the man, "You need to call it. I can't call it for you. It wouldn't be fair. It wouldn't even be right."

Chigurh himself is not a Texan, nor is he Mexican. His origins are as cloudy as his sense of fair play; he is not motivated by compassion cer-tainly, but neither is he motivated solely by greed. He executes his own associates even more summarily than he does unwary travelers, and he seems more interested in killing than in recovering the lost $2 million. When Moss first hears his name from Carson Wells, he mistakenly be-lieves the killer's name is Sugar, perhaps the film's greatest irony. No sweetness exists in Chigurh's life, and none exists in his wake. Even when Chigurh leaves his victims alive, like the gas station proprietor, they feel the chill of a brush with evil. Chigurh leaves few behind to describe him. By the conclusion of the film, Chigurh has walked away nursing a com-pound arm fracture and a few other injuries, but he has survived worse and the audience knows he will survive this as well. His injuries are a result of bad luck, not of the work of Sheriff Bell, who has already reached the end of his questionable usefulness.

Bell is not welcome at home. He invites his wife to go riding with him, and she tells him, "I'm not the one who retired." She further refuses his offer to stay and help her with household chores, since she has her own routine. Loretta Bell is no artifact or relic of the myth; she plays a woman with not only her own life, but also her own horse, which Bell instructs his deputy to ride:

> Ed Tom: You ride Winston.
> Wendell: You sure?
> Ed Tom: Oh, I'm sure. Anything happens to Loretta's horse, I don't want to be the party that was on board.

In traditional Westerns women are supportive, but their role was limited to waving good-bye as husbands and lovers rode away. They were regularly filmed from behind, crisp white aprons tied snugly around trim waists, as the pursuers departed in search of the bad guys. Loretta suggests that she'd like to see rental income from the county for the use of Winston, who is after all, privately owned. Her goodbye to Ed Tom is a slightly updated version of the classic parting:

> Loretta: Be careful.
> Ed Tom: I always am.
> Loretta: Don't get hurt.
> Ed Tom: I never do.
> Loretta: Don't hurt no one.
> Ed Tom: Well, if you say so.

On the verge of retirement, Bell tells Ellis that he had always assumed that as he got older "God would sorta come into my life somehow. And he didn't. I don't blame him. If I was him, I'd have the same opinion of me that he does." He no longer expects understanding or acceptance in this world or the next. The film ends with Bell relating a dream, wherein his much admired father is carrying fire, going on ahead in a cold and dark place, to start a fire and wait for him. Bell's life, spent mopping up once the violence is over, is nearing its futile end. The film is a powerful look into the heart of darkness, an acknowledgement that life is hard and then you die.

Nick James, editor of *Sight & Sound*, the British Film Institute's critical magazine, suggests that "if you were to consider Chigurh as the bad guy, Bell as the good guy, and Moss as the one caught between darkness and light, you wouldn't be far from the truth" (2007, 22). Yet this pronouncement can only be true if the film is viewed through the lens of the Old

West, for there's nothing heroic about Ed Tom Bell, nothing uncertain about the naïveté and greed of Llewelyn Moss, and no consistency in our understanding of evil as revealed by Anton Chigurh.

REFERENCES

Dillon, Richard, comp. 1993. *Western Quotations: Famous Words from the American West*. Tempe, AZ: Four Peaks Press.

Handley, William R. 2002. *Marriage, Violence, and the Nation in the American Literary West*. New York: Cambridge University Press.

High Noon. 1952. Dir. Fred Zimmerman. Stanley Kramer Productions.

James, Nick. 2007. "Blood Money." *Sight & Sound* 17: 20–22.

McCarthy, Cormac. 2005. *No Country for Old Men*. New York: Alfred A. Knopf.

McCarthy, Todd. 2007. "*No Country for Old Men*." *Variety*, May 18. www.variety.com/index.asp?layout=festivals&jump=review&reviewid=VE1117933677&cs=1&query=no+country+for+old+men.

McMurtry, Larry. 1987. "Approaching Cheyenne . . . Leaving Lumet. Oh, Pshaw!" In *Film Flam: Essays on Hollywood*, 125–31. New York: Simon & Schuster.

Mitchell, Jason P. 2000. "Louise Erdrich's *Love Medicine*, Cormac McCarthy's *Blood Meridian*, and the (De)Mythologizing of the American West." *Critique: Studies in Contemporary Fiction* 41 (Spring): 290–303.

Mitchell, Lee Clark. 1996. *Making the Man in Fiction and Film*. Chicago: University of Chicago Press.

No Country for Old Men. 2007. Dir. Ethan Coen and Joel Coen. Miramax Films.

Rosa, Joseph G. 1969. *The Gunfighter: Man or Myth*. Norman: University of Oklahoma Press.

Weitner, Sean. 2007. "Review of *No Country for Old Men*." *Flak Magazine*. www.flakmag.com/film/nocountry.

Yeats, William Butler. n.d. "Sailing to Byzantium." *The Literature Network*. www.online-literature.com/yeats/781.

9

+

Devil with a Bad Haircut: Postmodern Villainy Rides the Range in *No Country for Old Men*

Scott Covell

Girl: Which part were you reading, Billy?
Billy ("the Kid") Bonney: About how Cain killed Abel. Do you know
that was the first killing ever took place?
Girl: Oh yes, I know.
Billy: Sure has been a parcel of 'em since then . . .
Girl: Sure has.

—From *Chisum*

War is God.

—Judge Holden, *Blood Meridian*

What's this guy supposed to be, the ultimate badass?

—Llewelyn Moss on Anton Chigurh, *No Country for Old Men*

American cultural depictions of Western villains have come a long way
from the nineteenth century of the Deadwood Dick dime novels and
the bushy-mustacheoed killers of early silent screen melodramas. Gone
are the halcyon days of the Western as the number one film genre, but
certainly 2007 provided a sort of boon for Westerns of various types as
well as for diverse Western villains. The remake of *3:10 to Yuma* gave us
a fine revisioning of Elmore Leonard's Jim Kidd, thanks in part to Russell

Crowe. *The Assassination of Jesse James by the Coward Robert Ford* (based on the recent novel by Ron Hansen) provided both legendary outlaw villain Jesse James as well as his killer, Robert Ford, and begged the question of who, really, was the most "villainous": the famous outlaw killer or the "coward" who shot him in the back. *There Will be Blood* (2007; very loosely adapted from Upton Sinclair's *Oil!*) is situated in a Western milieu some forty years after death of James, but Daniel Day-Lewis's epic Daniel Plainview is no less a Western villain than Jesse James or *Yuma's* killer.

And then there's Anton Chigurh of *No Country for Old Men* (2007), and the late twentieth-century American West. We see him stalking about 1980s west Texas with his strange carbon dioxide–powered cattlegun kit, his white socks, his sardonic dark visage, his bad haircut. He flips a coin, acts as facilitator of the universe, has a strange way of opening doors, is impossible to trace, and exists without enemies because he doesn't "permit such a thing" (*No Country*, 253). Yet for all his oddness, the killer Anton Chigurh—as played by Oscar-winning Javier Bardem in Ethan and Joel Coen's Oscar-winning film adaptation of Cormac McCarthy's novel *No Country for Old Men* (2005)—shares traits of many murderous villains in Hollywood's Westerns and in American literature, as well as those of more contemporary pop culture characters. Nevertheless, it is Bardem's unique performance along with McCarthy's and the Coen brothers' "play" with and subversion of McCarthy's earlier bloodbath-on-the-border yarn, *Blood Meridian* (1985), and older Western texts and their killers as well as contemporary cult figures that leads to the brilliant collaborative creation of the postmodern Western villain, Anton Chigurh. In true postmodern fashion, Chigurh's multilayered character challenges and destabilizes the idea of a singular Western villain identity, as it continually "point[s] to a certain context, or to a certain story within which the character previously evolved," offering "a re-writing or hypertext where one . . . is able to recover the 'threads' of previous stories woven into the hypertext" (Musat 2006, 2). Chigurh emerges as a human palimpsest, wherein images and aspects of earlier texts and cultural artifacts may be perceived, morphing into an intriguing twenty-first-century depiction of the ultimate Western villain persona.

Initially, we may not know what to make of the filmic Chigurh. We first see him being brought into a police station by a Texas police deputy for reasons unknown. Javier Bardem's Anton Chigurh is imposing, powerfully built, replete with dark denim jacket and jeans, and sporting that infamous page-boy haircut that so many film critics and comedians have feted. Comedian Jon Stewart calls it a "Dorothy Hamill wedge-cut" (Nair 2008, 5); for David Denby, it is a "modified Prince Valiant" hairdo (2008, 1), while Michael Ordoña sees Chigurh as "alarmingly coifed" (2008, E6). David Letterman said, "The haircut alone is too creepy for Americans"

(Letterman 2008). Director Joel Coen explains, "We wanted somebody who could have come from Mars" (Turan 2007, C3). Apparently, Bardem agreed; reportedly he took one look at the cut and said, "Oh no, now I won't get laid for the next two months" ("Latest News" 2008, 1). There is something so incongruous about his odd hair and out-of-place clothing options, which is made all that more sinister by the nature of his face. But for the face, he could be anyone—the innocuous everyman. As a boy tells Sheriff Bell in the novel, "He looks like anybody. . . . He didn't look like anybody. . . . He didn't look like anybody you'd want to mess with" (*No Country*, 292). But there *is* the face. With his glum, dark, generally malevolent eyes and wide lips and nose, Bardem resembles some glowering Olmec god. His accent and his origins are "unplaceable," as Joel Coen says ("The Making of" 2008), but there's more than just a strange accent in Bardem's uncanny performance. Perhaps costar Josh Brolin puts it best: "He brings this soul to it that makes it very eerie" ("The Making of" 2008). And this eeriness even translates to his attire. Chigurh's boots, as the film's costume designer Mary Zophres states, "just sort of made you cringe if you look at them; . . . bumpy, gross and pointy—they could kill somebody" ("The Making of" 2008). He certainly wastes no time in "kill[ing] somebody," as the opening scene visit to the police station is punctuated by his brutal murder of the deputy. Chigurh stretches his manacled hands around the officer's neck, falls back onto the floor with the poor fellow pinned to his chest, and strangles him. The killing takes some time, and with his hair fanned out behind him on the floor, Chigurh appears weirdly gleeful in the process—like that Karen Black *Trilogy of Terror* Zuni fetish doll—staring up to the heavens with a bemused dazed look, a sinister priest delivering a twisted benediction.

It is when Chigurh stalks the forlorn motel sidewalk shoeless, his white socks glowing in the Texas night, the pneumatic cattlegun rig and the shotgun by his side, that the Coens' postmodern sensibility hits full stride—and Bardem only intensifies the feeling. Chugurh is at once so ponderous, so deadly, but yet so ordinary—with even a touch of what Chris Vogner calls "geek chic feel" (2004, 1). Nitin Nair alludes to this odd duality in "Chigurh: The Ultimate Psycho": "Here's a man . . . who is stoic and philosophical, someone who can be downright clumsy one moment, but can kill with a clinical nonchalance the next" (2008, 2). It is as if, like Brad Pitt's Tyler Durden floating about the head of the psychotic narrator of *Fight Club* (1999), behind the sinister assassin aspect of Anton Chigurh there looms the John Heder persona of *Napoleon Dynamite* (2004). There is a fragment of Anton Chigurh that is tinged with the nerdiness of such proto-twenty-first-century male geeks as Heder, Michael Cera's Paulie Bleeker from *Juno* (2007), and Christopher Mintz-Plasse's ultra-nerd Fogel in *Superbad* (2007), who epitomize what Peter Travers of *Rolling Stone* calls "geek perfection" (2004, 1). Such analogies to *No Country for Old Men* may be a bit hard to fathom at this juncture, what with Anton Chigurh's glowering face looming "ghost"-like before us. However, when Vogner in his review of *Napoleon Dynamite* talks about Napoleon operating "under a flag of deadpan weirdness," and of his friend, that "near-somnambulant Mexican kid," don't those comments suggest the solemn, yet, well, "geek[ish]" side of Chigurh? (Vogner 2004, 1). Chigurh's "deadpan weirdness" is one of the ways we might categorize his behavior, which approaches on occasion "near-somnambulan[ce]." And just as Napoleon Dynamite's appearance shouts "nerdy," off-kilter, eccentric, and geekish, with his "mangy nest of orange hair," sporting moon boots and an unknown action figure tied to a fishing line, so does Anton Chigurh's "look" (particularly in the motel assassination scene), with his gleaming white socks, his sawed-off mop of black hair, his slumberous Olmec god expression, and just his sheer against-the-code audacity in carting around the cattlegun with its clunky almost Victorian air canister—and to use that ridiculous thing to kill people! (Shannon 2008, 1). This killer's persona is twisted in a wonderfully Coen brothers' way, as they remain ever the trendsetters and trendcatchers, capturing a specific American *zeitgeist*, and fulfilling Michael Ordoña's claim of their being "leaders of American cinema" (2008, E6).

But how does Chigurh stack up against the leading cinematic villains, and those of strictly Western traditions? Nair claims, "As a cinematic villain, Chigurh is, arguably, at the head of a table that seats Anthony Hopkins' Hannibal Lecter, Jack Nicholson's Jack Torrance from *The Shining* and Anthony Perkins' Norman Bates from *Psycho*"—a formidable and highly recognizable bunch" (2008, 2). As for Chigurh's ranking in more Western, if lesser-known, circles of villainy, we must establish what exactly constitutes a "Western villain." While the geography and the times have changed for the bad men in American Western films and literature, one thing that hasn't changed is their adherence to the *ethos of violence*. The Western villain killer experiences life vis-à-vis violence. Whatever the tool for perpetrating it, and whatever his attitude and era, his weltanschauung is confirmed by his propensity for/joy in/intractable bent for destruction: a destruction that empowers and deifies him. In addition, his appearance is striking, often eccentric, sometimes horrible. A crack shot and death with any weapon (however strange it may be), the Western villain killer's greatest joy is to toy with his victims. This character is what students, gamers, online film review bloggers (and even Llewelyn Moss, ultimately) call "the ultimate badass." There have been many greats of this type, but best old-school version remains the immortal Jack Palance and his portrayal of the murderous gunfighter Jack Wilson in *Shane*, George Stevens's 1953 film version of Jack Schaefer's novel. The obvious archetype of the evil Western gunslinger, Wilson drips crafted malevolence. With his towering height, his black gunfighter's regalia, his wide and massive brown leather gunbelt and twin-holstered Colts, Wilson evokes images of mercenary medieval knights, like the Black Knight of Ivanhoe; even his spurs jangle or "clink" like armor when he moves. Lean, bent, and dangerous as a snake, he's like some vicious bird of prey, hovering. Beyond that, there is Wilson's face (Palance was hit in a World War II bombing run), which strikes one as über sinister: puffy and malleable as an ancient gremlin, yet hard and chiseled like it was sledge-hammered out of granite. One remembers Billy Crystal's classic quip about the older Palance (as Curly Washburn) in *City Slickers* (1991): "Did you see that guy? That was the toughest man I've ever seen in my life. . . . He was like a saddlebag with eyes!" And always the satanic grimace of glee on Wilson's face in *Shane*, the anticipation of mayhem. Nowhere is this more evident than in the pitiable slaughter of the farmer, Torrey. Waiting for the poor man, like a grinning Jack o' Lantern on a barrel, Wilson baits him into a fight as—vulture-like—he then stalks Torrey's slow, forlorn, and hopeless mud-lane journey:

"They tell me they call you 'Stonewall,'" sneers Wilson at Torrey.
    "Anything wrong with that?"
    "I guess they named a lot of that . . . southern trash after old Stonewall," he says, putting his gloves on deliberately.
    "What did they name you after . . . or do you even know."
    "I'm saying that Stonewall Jackson is trash himself. Him, and Lee, and all the rest of them Rebs. You too." [Add vulture smirk.]
    "You're a lowdown lying Yankee."
    "Prove it." (*Shane* 1953)

Torrey draws his gun pathetically and is easily outgunned by the lightening-quick Wilson and killed, collapsing with a thud deep into the mud. Wilson gives us his evil grin, and as an onlooker quips, "One less sodbuster," we hear Wilson's bodiless snicker eerily float the air. Wilson's enjoyment of the killing is common with the Western killer, and it reminds one of the glee of Poe's revengeful Montressor in "The Cask of Amontillado" or perhaps that of the archetypal gleeful literary killer: Aaron the Moor in Shakespeare's *Titus Andronicus* (2000). (After conning Titus into cutting off his hand to save his sons—a promise Aaron has no plans of fulfilling—we see him in Julie Taymor's film version [1999] joyously proclaiming, "Oh, how this villainy doth fat me with the very thoughts of it!" [3.1.202–3].)

There are many iconic "badass" Western killers of this nature in American film and literature, from *The Virginian*'s nemesis Trampas (novel in 1902, first film version in 1914) to Russell Crowe's Jim Kidd of 2007's *3:10 to Yuma*. Many of these were of course, psychotic and little weird;

however, it was Marlon Brando's Robert E. Lee Clayton in Arthur Penn's *Missouri Breaks* of 1976 that set the standard for a new type of Western killer portrayed in late-twentieth-century works: the more eccentric, flamboyant, and horrible villain. Brando plays the bizarre, apparently Irish, hired assassin Lee Clayton, who, with his long stringy blonde hair descending from a partially bald dome and his propensity for extremely odd clothing, is strange, goofy, flamboyant: obviously psychotic but in a happy way. He sings little ditties. His best friends are his horse and mule, with whom he argues and nibbles carrots. Critic Philip French suggests that his "extravagant manner and accent seem to be sending up Richard Harris" (2003, 1). Yet Clayton is a brilliant assassin, and proclaims such. Observing a recent corpse, he suggests, "If you had me around in the first place, this poor man wouldn't have lost his life." His assurance and aura of invincibility and control are important factors in this type of Western killer. Another way Clayton stands out is by unusual weaponry, including a rare Creedmore rifle, which, according to Jack Nicholson's Tom Logan, "Must make a pretty good mess of a human"—and it does. He also owns and utilizes a strange handmade cross-shaped tomahawk weapon composed of four thin "blades" held together by what appears to be a Native American–type binding: leather and little trinkets and bones hanging off of its center which "jingle" uncannily when the weapon finds its target. We first see this in use when Clayton tracks down a wild hare and spears the tiny creature with a perfect toss of the tomahawk, all the while screaming, hollering, and laughing like some deranged Plains warrior of times past. Like Wilson in *Shane* and other Western killers, Clayton enjoys toying with his victims. He pretends to befriend Randy Quaid's character, Little Todd, one night, speaking in a down-home Western dialect to fool him, harassing him around a campfire, and later dropping a giant beetle into his snoring mouth. The next day he sends Todd out into raging river tied to a rope, making quite a game of it, only to pluck him off his horse and watch him slowly drown. "Adios amigo," he says smirking, in yet his third accent, as Todd disappears beneath the current. Later he toys with Harry Dean Stanton's Calvin, who, mortally wounded, is asked by Clayton—now dressed as "poor ol' granny"—to stare up at the heavens to find the "Star of Bethlehem." As he looks up, Clayton then hurtles his own little "Star of Bethlehem" at Calvin, catching him square in the right eye, while the trinkets jingle. He has been told that he is "out of control" and ordered "off the job!" by the rancher, but Clayton won't "get" until the job is done and all are dead and his mastery over them is complete.

In terms of more contemporary film and literature, perhaps the most intriguing, sinister, powerful, and eccentric Western killer is Judge Holden, from Cormac McCarthy's brilliant earlier novel, *Blood Meridian, or, The Evening Redness in the West* (1985), which relates the massacres that took place south of the Mexican border in the 1840s between Americans, Mexicans, and various indigenous tribes. If Jack Wilson resembles the Black Knight in *Ivanhoe* (Scott and Tulluch 2000), the judge resembles the Green Knight in the medieval romance *Sir Gawain and the Green Knight* (1957). The judge is gigantic—he stands close to seven feet tall and weighs in at over three hundred pounds. However, he is somewhat of a contradiction in appearance: both massive and childlike, with his "oddly childish lips" (*Blood Meridian*, 140). He's "bald as a stone" (6), and when he enters a public bath to wash off the carnage of battle, he does so "with a cigar in his mouth and a regal air, testing the waters with one toe, surprisingly petite." As McCarthy describes him, "He shone like the moon so pale he was and not a hair to be seen anywhere upon that vast corpus. . . . The immense and gleaming dome of his naked skull looked like a cap for bathing pulled down to the otherwise darkened skin of his face and neck" (167). Despite his oddness, the judge is multitalented, can converse in many tongues and play any instrument, and is a "deadeye" with any weapon. At one point he faces down an entire tribe of Yumas with a small howitzer clasped to side. There is no question that the judge is some sort of primeval incarnation of war, of violent destruction, and if not the Devil himself, then a "devil" summoned up from hell's realm to carry on what he feels is the destiny and true talent of men: to kill each other. Tobin's tale of how the judge rescued his troop one time before the arrival of "the kid," the novel's protagonist, helps illustrate the judge's character, powers, and deadliness. Out of powder and running from hundreds of native warriors, Tobin recounts how he and his fellow merry band of killers, faced with disaster out in the desert, suddenly come upon the judge, "on his rock there in the wilderness by his single self" (125). After a deal is struck with head psycho Glanton, the judge immediately sets out exploring the countryside and compiling various raw materials from the desert wastes—for what purpose, the men don't know. As the Apaches close in for the kill, the judge mixes together the ingredients he has compiled: nitre, saltpeter, charcoal, and sulfur. He dumps them in a "cupped place in the rock" and stirs the mixture about with his hands; as Tobin relates it,

All the while the savages down there on the plain drawin' nigh to us and when I turned back the judge was standin, the great hairless oaf, and he'd took out his pizzle and he was pissin into the mixture, pissin with a great vengeance and one hand aloft and he cried out for us to do likewise. We were half mad anyways. . . . We hauled forth our members and at it we went and the judge on his knees kneadin the mass with his naked arms and the piss was splashin about and he was cryin out to us to piss, man, piss for your very souls for cant you see the redskins yonder, and laughin the while and workin up this great mass in a foul black dough, a devil's batter by the stink of it and him not a bloody dark pastryman himself. (131–32)

After drying the mixture and loading it into their guns, the judge then puts on quite the performance—pretending to be alone and desperate, and suckering the natives into a foolish assault. And as the Apaches charge up the hill, the judge "drew one [pistol] in each hand and he is as either handed as a spider . . . he commenced to kill Indians," as does the rest of Glanton's gang, until "there was fifty-eight of [the native war party] lay slaughtered among the gravels" (134).

Here we also see the judge's malevolent trickster impulse, a trait that informs his playing or toying with members of his own gang, for he knows they will all die soon. His conversations with Toadvine, Tobin, the kid, and Brown all bare a sense of his knowing something they don't which angers them all: "You're crazy Holden. Crazy at last," finally utters Brown (*Blood Meridian*, 249). But if he's crazy, there appears to be a method to his madness. His madness accompanies his *play*, his joy at empowerment and true knowledge of the human experience. This is particularly resonant when he toys with the kid at the climax of the novel, speaking of his disappointment with the young man when he meets up with him by chance at a crowded Western saloon: "I recognized you when I first saw you and yet you were a disappointment to me. Then and now. Even so at the last I find you here with me" (331). "I ain't with you," the kid tersely replies, once again making his stand against the judge and all he represents. The judge continues lecturing the kid on the forces of the world, as is his want, to which the kid finally responds with the usual appropriate response to these villains, "I don't like craziness" (330). Like it or not, the kid is stuck with it, and with the judge's judgment of him, and it is only a matter of a few hours before the judge ambushes the kid in a "jake" and murders him, having judged him unfit for his morbid ministry. Moments later we find the judge breaking into a merry jig on a saloon stage to the delight of all.

What also makes the judge intriguing, in a postmodern sense, is the way in which he appears to lay the foundation for McCarthy's Anton Chigurh character in *No Country for Old Men*. There are certainly some interesting correlative elements between the judge and Chigurh: both can't be defeated; gamble with people's lives; use coins and coin imagery to make their points; and as is common with other Western killers, utilize strange weaponry, toy with their victims, and perhaps most significantly, relish their moments of destruction—like Aaron the Moor, their "villainy doth fat [them] with the very thoughts of it." This last point is key to understanding an important aspect of American history and all of the Western villains surveyed here. When historian Richard Slotkin speaks of our nation's "regeneration through violence," he is referring to how our many outbreaks of "peculiar violence"—while horribly destructive on one hand—have furnished a regenerative condition wherein we

Americans have prospered as individuals and as a nation, and indeed, how this has led to our inescapable status as a "Gunfighter Nation" (1998, 12). In the same manner, for these gunfighting villains of the West, killing is the ultimate empowerment, and their horrific ontology is symbolized in many of these texts by the brutal slaying of innocents and innocent animals: Clayton and his tomahawking of the wild hare, Chigurh with his sudden drive-by annihilation of the crow on the bridge, and the judge with his drowning of the puppies and his shocking murder of the little boy, which even the ghastly Toadvine finds alarming. In the judge's case, this sensibility is compounded by his strange cataloging and ordering of all things. "Whatever in creation exists without my knowledge exists without my consent," he utters (*Blood Meridian*, 198), periodically collecting, cataloging, and then destroying his multifarious collections, as "he seeks to master and appropriate" (Shaviro 1999, 152). His ethics of control and domination embraces McCarthy's jab vis-à-vis *Blood Meridian* at the Manifest Destiny ideology of nineteenth-century America (one of Slotkin's main targets as well), but it also suggests the murderer's credo: to kill it is to own it. Chigurh's ethos of domination and control is also apparent when he states to the oil executive in the novel, "I don't have any enemies. I don't permit such a thing" (*No Country*, 253). These killers maintain an aura of invincibility and control that verges on the egomaniacal. When asked by the oil exec how he knows no one else is coming to join in the deathly madness, Chigurh responds, "Because I am in charge of who is coming and who is going" (251).

However, while Chigurh shares many of the judge's characteristics, he is not the reincarnation of the judge: Chigurh is more the kid, reborn, having chosen the judge's path. For one thing, unlike the judge, who appears invincible no doubt due to his hellish supernatural origins, Chigurh can be wounded, as he is twice in the story, so he must be at least *somewhat* human. As the *New Yorker*'s David Denby says, "He is not quite the ineffable spirit of Evil" (2008, 5). More particularly, Chigurh can be read as a revisioning of the kid in *Blood Meridian*—the kid gone bad, a kid who made a different choice, who picked a different talisman of the coin: McCarthy's twentieth-century alternative to the surrogate son, the kid was supposed to be to the judge. The novel, in this manner, functions palimpsestically. We can peer through the hypertext of *No Country for Old Men* to glimpse the vivid killers of an earlier McCarthy text—devious human "threads" informing the newer version, with an inversion of his former protagonist (the kid) into the very type of killer (Chigurh) his surrogate father (the judge) would have wanted him to be. There is a sense in McCarthy that in a conflict-corrupted world—one which the judge likens to "a migratory tentshow whose ultimate destination after many a pitch in many a muddied field is unspeakable and calamitous beyond reckoning" (*Blood*

Meridian, 245)—the dogs of war will be summoned forth by the darkness, the evil, the death that plagues the earth. While the demonic judge has been summoned forth out of some hellish netherworld to enact his thralldom upon those who would serve under his leadership—like one of "the sinners so notorious evil that the fires coughed em up again" that Tobin speaks of (*Blood Meridian*, 130)—Chigurh and the kid are human killers. But though the kid certainly participates in orgies of violence during *his* Western sojourn, he eventually demonstrates his difference from the others, and from what the judge would want him to be, with his subtle compassion for several comrades in arms and apparently by not joining into the gang's relentless festive slaughtering as much as the judge would have hoped. Both novels are all about choices, and the kid disappointed judge with his choices: "You alone reserved in your soul some corner of clemency for the heathen" (*Blood Meridian*, 299). Now, Anton Chigurh would certainly *not* have "reserved" *any* "clemency for the heathen." Whatever choices Chigurh may have made in his time led him to subscribe to the judge's religiosity of war, though 140 years later. The kid is not the real "coinage" the judge seeks in *Blood Meridian*, nor is he the real "dancer," for, as the judge proclaims, "Only that man who has offered up himself entire to the blood of war, who has been to the floor of the pit and seen horror in the round and learned at last that it speaks to his inmost heart, only that man can dance" (310, 331). Ultimately, "the blood of war" does not speak to the kid, but it does resound to the depths of Anton Chigurh. Chigurh would have been the perfect "son"/disciple/novitiate for the judge. Thus McCarthy, through his palimpsest of *No Country for Old Men*, revises his killers with a postmodern sensibility intensified by the work of Bardem and the Coens in the film version.

As David Denby puts it, "The Coens' work merges with McCarthy's lethal cool" to create Chigurh (2008, 5). This McCarthy/Coen brothers' collaborative film hypertext is particularly resonant with the work of Javier Barden in the conversation with the "filling station" proprietor (*No Country*, 52). Of this scene Nair says, "Not since Hannibal Lecter's casual admission to dining on an inquisitive census taker's liver with fava beans and chianti in *The Silence of the Lambs* has a conversation in Hollywood history invoked such terror" (2008, 3). Though the lines of the scene are specifically McCarthy, the presentation is all Bardem and Coen brothers. "Duel with the Desert Dimwit" features a lone gas station attendant suddenly realizing he's battling for his life, flummoxed by the intensely interrogatory cashew-eating Chigurh, who toys with him in the best tradition of the psychotic Western killer readying his victim for the kill:

> "You all getting any rain up your way?" the proprietor asks.
> "Which way would that be?"

"I seen you was from Dallas."
"And what business is it of yours, where I'm from . . . friendo?"
"I didn't mean nothing by it."
"Didn't mean nothing . . ." [Accompanied by a sardonic smirk.]

How such a simple innocuous question could lead to the verbal grilling to come and to darker concerns definitely befuddles "friendo," especially when Chigurh asks him,

"What time do you go to bed."
"Sir?"
"You're a bit deaf aren't you? I said what time do you go to bed."
"Well . . . Somewhere around 9:30. I'd say around 9:30."
"I could come back then." [Accompanied by another bizarre smirk.]
"Why would you be coming back? We'll be closed."
"Yea, you just said that." (*No Country* 2007)

Rather than call him—à la Jack Wilson—"white trash," or perhaps "big white dummy," Chigurh insults him in a more subtle underhanded way. Chigurh's comments are punctuated by his little sinister smirkings, which lends to the whole scene even more strangeness and more of a sense of black comic ridicule. Trickster-like, Chigurh's dark and heavy malevolent face often becomes suffused with such a sly sinister smirk reminiscent of Palance's evil sparkle, but Chigurh's private little grim grinnings are somehow stranger. In any case, the Texaco owner's biggest mistake was certainly suggesting that he knew where Chigurh was from, which wouldn't go over well with a killer trying to continually cover his tracks—to remain ghost-like. Still, Chigurh gives him a chance, apparently putting the owner's life up on the toss of a coin: "What's the most you ever lost in a coin toss?" The guy guesses right, despite his reluctance. In this story, some will get the coin toss and some won't; it appears Chigurh reserves the coin for the innocent whom he allows a choice. The guilty have made their choices already, and must die for them: the two hit men working for the Matacumbe Petroleum Group, the hit man Carson Wells who was paid to find Chigurh and dispense with him, the owner of the company who sicked Wells onto Chigurh, and the three Mexican drug cartel hit men blown away in their motel room. He particularly enjoys toying with Carson Wells (played by Woody Harrelson)—his counterpart, his proposed executioner—in one of the three pre-killing chats he has with prospective victims: "I do know to a certainty," he says to Wells, referring to future events, as they sit across from each other in the hotel room, Chigurh with the massive shotgun on his lap pointed directly at Wells. "And do you know what's gonna happen now Carson? You should admit your situation. There would be more dignity in it."

Carson shakes his head slowly. "You go to hell."

Chigurh sniggers, smirks, and responds, "All right. Let me ask you something: if the rule you followed brought you to this, [sinister smirking] of what use was the rule?"

Wells can only respond, "Do you have any idea how crazy you are?" (*No Country* 2007).

Anton's craziness is just another way for him to degrade Wells and empower himself in the best tradition of the Western "toying" killer. Just as Jack Wilson defiles the Southerner's deeply coded ideological construct when he insults Stonewall Jackson, so does Chigurh in his abasement of the "rules" Wells followed: the Western killer doesn't just humiliate the victim but assures that everything the victim had lived for—his rules, his heroes—is meaningless and suggests the wrong choices. Wells' life ends shortly thereafter, but not before his penultimate comment to Chigurh about his madness, which certainly embraces a commonality with all of these killers and how we perceive them.

In terms of his weaponry, like all badass Western killers, Chigurh is proficient with any weapon and often with whatever is available: the deputy is strangled with his own handcuffs; the innocent car owner on the freeway is popped in the skull with the cattle gun; the two oil company hit men are jarringly executed with a 9mm picked up off the ground, courtesy of the blown drug-deal shootout victims; the three Mexican killers in the motel are taken out with a silencer-clad shotgun; and as he flees, Moss is winged from the second floor of the hotel with a .45. "Damn," thinks Moss at that point in the novel, "What a shot" (*No Country*, 114). The silencer on the shotgun is itself fascinating; it looks like a giant spray can painted black. In the novel McCarthy tells us that the gun is "fitted with a shopmade silencer fully a foot long and big around as a beercan" (103). But his most intriguing weapon (and door-opening unit) is also one of the most perfect McCarthy/Coen brothers postmodern elements to the film and novel: the carbon dioxide–powered captive-bolt pistol. Here is a weapon—the signature weapon and utility usage instrument of our twenty-first-century Western killer, Anton Chigurh—which, besides referencing the odd weaponry of the more eccentric Western killer, in itself represents a stunning parody of the classic Western gunslinger with his Colt .45 and Winchester .73, for the air "gun" offers an inversion or subversion of the usual manly *implementia* carted about by our Western villains: it suggests a subversion of the ubiquitous cowboy and his use of a rifle to guard the vast herds of steer back in the "Wild West" days. This gun is used to *kill* the steer—not guard them—and its usage is promulgated not by its firepower but by its functional simplicity and effectiveness. As Bell states to another sheriff in the novel, referring to the old ways of knocking cattle "in the head with a maul," "They don't do it thata way no more.

They use an air-powered gun that shoots a steel bolt out of it. Just shoots it out about so far. They put that thing between the beef's eyes and pull the trigger and down she goes. It's that quick" (*No Country*, 105). Using the gun as a weapon of destruction serves as a rebuff, a spoof, a dissing of conventional manly ordinance. Even Brando's strange cross tomahawk implement in *The Missouri Breaks* resonates with a strong sense of Native American culture and the wildness of the frontier, but Chigurh's cattle-gun rig is odd, and smacks of the advent of technology and the death of the Old West and its natural and wild sensibility. Just as the onslaught of the drug cartels and their machine gun–prone killers signifies the end of the code of the West that Bell has known and reveres, so does Anton Chigurh's choice of weapons—and yet, well, there's something different, something perhaps "lethal[ly] cool" about it (Denby 2008, 5).

In the film version of *No Country for Old Men*, the Coen brothers and Javier Bardem have combined with Cormac McCarthy to create a new type of killer. He is postmodern; he is perhaps the figure of Death, or "the ineffable spirit of Evil" (Denby 2008, 5); he is possibly "the true and living prophet of destruction" Sheriff Bell sees mutating out there in the waste lands of the Americas (*No Country*, 4); he is "geek perfection" meets grim psychotic assassin, or as a student of mine put it, "Creepy as shit." We are drawn to such killers. Sure, we may revere the good people—what McCarthy calls in *The Road* (2006) the "godspoke men" [and women] out there who "carry the fire" (27, 83): people like Sheriff Bell, his dad, and his wife, Loretta, in *No Country for Old Men*; people like Carla Jean, old uncle Ellis, and even those who make some poor choices, like Llewelyn Moss—but it is the Anton Chigurhs who mesmerize us, with their deadliness, their craziness, and their ability to make us ask questions about our increasingly complex world and the role of good and evil in it. Recent Westerns surprisingly have fashioned some of the best ruminations into these questions, offering new villains with intriguing moral, behavioral, and ontological complexities and nuances. The twenty-first century calls for new villains in our films and literature. The great irony is that the most intriguing twenty-first-century depiction of the Western villain killer is not Brad Pitt's Jesse James, Russell Crowe's Joe Kidd, or Daniel Day-Lewis's Daniel Plainview, but Javier Bardem's and the Coen brothers' Anton Chigurh of the 1980s American West, with his evocations of such great American legends as Palance's Jack Wilson, Brando's Robert E. Lee Clayton, McCarthy's Judge Holden, and yes, even Napoleon Dynamite.

On the popular cultural landscape and among his Western brethren, Anton Chigurh holds the title for terrors both familiar and new. Before we last see him in *No Country for Old Men*, there is a scene where Sheriff Ed Tom Bell visits his uncle, who lives alone in a remote western locale. Windmill, cowboy hat, overalls, rocking chair—the synecdoche is in full

force to conjure up the Old West. Throw in a story about an Indian attack
and reference to old Uncle Mac's shotgun, which was used defensively
in said attack circa 1909 and ended up on display in a museum, and you
have the perfectly incongruous lead-in to Chigurh roaming the suburbs.
He, unlike, the gun, is no relict. He is the new Western villain palimpsest,
the volatile and ever-evolving collection of artifacts and guises and identi-
ties who rides the range of the self. "*Some new kind* [of killer] *coming down
the pike*," Sheriff Bell laments in the novel (*No Country*, 4). He entertains
us, creeps us out, even as he reminds us of where we've been, where we
are, and where we might be headed, the horizon reddening as we speak.

NOTE

Special thanks to my colleague, Mark Hoffer; his assistance was invaluable.

REFERENCES

3:10 to Yuma. 2007. Dir. James Mangold. Lionsgate Entertainment.
The Assassination of Jesse James by the Coward Robert Ford. 2007. Dir. Andrew
    Dominik. Warner Bros. Pictures.
City Slickers. 1991. Dir. Ron Underwood. Castle Rock Entertainment.
Denby, David. 2008. "Killing Joke: The Coen Brothers Twists and Turns." *New
    Yorker*, February 25. www.newyorker.com/arts/critics/atlarge/2008/02/25/
    080225crat_atlarge_denby.
Fight Club. 1999. Dir. David Fincher. Art Linson Productions.
French, Philip. 2003. "It Was a Classic Year for Western Heroes." *Observer*, May 25.
    www.guardian.co.uk/theobserver/2003/may/25/features.review47.
Juno. 2007. Dir. Jason Reitman. Dancing Elk Productions.
"Latest News: *No Country for Old Men*." 2008. *Cinestar*, June 9. www.cinestarcinemas
    .com/english/cs_cut.aspx.
Letterman, David. 2008. *The David Letterman Show*. NBC. November 14.
"The Making of *No Country for Old Men*." 2008. *No Country for Old Men*, special
    features. DVD. Dir. Ethan Coen and Joel Coen. Buena Vista Home Entertain-
    ment, Inc., and Paramount Vantage.
McCarthy, Cormac. 1985. Blood Meridian. New York: Vintage.
———. 2005. *No Country for Old Men*. New York: Vintage.
———. 2006. *The Road*. New York: Random House.
The Missouri Breaks. 1976. Dir. Arthur Penn. Devon/Persky-Bright.
Musat, Carmen. 2006. "Rewriting, Overwriting: The Palimpsest Effect in Contem-
    porary Literature." www.inst.at/trans/16Nr/09_6/musat16.htm.
Nair, Nitin. 2008. "Chigurh: The Ultimate Psycho." February 10. www.gulfnews
    .com/4men/Celebrities/10204500.html.
Napoleon Dynamite. 2004. Dir. Jared Hess. Fox Searchlight Pictures.

No Country for Old Men. 2007. Dir. Ethan Coen and Joel Coen. Miramax Films.

Ordoñā, Michael. 2008. "Coen Brothers Road Less Traveled Leads to *No Country for Old Men.*" Special to *Los Angeles Times*, February 10. www.theenvelope.latimes .com/news/env-ca-coens10feb10,0,6063571.story?page=1-2.

Scott, Sir Walter, and Graham Tulluch. 2000. *Ivanhoe.* New York: Penguin.

Shakespeare, William. 2000. *Titus Andronicus.* New York: Penguin.

Shane. 1953. Dir. George Stevens. Paramount Pictures.

Shannon, Jeff. 2008. Review of *Napoleon Dynamite. Elasticdog's DVD Library*, May 28. http://elasticdog.com/movies/page15.

Shaviro, Steven. 1999. "'The Very Life of Darkness': A Reading of *Blood Meridian.*" In *Perspectives on Cormac McCarthy*, ed. Edwin T. Arnold and Dianne C. Luce, 145–58. Jackson: University Press of Mississippi.

Sir Gawain and the Green Knight. 1957. In *Medieval Romances*, ed. Roger Sherman Loomis and Laura Hibbard Loomis. New York: Modern Library.

Slotkin, Richard. 1998. *Gunfighter Nation: The Myth of the Frontier in 20th-Century America.* Norman: University of Oklahoma Press.

Superbad. 2007. Dir. Greg Mottola. Columbia Pictures.

There Will be Blood. 2007. Dir. Paul Thomas Anderson. Ghoulardi Film Company.

Titus Andronicus. 1999. Julie Taymor. Clear Blue Sky Productions.

Travers, Peter. 2004. Review of *Napoleon Dynamite.* www.rollingstone.com/reviews/movie/6085489/review/6085490/napoleon_dynamite.

Turan, Kenneth. 2007. "O Brothers, What Hath Thou Wrought?" *Los Angeles Times*, May 19. http://articles.latimes.com/2007/05/19/calendar/et-coen19.

The Virginian. 1914. Cecil B. DeMille. Jesse L. Lasky Feature Film Co.

Vogner, Chris. 2004. "*Napoleon Dynamite*: Movie Review." *Dallas Morning News*, June 25. www.guidelive.com/portal/page?_pageid=33,97283&_dad=portal&_schema=PORTAL&item_id=21557.

Wister, Owen. 1902. *The Virginian.* New York: MacMillan.

10

✞

For Every Tatter
in Its Mortal Dress:
Costume and Character in
No Country for Old Men

Sonya Topolnisky

Three posters preceded the release of the Coen brothers' film *No Country for Old Men* (2007). In the first, we see a man against a dry sun-baked ground, facing forward and gripping a shotgun with knees bent in a ready stance. There is no indication as to what he is aiming at, but the tension in his limbs and his slightly hunched position imply that he is sneaking up on something. The image is tightly framed and cropped just above his waist. He wears a nondescript brown and white plaid shirt with the sleeves rolled up, blue jeans, and dusty cowboy boots. The second poster is similar in composition. This man wears cowboy boots, dark brown pants with a pressed crease down the leg, a brown tooled leather belt, and a tan shirt. His pose could reflect either surprise or a moment's pause before springing into action. He holds a gun in his right hand, a black pistol aimed down. As in the previous image, the clothing blends into the dun-colored background of sand, pebbles, and dry grasses. The last poster shows another man against a similar setting, but the palette is different. Blue-grey tones dominate, and the central figure is dressed in dark colors. His wide-legged pants flare slightly and are worn with a black belt and a dark brown long-sleeved shirt. His arms are relaxed, and he grips something in his right hand that resembles a gun with a strange chrome cylinder on its end. This image is more ominous and off-putting, largely because it is hard to discern what kind of weapon this is.

The posters depict three main characters of *No Country for Old Men*: Llewelyn Moss, played by Josh Brolin; Sheriff Bell, played by Tommy Lee Jones; and Anton Chigurh, played by Javier Bardem respectively. Moss is paired with the caption "There are no clean getaways," Bell with "There are no laws left," and Chigurh with "You can't stop what's coming." The images are intriguing because even though they exclude the characters' faces, they succeed in presenting three distinct and compelling types, at once strange and familiar. Isolating and reducing the characters to an amalgam of garments and weapons, these images served as the public introduction to the film. But what exactly are the implications and complications of the archetypal Western materiality that the posters so prominently project?

In interviews, the actors and the Coen brothers themselves have difficulty classifying *No Country for Old Men*, using the terms *chase, horror, comedy, Western*, and *noir* interchangeably. Categorizing it is no easy task, nor is it necessarily a desirable one. Of the assorted genres listed above, the Western is not only the most distinctive, but the most ideologically wrought. I do not seek to recast *No Country for Old Men* as a Western per se, but it bears a strong "family resemblance" to the genre through its preoccupation with violence and manhood.[1] Much of *No Country for Old Men*'s visual language borrows from that of Western films, setting up expectations and assumptions for the audience only to challenge or contradict them, some more immediately than others. Drawing on Cormac McCarthy's detailed and intimate descriptions in conjunction with the Coens' vision, I will explore how established conventions in costume and character are employed and complicated.

No Country for Old Men, both the novel and the film, tells a rich story set on barren terrain. It is a modern setting, yet this part of west Texas remains a wild and treacherous landscape that has yet to fall victim to the romantic nostalgia of the Old West. Nevertheless, ideas about the West as a place and the Western as a genre are bound to the narrative and the construction of characters. Here the cinematography lingers on the landscape long enough to bring to mind notions of cowboys and Indians, a patchwork of memories culled from fictional accounts of the last frontier. For an arid, nearly uninhabited landscape, the West as represented in literature and Western films is densely populated with myths and with concerns over American identity. In an interview following the film's release, Joel Coen noted, "It's hard to know exactly what a traditional western means. . . . We didn't particularly look at this movie as a Western in quotation marks" (Rich 2007, 2). Amid the disputed and reconstructed definitions of the genre, all that can be stated with any certainty is that the Western is not a monolithic rigidly defined category, but rather one that shifts with the changing winds of cultural anxieties (Mitchell 1996, 4–5).

The diverse assortment of films that have been defined as Westerns
are unified by iconography and their settings. *No Country for Old Men*,
however takes place in the west Texas borderlands in 1980. The recent
past can often be difficult to represent on film. From the standpoint of
production design the material artifacts are not always available, as few
people think to preserve what is recently outmoded. Rural locales also
present a challenge for audiences trying to position it chronologically
because they are not always up to date in terms of fashionable dress,
buildings, or interiors. Despite these caveats, the aesthetic sensibility,
and historical accuracy in *No Country for Old Men* is flawlessly rendered. The relative dearth of material indices adds an ageless quality
to the picture and allows for the overarching tone, the bleakness, and
the destruction to penetrate beyond the confines of a story bound to a
specific moment in time.

Objects, including costume, help position the narrative geographi-
cally and socially. Costume is particularly relevant when considering *No
Country for Old Men* in light of the Western tradition, a genre steeped in
iconic tropes and symbols connected to regional identity. Costume trends
in Western films have changed over successive generations, often subtly,
and covering a wide range of historical specificities. It is near impossible
to examine the shifting conventions in Western costume without getting
existential over definitions of authenticity. Jane Gaines and Charlotte
Herzog summarize this problem in their essay "The Fantasy of Authenticity in Western Costume," insisting that nowhere in other American
genres does nature flow into culture with greater ease, making the mythic
and the authentic virtually indistinguishable (1998, 172). Regardless of the
specifics of any particular film, the mention of "a Western" never fails to
bring to mind a cowboy. The cowboy aesthetic can fall anywhere across
a continuum from the dirty, worn, and unembellished to the ostentations
examples, with lavishly embroidered shirts, chaps, fringe, spurs, and
lasso. Dress also functions as shorthand for understanding the characters
in ways legible to those with even a cursory experience of Western films.
The cliché of hero in the white hat and villain in the black hat has served
well in many movies, though the visual codes for good and evil are often
more nuanced, even in the formulaic B Westerns.[2]

The posters indicate just how immediately and seemingly instinctively
impressions can be drawn about a character even when clothing is the
primary evidence available. In art, as in life, clothing signifies. In a meager setting such as the West, which frequently lacks conventional social
framework or architectural landmarks, garments on the body are among
the few possessions and markers of identity. As such, it can be argued
that dress signifies more in a Western than in other genres. The wealth of
tacit knowledge and assumptions that the viewer brings concerning, for

instance, what rugged work wear or a sheriff's uniform ought to be, have been molded and refined largely through experience with Westerns.

Mary Zophres designed the costumes for *No Country for Old Men,* and she describes working with the directors as an organic collaborative experience. This was her seventh picture with the Coen brothers but the first to have been adapted from a novel. An adaptation presents its own set of challenges, and in this case the author had described some dress details with exacting specificity while others were unspecified. The former gave her something to build on, while the latter left her ample room for interpretation. A costume designer needs to be attuned to the subtleties of functional dress and how each character wears their clothing. And Zophres' costumes are both strong and subtle for the three distinct types, defined by the directors as a "good guy" a "bad guy" and a "guy in between" ("Interview with Mary Zophres" 2008).

Anton Chigurh's character was the most ambiguous in the novel, but ironically Javier Bardem's physical instantiation of Chigurh is the most distinctive of the main characters. Chigurh has already become a familiar villain and the subject of popular parody. With his dark clothing and unmistakable haircut adding to his threatening demeanor he is a commanding presence whose look is more easily called to memory than his name. Anton Chigurh is described in many ways, but he never comes close to being explained. In some ways he is a quintessential Western villain: evil, relentless, and dressed in black. But, that fails to do justice to the extent of his malevolence and the twisted logic he expounds. In Sheriff Bell's first monologue, he fears the presence of a living prophet of destruction and is wary to put his soul at hazard by confronting something he does not understand. Chigurh is impossible to understand. He defies classification, nationally or ethnically, speaking in an unplaceable accent and walking with a steady looming gait. The cruelly efficient pressurized air gun is Chigurh's most distinctive accessory. He carries it at his side in broad daylight and no one, not even the ill-fated deputy who arrests him, recognizes what it is. His firearms define him because they are as incomprehensible and dangerous as he is, but they offer no deeper understanding as to his interior life or motivations.

Chigurh also resists classification because he operates on different levels, yet never seems to be completely committed to any one code of behavior other than his own warped conception of fate and justice. He is a hired gun, but not entirely, preferring instead to manipulate the situation to his own advantage. McCarthy painted a deep and disturbing picture of Chigurh, with one of his most chilling lines spoken to Carla Jean moments before murdering her: "Even a nonbeliever might find it useful to model himself after God. Very useful in fact" (*No Country,* 256). Chigurh possesses a sense of justice and duty that bears no relation to established social mores and is compelled to follow through on his word. Chigurh is more than a murderous madman; he is the personification of violence itself. Javier Bardem aptly describes him as "everything but a human being. It's more an idea of what violence means" (Sunshine 2008, 1). His ruthlessness is pure and unadulterated. There have been despicable villains in the Western tradition, but they get their comeuppance, and, what is most significant to the present analysis, they execute violent acts with a sense of flair.

In *Gunfighter Nation*, Richard Slotkin points out that even though the villain is the dangerous product of a harsh environment, there exists a kind of professionalism and artistry to his actions, thereby making the gunfighter a worthy opponent to the Western hero (1993, 384). Again, Chigurh fails to adhere to convention. The problem is not that Bell and Moss are incapable of winning against him, but that no man would succeed. Seeing Chigurh in action is somehow otherworldly, like watching a technologically superior machine. His violent acts are committed coldly and methodically without style or bravado. As violence personified, lacking conscience and glamour, Chigurh is a terrifying distillation of the preoccupation with the violence that runs through all Westerns and through contemporary society. An aspect of Slotkin's view of the gunfighter that seems particularly appropriate to Chigurh's role in *No Country for Old Men* is the notion that "the 'progressive' rationale for both political action and violence may in fact be a chimera. The gunfighter enters the narrative knowing that the wild west's promise of fame and power is an illusion" (Slotkin 1993, 390). Paradoxically, a figure like Chigurh demonstrates the pragmatism behind violence, insofar as he gets what he wants, while demonstrating that violence may work in service of a higher order even if it is outside "reasonable" bounds. Indifferent to social motivations such as fame, glory, or wealth, his adherence to his own convictions and sheer force of will help him operate undetected.

If one were to describe Chigurh's appearance at a superficial level— black jeans, black denim jacket, brown or black shirts with dark cowboy boots—it would seem generic and unimpressive. Other than the boots, there is nothing particularly Western about his style. Indeed, he is characterized in part by the lack of the characteristic Western belt buckle, and his bizarre haircut is not concealed by a cowboy hat. His look makes him stand out in any setting, and is a strong contrast to each of the other main figures. In describing Chigurh's appearance in detail it is best to start from the top, with the hair. In her review for the *Guardian*, Chrissy Iley labeled it "method hair, the power behind the performance" (2008, 1). Bardem's response to the hair suggests that Iley's remark is not an overstatement, the choice of hairstyle was evocative and had a great deal of impact on his performance. Explaining how the character came to be defined from the visual blank slate McCarthy provided, Bardem commented, "Then the haircut came along. And that helped us [the Coens and Bardem] a lot. It was a big deal to all of us because then we now have something that is very uncomfortable and weird to watch and that says a lot about him, which is that he is a guy who is a little bit out of sync. There's something that doesn't work there. So that was the high note and from there we have to go to a still place where the guy is almost neutral. The spotlight is the haircut" (Sunshine 2008, 2). "Uncomfortable and weird to watch" perfectly describes of the effect of the hair. It jars with the rest of his look, which is quite neutral, in an unsettling way. The hair is the physical representation of Chigurh's antipathy toward social convention. He stands out, but gives no indication that he is trying to do so and even less indication that he cares.

The hair is long and strangely unmoving. One hairdresser described it as a barber's short back with sides that have been neglected and grown out. The fact that the wearer seems unconcerned with what it has grown into adds to what makes it so unnerving (Mark Smith qtd. in Iley 2008, para. 6). A comparable convention in traditional Westerns might be that of a villain sporting a beard or moustache as a foil to a clean-shaven hero, with facial hair indicating a wild and uncivilized nature (Pumphrey 1989, 83). Chigurh's hair is long and thick, and covers Bardem's head like a helmet. Paul LeBlanc, the stylist responsible for the cut, likens it to those sported at the time of the Crusades, evoking the slaughter in the Holy Wars depicted in illustrated medieval manuscripts (LeBlanc, qtd. in Iley 2008, para. 4). Whether one accepts this analogy or not is inconsequential; what matters is that a single element of style incites a huge amount of commentary and conjecture that this haircut has elicited. It is not only tremendously effective in inducing a sense of oddness, lending extra "creepiness" to the overall look of the character. The look gets under the viewer's skin and stays there, solidifying Chigurh as a contemporary iconic villain.

The specifics of his look were inspired by a photograph that the Coens saw of a man sitting in a border town brothel in 1979. Zophres and Paul Le Blanc the hairstylist used this image to pattern a look for Bardem ("Interview with Mary Zophres" 2008). Zophres saw Chigurh as a character who attempts to blend in with his surroundings but fails. He wears jeans and a denim jacket, but their color and fit are not the same as the others in the picture. His clothing is in fact more up to date stylistically than that of the other characters. Yet, I would not go so far as to say it is fashionable; Chigurh's clothes are nothing if not practical and understated. The only Western flourish he appropriates is the cowboy boots. His boots are darker and somehow sharper than the others. Zophres took care to ensure that they had a colder, harder edge to them. She wanted the boots to cohere with his persona and have the threatening look of a weapon ("Interview with Mary Zophres" 2008). If wearing cowboy boots can be conceived as an attempt to assimilate with his surroundings, Chigurh's selection of expensive black ostrich boots impedes this because the other characters favor more conservative styles.

Conversely, Llewelyn Moss exemplifies the prototype of blending in with his environment. In terms of representing the region, Moss and Sheriff Bell have a great deal in common, and I will discuss them in relation to each other. Both men are Texans and war veterans, albeit from two very different conflicts. In Bell's case, it is possible to form a mental image of him before he appears on screen. A sheriff's uniform is utilitarian and authoritative, in shades so neutral and unremarkable they meld with the background like camouflage against the desert sand. In a mixed social group the effect is the opposite, instead of blending in the uniform stands out, demarcating its wearer as a figure of authority.

Moss's appearance is in many respects the hardest to define because it is the most nondescript. The sheriff's uniform may be the only example of what is considered "fossilized" clothing, but Llewelyn Moss's comes close.[3] Compared to Bell's uniform or Chigurh's dark ensembles, Moss's garments carry less obvious symbolic weight. Yet, it is precisely the generic qualities that make them believable on film and revealing about Moss himself, a character whom Josh Brolin describes as a "backwoods country boy who never had any money" ("Interview with Josh Brolin" 2008). We first encounter Moss in the film taking aim with his Remington 700. The gun is a sniper's weapon, and as he points it toward a herd of antelope, he echoes the words "hold still," last spoken by Anton Chigurh before killing a man with his air gun. Moss wears snug-fitting blue jeans with a Western-style button-down shirt in neutral tones and a straw cowboy hat. He is always wearing some variation of this ensemble, making it ostensibly a uniform—predictable garb for a man in his position. His garments vary little over the course of the film and they are not bound to a particular moment in time, nor are they indicative of fashionable trends. As such, they bring to mind a certain type of man: working class and Western. Moss's independent, daring nature fulfills what the viewer has come to expect from a Western hero. Moss initially comes across as a sympathetic character in the vein of the cowboy. Although we learn that he is a welder by profession, he is never shown working. Instead, we see him mastering the terrain, outrunning the bad men, and dexterously manipulating his firearms. It is easy to identify with Moss during the chase sequences, which his predictable no-frills aesthetic facilitates.

However, it is vital to keep in mind that although they may come close, Moss's clothes are not in fact a uniform. They are suited to his occupation and lifestyle but are not mandated by protocol the way Bell's are. Moss dresses this way because he chooses to. This agency is made apparent when he is shopping at the Western wear store after leaving the hospital. His exchange with the store's employee demonstrates that Moss is clearly conversant in the familiar brands and styles and knows exactly what he wants:

Do you carry the Larry Mahans?

No sir, we don't.

That's alright. I need a pair of Wrangler jeans thirty-two by thirty-four length. A shirt, size large. Some socks. And show me some Nocona boots in a ten and a half. And I need a belt. . . . You got any of them stockman's hats with the small brim? Seven and three eighths?

Yes we do. We have a three X beaver in the Resistol and a little better grade in the Stetson. A five X, I think it is."Let me see the Stetson. That silverbelly color.

All right sir. Are white socks all right?

White socks is all I wear. (*No Country*, 190–91)

At this juncture in the plot, after leaving the hospital, Moss literally has nothing. The scene in the store shows him putting himself back together. The garments themselves, Wrangler jeans, Stetson hat, and white socks are all items the audience has seen on Moss up to this point, albeit in varying stages of wear and disrepair. His new clothes are consistent with a formula. Gravitating toward what is familiar suggests force of habit, and also speaks to Moss's inflexibility. He chooses to build himself back up in a very deliberate methodical way, never straying from his preferences. Therefore, if Moss fits the Western working-class "type," he does so by choice.

After making his purchase, Moss is evidently content with his new clothes and exclaims, "I ain't been dudded up like this since I got out of the Army" (*No Country*, 192). This remark is revealing because unlike when he left the service, he has a satchel full of money and could buy whatever he wants. He could have purchased more expensive variations of his usual garb, or reconfigured himself completely in high-end clothing, or even selected something unexpected to disguise himself from his pursuers. He chooses none of these options. One would expect that money would change Moss; if he did not believe that it could improve his material situation it is unlikely that he would have risked everything the way he does. This scene demonstrates how money has changed him, and also how it has not. On one hand, money grants the freedom to be outfitted in a new set of clothes from head to toe; on the other, it shows his inability to think beyond the familiar.

Moss's preferred footwear, Larry Mahan boots, reinforce his position as a dyed-in the-wool Texan. Mahan is a celebrated rodeo champion who was also the subject of *The Great American Cowboy*, a documentary film whose evocative title requires no elaboration. After retirement, Mahan extended his legacy by endorsing a line of cowboy boots, fabricated in Texas. The exchange in the store is not the first time Larry Mahan boots are mentioned. In the novel, when Moss leaves Del Rio for a brief visit to Ciudad Acuña he visits a boot shop. One can assume that he is considering treating himself to new boots with some of the money. McCarthy described how Moss "went into a boot shop and looked at the exotics—crocodile and ostrich and elephant—but the quality of the boots was nothing like the Larry Mahans that he wore" (*No Country*, 85), a passage that implies that the foreign skins, the exotics, piqued his curiosity but did not meet Moss's specific standards.

The cowboy boot projects all the romanticism associated with the cowboy image more explicitly than any other piece of Western costume (DeLano 1981, 12). They are the sartorial embodiment of everything rugged and individualistic about the American frontier. Western wear, generally speaking, is the perfect example of clothing originally conceived to be functional turned fashionable. This shift cannot be mapped onto a linear chronology, nor does Western wear ever fall neatly into the disparate camps of "fashion" or "function." As is the case with any style that has endured over a century, the boundaries are permeable and always in flux. A variety of decorative flourishes can be applied that transcend the realm of utility, but do not take away from what the boot represents. A pair of cowboy boots originally designed to be durable, brace the foot, and hold it in a stirrup can be worn with all or none of these functions in mind. Llewelyn Moss's chosen boots certainly lean more toward practicality than fashionability, and it is clear from the text that he is concerned more with quality than style. Moss's footwear is glimpsed rarely, and the weathered brown leather boots, though carefully considered, blend seamlessly with his overall appearance.

Moss is not the only figure in cowboy boots. In fact, all the characters, including the Mexican drug dealers, the deputies, and most of the extras, wear them as well. Different boots surface again and again in McCarthy's descriptions: Moss's Larry Mahan's, Chigurh's "expensive" pair, the dealer's good crocodile boots, and Carson Wells's "expensive Lucchese crocodile boots." Such details would not be included in McCarthy's quick-paced and spare prose if they were not significant. The specific style of boots reflects the individual in terms of his personal tastes and social position. In a wider context, wearing cowboy boots functions as a kind of visual shorthand, an indication of being local. It is a connection that is made conspicuous throughout the narrative. After Chigurh has suffered the car accident and Bell comes as close as he will ever get to apprehending him, the sheriff interrogates a young witness:

Was he wearing boots?
Yeah. I think he was wearin boots.
What kind of boots?
I think they might have been ostrich.
Expensive boots.
Yeah. (*No Country*, 290)

At this juncture, Bell is seeking any scrap of evidence that might help him catch Chigurh, or at the very least define him better. There is something slightly desperate in Bell's grasping on to this clue. It is as though he hopes that this villain was not wearing boots, which would imply that he was from somewhere else. Bell's discomfort with the notion that such a man could be a product of this world, and even more unsettling, his own community, is palpable.

Sheriff Bell never comes across as a man who devotes much attention to dress or appearance. He does not acknowledge his own looks or those of others, unless it is in service of identifying a suspect. However, it is fascinating that he is compelled to address clothing at significant moments. Bell makes reference to dress precisely when such "superficial" matters ought to be of little interest. For instance, in the novel when reminiscing about the execution of death row inmates, he explains, "*You remember certain things about a thing like that. People didn't know what to wear. There was one or two come dressed in black, which I suppose was all right. Some of the men come in just their shirtsleeves and that bothered me. I aint sure I could tell you why*" (*No Country*, 63). Bell is perturbed by sartorial details moments before a man's life is about to be extinguished, and he thinks about it still. He assumes black is alright, no doubt because of its symbolic connections to death and mourning. We cannot know with certainty whether the color alone makes an impression or if it is the conscious decision to wear black, to address the gravity of the situation with a degree of formality, that impresses Bell. He is a man who not only respects decorum but also expects to see it in others, even at the most despairing moments. Although he does not articulate it precisely, this is why the shirtsleeves bother him. The lack of formality implies a lack of respect for life, whether it be out of ignorance or malice. Bell's careful consideration of the men's choices speaks to his larger concerns over decency and fair play and ultimately, even in the very last moments of life, appearance enters into the equation.

It is Bell's sense of honor that is offended by the informality. As the "old man" the title alludes to, Bell possesses an antiquated sense of honor and virtue. He is bound to the region by his service to the state, confirming his status as an ideal "Westerner" as defined by Robert Warshow in his 1954 essay, an analysis that is itself appropriate to Bell's generation and his conception of the nation. According to Warshow, honor as conceived in the Western tradition is more than justice and virtue; it is a style. As a style it is "concerned with harmonious appearances as much as with desirable consequences, and tending therefore toward the denial of life in favor of art" (Warshow 1998, 38). This is not to say that a figure like Bell prefers appearances to reality, but that harmonious appearances are a necessary component of reality for him. If he does not go so far as to deny life in favor of art, he does refuse to confront the truth about the brutality of the world he inhabits, favoring a code of honor and a set of laws that do not apply.

Bell does not deny that there is violence in the world and is admittedly willing to sacrifice his life in the line of duty. Yet, he recalls with fondness a time predating his own experience when some sheriffs did not require guns, meaning that the past was either a less violent time or that the title of sheriff, what the uniform represents, garnered more respect. Warshow effectively summarizes the connections between guns, honor, and the law as they function in the Western genre: "The gun tells us that he lives in a world of violence, and even that he 'believes in violence.' But the drama is one of self-restraint: the moment of violence must come in its own time and according to its own special laws, or else it is valueless. . . . Really it is not violence at all which is the 'point' of the western movie, but a certain image of a man, a style which expresses itself most clearly in violence" (1998, 47). Bell accepts a certain kind of violence, violence with boundaries. He therefore corresponds to the image described by Warshow. Bell is a man of laws, and he expects others to be equally reasonable, if they are not his role is to enforce the law. Yet, because *No Country for Old Men* is not a typical Western, such a figure does not fit comfortably into it. In fact this concept of humanity goes beyond the anachronistic and is exposed as flagrantly misguided. Bell's devotion to law and discipline does not impart a heroic status. Furthermore, he is denied the opportunity to express himself through violence; instead his scenes and meditative monologues offer respite from the fast-paced chase between Moss and Chigurh. Though Bell resembles the quintessential Westerner in many ways, he is not a man of action, and always arrives after the violence has taken place. Bell's helplessness is conveyed most poignantly when he and the deputy survey the gruesome aftermath of the initial drug deal. Arriving on horseback, for an added touch of anachronism, he assesses the site of not one but two instances of multiple murder that occurred under his jurisdiction—atrocities that he was powerless to stop. He does not come across as completely inept, but as someone simply beyond his depth.

Bell explicitly mentions appearances on another portentous occasion, after Moss is dead and he has decided to quit his job. Bell recalls the changes in his life and attitudes that have brought him to this point and, as is his custom, relates his experiences to ideas about the past: "*These old people I talk to, if you told em that there would be people in the streets of our* *Texas towns with green hair and bones in their noses speakin a language they* *couldnt even understand, well, they just flat out wouldnt of believed you"* (*No* *Country*, 295). In the novel, this line appears after Bell speaks with Moss's father and thinks ahead to his last day at the office, and in the film it surfaces in conversation between Bell and the sheriff in Van Horn. This statement is emblematic of Bell's character on a number of levels, the first being the obvious pejorative tone conveyed by the use of "green hair and bones in their noses speakin a language they couldnt even understand." It is clear that Bell's dismissive generalizations refer to young people specifically, and paired with the suggestion that the adoption of this aesthetic is tantamount to "signs and wonders" leaves no room for doubt that he believes the downfall of society is mirrored by the way people look. Yet, no one responsible for the death and devastation witnessed throughout the narrative bore any resemblance to the "signs and wonders" Bell describes. No people with green hair, under the influence of outside forces, enter into the plot. If anything, the men committing atrocities and dealing drugs are the ones who fit in best in terms of appearance. Chigurh may have looked unusual in the film, but his was not an expressive stylistic affectation, and in the novel he does not stand out in the least. Even the Mexicans, who are technically foreigners, are very much one with the area, with a language and aesthetic that is familiar to the other characters. A clash with the material and cultural landscape represented by the novelty of the green-haired kids is distressing to Bell, when in fact characters who are capable of blending into his environment prove much more dangerous.

For Bell, conflicting iconography upsets his worldview. It shatters his expectations in much the same way as *No Country for Old Men* complicates our expectations of the Western genre. Cormac McCarthy's work has frequently served as a critical foil to the Western tradition. Though some scholars go as far as to label it "anti-Western," I hesitate to adhere to a term that suggests such a rigid binary, as no work can be purely faithful or purely critical.[4] *No Country for Old Men* is no crude parody or spoof of the Western genre; it works subtly to erode expectations that the viewer or reader has already internalized about its central characters.

As we have seen with Bell, coherent formulations of right and wrong are complicated by preoccupations over propriety and style that are grounded in an idealized past. These overarching concerns are expressed at the material level throughout the narrative, giving added dimension to the doubt and disillusionment. Dress is an aesthetic reflection of the nuanced and effective ways that archetypes are evoked, only to be torn down. Moss approximates the cowboy archetype best in terms of dress and persona. He may be physically daring and headstrong, but he is fatally bound to the familiar and lacks the creative capacity that might have saved him and his wife. When presented with the opportunity to exceed material boundaries, even at a mundane level, he fails to do so. In the case of Chigurh, his attire and personal philosophy work both with and against what is expected from a Western villain. He is not greedy, rash, or lustful and adheres to a code of ethics with a personal dedication and force of will that are conventionally the traits of a hero. *No Country for Old Men* is a dark and multivalent tale, alternately brusque and reflective. The costumes adhere to the style of the time and cohere with the overall look of the film, but they also bear the additional weight of iconic significance molded over generations of Western cinema.

NOTES

1. Lee Clark Mitchell borrows Wittgenstein's term "family resemblance" to describe how the broad range of Westerns tend to cohere (Mitchell 1996, 7).

2. A popular example is seen in *Shane* (1953). The hero, played by Alan Ladd, dons a white Stetson, while the villain, played by Jack Palance, is in black. However, the application of this convention is largely exaggerated (Everson 1969, 11).

3. Costume historian Alexandra Palmer uses the term *fossilized clothing* to refer to garments that do not change in accordance with trends and continue to signify the same meaning over time (Palmer and Clark 2005).

4. Susan Kollin examines the specifics of the "anti-western" and draws similar conclusions (Kollin 2001, 557–88).

REFERENCES

DeLano, Sharon. 1981. "The History of the Cowboy Boot." In *Texas Boots*, 12–35. New York: Viking Press.

Everson, William K. 1969. *The Hollywood Western*. New York: Citadel Press.

Gaines, Jane Marie, and Charlotte Herzog. 1998. "The Fantasy of Authenticity in Western Costume." In *Back in the Saddle Again: New Essays on the Western*, ed. Edward Buscombe and Roberta E. Pearson, 172–82. London: BFI Publishing.

Iley, Chrissy. 2008. "The Method Haircut That Won an Oscar." *Guardian*, Film Features, February 28. www.guardian.co.uk.

"Interview with Joel and Ethan Coen." 2008. *No Country for Old Men*, special features. DVD. Dir. Ethan Coen and Joel Coen. Buena Vista Home Entertainment, Inc., and Paramount Vantage.

"Interview with Josh Brolin." 2008. *No Country for Old Men*, special features. DVD. Dir. Ethan Coen and Joel Coen. Buena Vista Home Entertainment, Inc., and Paramount Vantage.

"Interview with Mary Zophres." 2008. *No Country for Old Men*, special features. DVD. Dir. Ethan Coen and Joel Coen. Buena Vista Home Entertainment, Inc., and Paramount Vantage.

Kollin, Susan. 2001. "Genre and the Geographies of Violence: Cormac McCarthy and the Contemporary Western." *Contemporary Literature*, no. 3: 557–588.

McCarthy, Cormac. 2005. *No Country for Old Men*. New York: Vintage International.

Mitchell, Lee Clark. 1996. *Westerns: Making the Man in Fiction and Film*. Chicago: University of Chicago Press.

Palmer, Alexandra, and Hazel Clark. 2005. *Old Clothes, New Looks: Second Hand Fashion*. Oxford, New York: Berg.

Pumphrey, Martin. 1989. "'Why Do Cowboys Wear Hats in the Bath?' Style Politics for the Older Man." *Critical Quarterly* 31, no. 3: 83.

Rich, Katey. 2007. "NYFF: *No Country for Old Men*." Cinema Blend.com, October 8. www.cinemablend.com.

Shane. 1953. Dir. George Stevens. Paramount Pictures.

Slotkin, Richard. 1993. *Gunfighter Nation: The Myth of the Frontier in Twentieth Century America*. New York: HarperPerennial.

Sunshine, Jen. 2008. "Javier Bardem—*No Country for Old Men* Interview." UGO.com, April 21. www.ugo.com

Warshow, Robert. 1998. "The Westerner." In *The Western Reader*, ed. Jim Kitches and Gregg Rickman, 35–49. New York: Limelight Editions.

11

✛

"Hold still":
Models of Masculinity
in the Coens'
No Country for Old Men

Stacey Peebles

In the Coen brothers' *No Country for Old Men* (2007), Anton Chigurh carries an unusual weapon. The captive bolt pistol, commonly used to slaughter cattle, looks more like an oxygen tank to one doomed deputy, and its lethal effects confound other pursuing law enforcement as well. Early in the film, an unsuspecting motorist is confused when Chigurh approaches him. "What is that?" he asks. "What is that for?" Chigurh responds, "Would you hold still, please?" as he places the barrel of the bolt pistol on the man's forehead. Then he fires. The scene cuts to Llewelyn Moss painstakingly aiming his long-range rifle at an antelope on the plain below. "You hold still," he intones before pulling the trigger. Unlike Chigurh, Moss misses—he injures, but fails to kill, the animal he shoots. As these sequences emphasize, *No Country* follows its male protagonists in their varied efforts to make things "hold still" and conform to their will.

The three major characters in *No Country for Old Men*—Sheriff Ed Tom Bell, Moss, and Chigurh—are quite different, and these differences are emphasized during the course of the film. Each, however, embodies a version of the masculine ideal and displays traits that, in American narrative generally and Westerns in particular, are celebrated markers of manhood. Moss is the consummate opportunist, ready to seize good fortune when it comes by and (literally) run with it. He is clever and backs up that resourcefulness with formidable determination and optimism. Though Chigurh displays a similar ability to improvise and make productive use of his surroundings, his own character is more appropriately described as rational. His actions are not motivated by optimism, pessimism, or indeed by any emotionally inflected view of the world. He begins with his principles, and his actions follow in what he considers an entirely reasonable manner. Finally, before we even see him, Sheriff Bell's opening voice-over makes clear his respect for and adherence to tradition, particularly the tradition of Texas law and leadership. He laments, however, the changing times and what he sees as the general erosion of that respect. Bell, then, also wants things to "hold still."

Stories of masculine adventure and risk-taking often end with a protagonist bloodied and beaten but yet unbowed by adversity. Ultimately, the male hero is a triumphant figure of phallic mastery. Think of *Shane* (1953), or *Lethal Weapon* (1987), or even *In the Valley of Elah* (2007), a film released the same year as *No Country* that follows Tommy Lee Jones as a father trying to uncover the circumstances of his son's death. His discoveries are horrific and painful, but they still enable him to piece together precisely what happened. In the end, he prevails—he uncovers, untangles, and solves the mystery of the murder of his son. *No Country*, however, gives us a different kind of masculine portrait. Here, the three main characters are indeed variously bloodied and/or beaten down during the narrative, and yet in the end they do *not* prevail. Each of the three models of masculinity fails in his attempt at mastery, failures that are ironically emphasized by the Coens' choice of actors. Particularly in the case of Jones and Josh Brolin, their appearances and previous roles tag them as classic masculine icons. By its conclusion, however, the film has de facto presented us with an alternative mode of engaging with the world, one that doesn't rely on the need to take control with the use of cleverness, stubbornness, rationality, tradition, or lethal force. Instead, this alternative practice is based on renunciation and the surrender to those forces that are beyond one's control rather than in service of it.

By virtue of its geographical setting in west Texas and this emphasis on masculine action devoted to both the enforcement and defiance of the law, *No Country for Old Men* is a Western. The Coens draw our attention to these generic markers right away, as the movie opens with shots of the landscape, all open spaces and slanting sunlight. A lone windmill turns lazily. Sheriff Bell's voice-over narration complements these images with a history of local law enforcement in the region and his own family's history serving as sheriff. Bell reveals his strong nostalgia for the "old timers," and thus from the outset the film raises a lingering question about what constitutes this modern West. When we talk about Westerns, however, whether they are set in the Old West or the New, we talk about the representation of masculinity and the assignation of power, since the genre is perhaps the ultimate venue for the display of male power as evidenced by the ability to overcome the wilderness as well as the bad guy. A number of critics have commented on this association, including Steve Neale, for example, who notes in his discussion of "masculinity as spectacle" that the male protagonists of the Western often rely heavily on narcissistic fantasies of power, omnipotence, mastery, and control; Neale draws our attention to icons like Clint Eastwood in *A Fistful of Dollars* (1964) and *The Good, the Bad, and the Ugly* (1967), Tom Mix in his Westerns, and even Mad Max, a kind of futuristic, Australian Western hero (Neale 1993, 11). Framing her claim against those of scholars like John Cawelti (1984), Will Wright (1975), and Martin Pumphrey (1988), Wendy Chapman Peek has argued that postwar Westerns celebrate a variety of masculine behaviors and character types rather than a single masculine ideal, just as long as the character in question is (1) male and (2) successful: "In Westerns, then, the most important thing is to be a man. The second most important thing is to be successful. Ideal masculinity matters only to the extent that it supports the other two, which may be not at all" (Peek 2003, 211). Control matters. *Winning* matters, and the ability to achieve that victory becomes the Western hero's defining characteristic, regardless of how—or even *if*—you wear your gun, hat, and boots. Men in Westerns are made of variously tough stuff. They get the job done and they do it with flair, to such a degree that their stories often have the qualities of myth and epic. They are fun to watch, but perhaps more difficult to imitate. The Coens, however, are after something different.

Though *No Country* begins with Sheriff Bell's voice-over and soon shows us images of Chigurh, Llewelyn Moss—the third man to be introduced—initially seems to be our erstwhile protagonist. His actions, and particularly his theft of the money left over from a drug deal gone bad, drive the film's plot and propel the two other men into pursuit. Josh Brolin, who plays Moss, is recognizable for his turn as the iconic Wild Bill Hickok in the television Western *The Young Riders*, which ran from 1989–1992. The association emphasizes Moss's physical stamina and his intelligence.

While tracking that wounded antelope that didn't hold still after all, Moss happens upon a circle of cars and bodies where a drug deal was to have taken place. He moves carefully through the scene with his gun at the ready, calm and unruffled by the carnage. When he finds one man barely alive and begging for *agua*, Moss asks him curtly about the *ultimo hombre*, the last man standing. Moss finds the drug money by tracking that last man, who also failed to hold still and took the satchel that contains it to a stand of trees before dying from his wounds. From a distance, Moss crouches and watches patiently for any movement, then approaches with caution. When he opens the satchel and gets his first look at the money—a considerable amount, even at a glance—he remains largely unaffected. "Yeah," he grunts under his breath, thoughtfully affirming that the money isn't really too much of a surprise. Later, he returns home and hides the satchel under his trailer. His mood, as he sits next to his wife, Carla Jean, on the sofa, is light and confident. He deflects her questions about the satchel, the pistol he also took from that last man, and where he's been all day. "You don't need to know everything, Carla Jean," he chides her, and emphasizes his role as the phallic indicator of the narrative when he warns, "You keep running that mouth of yours I'm going to take you in the back and screw you." But later that night, he makes the decision to return to the circle of cars to give water to the wounded man who had begged him for it. He admits to Carla Jean that he's about to do something "dumber'n hell," but that he has to do it anyway. Moss has demonstrated his opportunism as well as his caution, and here he shows himself to be principled, even though putting those principles into action conflicts with his highly developed pragmatism.

When he arrives at the scene of the carnage, he's not the only one there. Other men in pursuit of the drugs and the money pursue him as well, and he runs desperately from men in a truck and from a very determined and nasty-looking pit bull. He shoots the dog, but not before he is shot himself. When Moss returns to Carla Jean, he is bloody and beaten up, yet unrepentant about these new developments. "Baby, things happen. I can't take them back," he tells her. Moss is dismissive of the past, but he does have a plan for the future. On the bus, as he sends Carla Jean along to her mother's, he remains optimistic, telling her that his "good feeling" ought to balance out her bad one. "I shall return," he says with a smile, echoing that most masculine of military icons, General Douglas MacArthur, speaking of his leadership in the Philippines in World War II. At this point in the story, Moss is still confident he can remain on top, eluding his predators to return to Carla Jean in triumph. Carla Jean wants to believe him. When Bell speaks with her, she tells him that "Llewelyn can take care of himself," that he never quits, that he can "take all comers." But as the sheriff notes, Llewelyn has gotten involved with some "pretty bad people," notably Anton Chigurh.

Chigurh indeed poses a threat, and once he enters the scene, Moss's confidence begins to waver. In Eagle Pass, Chigurh follows the signal of the transponder hidden in the satchel of money to Moss's hotel room, where Moss waits tensely on the other side of the door. We hear Chigurh carefully removing the light bulb out in the hall, and as the sound of the bulb being unscrewed comes faintly to Moss's ears, he seems to realize that he, in fact, is the one who's screwed. Chigurh fires his captive bolt pistol to blow out the lock, Moss responds by firing his shotgun through the door, and there ensues a running gun battle between the two men that wreaks havoc on the quiet town. Neither man makes the kill, but each manages to wound the other seriously. Moss suffers a debilitating wound in his side that gradually slows his movement from quick but considered action to literal unconsciousness. The wound is emasculating—Moss can no longer act with his characteristic speed and cleverness. Instead, he is reduced to bribing a trio of young men for a jacket to cover his bloody torso on the bridge into Mexico, and later weakly offers a bloodstained bill to some surprised mariachis serenading him at dawn in exchange for *médico*, or help finding a doctor. Instead of operating with masculine efficacy and power, Moss now has to rely on money as his only currency.

As a result of that wound, Moss is forced to spend valuable time recovering in a Mexican hospital, and eventually crosses the border back into the States in his hospital gown. The border guard asks him how he "come to be out here with no clothes," and when Moss returns to the boot shop in Del Rio that he had recently patronized, he sheepishly asks the clerk, "You get a lot of people come in here with no clothes on?" The clerk affirms that it is, in fact, unusual. Moss is, of course, wearing clothes—he's just not wearing the utilitarian shirt and jeans that would mark him as a proper Texas man. He wears what is effectively a dress, and an insubstantial one at that. The imposed femininity of his outfit is so glaring in the masculine ethos of the Western that the border guard, Moss, and the clerk all refuse to refer to it as any kind of garment at all. If you're wearing a dress, you might as well be naked. His predicament is played for a joke, but the implications for Moss's masculinity are serious. As Peek notes, Western heroes may indeed have recourse to a range of variously domestic, intellectual, and violent abilities in order to achieve success, and thus don't necessarily need to wear a particular masculine costume and behave in a particular masculine way, but here Moss's attire signals his loss of control—over his body, his clothes, and his appearance. If, as the title of Peek's article (2003) suggests, Westerns are a "romance of competence," Moss's gown does not indicate his proficiency. According to Moss's own way of seeing the world, he has been subtly coded as feminine in this highly masculinized environment. This, Moss seems to sense, is a bad sign.

When Carla Jean speaks to Bell again, her estimation of Moss has changed. This time, she tells Bell that "Llewelyn would never ask for help. He never thinks he needs any." She implies, of course, that he does need help now and needs it badly. But he doesn't get it. Before Bell can track him, Moss is shot down by an anonymous gang of pursuers while waiting for Carla Jean in the El Paso Desert Sands Motor Hotel. Bell arrives at the scene, and the camera frames the aftermath of the shooting from Bell's point of view. We see a seriously wounded Mexican man crawling on the ground, and then we see Moss's body, inert and bloody, inside a hotel room door. It comes as a shock, to Bell and also to the viewer. We are not accustomed, while watching Westerns, action movies, or masculine adventures of any kind, to seeing a scrappy, clever underdog succumb to his pursuers, especially not without a long, dramatic showdown. Here, Moss dies inelegantly, late in the story (though his is not the final death in the film), and because the exchange of bullets happens offscreen, is not permitted to utter any memorable final words. Neither does the film permit him a *Butch Cassidy*–style freeze-frame glorifying his passing. He just ends up as a staring, broken corpse, one among others. In the end, his cleverness and optimism have failed to pay off.

Javier Bardem, the actor who plays Anton Chigurh, has an admittedly different history of film roles than Josh Brolin or Tommy Lee Jones, who have, after all, played rough Western icons like Wild Bill and Woodrow Call. Most American viewers had not heard of Bardem before this film, although he became much more recognizable after he won the 2007 Academy Award for Best Supporting Actor for his performance as Chigurh. But those who did know the actor were perhaps familiar with his role in *Before Night Falls* (2000) as the gay Cuban poet and novelist Reinaldo Arenas, for which he received a Best Actor nomination. Bardem has also received accolades for his performance in *Mar adentro* (*The Sea Inside* [2004]) as a quadriplegic who fights a twenty-eight-year campaign in support of euthanasia and the right to end his own life. That film won the Oscar for Best Foreign Film.

Considering these roles, and inasmuch as American audiences recognized Bardem, he is cast against type as Chigurh, a coldly principled— some would say merciless—killing machine. That sense of intertextual juxtaposition, however, suits the role well, as Chigurh is a character who is in many ways unknowable. He presents himself as strictly rational, someone who plays by the rules of the game as he sees them. Those rules, however, are lethal. In the opening minutes of the film, a deputy takes him into custody. Back at the station, the deputy makes a phone call, assuring the sheriff on the other end of the line that he has things under control. He may think so, but as is so often the case, that control is just an illusion. Immediately after the man puts down the phone, Chigurh approaches him from behind and wordlessly strangles him with his handcuffs. The two fall to the floor, Chigurh struggling with the flailing deputy in a perverse and physically intense embrace. After a climactic spurt of arterial blood, the deputy goes limp and Chigurh slumps post-coitally, apparently pleased at his successful domination. This is one of the very few hints of emotion that we see on Chigurh's face during the film.

When he kills an unsuspecting motorist a few moments later, he does so with as few words as possible. The next time we see Chigurh, however, we have a chance to hear him talk in more detail about how he sees the world. Chigurh enters a gas station whose middle-aged proprietor stands

behind the counter. Chigurh seems uninterested in that proprietor until
the man asks in passing if he's been "gettin' any rain up your way." He
further indicates that he has noticed Chigurh is from Dallas, gesturing
at his car. When Chigurh responds that his whereabouts are none of the
man's business, the man apologizes, but Chigurh does not accept the
apology and extenuates the discussion in hostile and challenging terms
to such a degree that the proprietor grows more and more uncomfortable.
The man, clearly anxious to be rid of Chigurh's ominous presence, says he
needs to close the station for the day. He admits, however, that he usually
closes "about dark, at dark," though outside the sun still shines brightly.
This prompts Chigurh to comment, "You don't know what you're talking
about, do you?" He probes the man on his bedtime, his house, his marriage, and the details of his ownership of the station, and then suddenly
asks, "What's the most you ever lost on a coin toss?" Chigurh insists the
man call the toss and pick heads or tails. In explaining the value (or the
necessity) of the coin toss, Chigurh emphasizes the coin's agency, the fact
that "it's been traveling twenty-two years to get here. And now it's here.
And it's either heads or tails." Indeed, the coin works as a proper divin-
ing tool because it *is* either heads or tails, and the man is free to choose
either outcome. Regardless of this equal probability, one of those choices
is clearly the better one for Chigurh. "Heads," or the use of reason, is
far superior to "tails," the reliance on baser or more "animal" motivations, like emotion, passion, or desire. The proprietor's fear leads him to
speak as if he "didn't know what he was talking about," and that earns
Chigurh's disrespect. When the man calls "Heads then," Chigurh uncovers the coin and responds, "Well done." Heads is clearly the right answer
in several senses.

Chigurh operates largely unopposed for much of the film, although
Moss manages to wound him with his shotgun during the battle in Eagle
Pass. Chigurh pursues Moss into the streets, and when cornered behind
a car, simply disappears. We next see him methodically gathering the
resources he needs to attend to his wound. He steals medicine and first
aid equipment from a pharmacy, rents a hotel room with a television for
audio "cover," and lays plastic sheeting on the floor. Then we watch as
Chigurh methodically cleans and disinfects the gaping wound in his leg.
The camera lingers on it, making sure that we notice its severity. Chigurh
is naked and perforated, clearly experiencing pain, and yet remains in
total control. His expression is one of concentration, with perhaps a scant
amount of irritation at having to attend to himself in such a way. Bodies,
like emotions, are simply secondary to the mind and the will. He expresses the same kind of irritation with the Houston businessman whom
he summarily dispatches in his office. The man gave the receiver to two
"executive types" who were also hunting Moss, and whom Chigurh also

shot. "That's foolish," he says of the decision to employ others and to give them the receiver. "You pick the one right tool."

Chigurh, as played by Bardem, is not obviously coded as masculine by his physical appearance. He wears a denim jacket and jeans that would seem to be an attempt at Western attire, but their newness and neatness stand out in a region where well-used boots and broken-in clothes are more common. The oddity of his Prince Valiant haircut has, of course, been commented upon extensively in reviews and elsewhere, but its exacting arrangement makes sense on a man who has everything under control—emotions, employers, coiffure. And yet despite these deliberately off-center masculine tags, and despite the associations Bardem brings from his previous roles, Chigurh is nevertheless a hypermasculine figure. The emphasis on his rationality in all situations, his emotionless responses, and the impressive exertion of his will make this possible. His kill ratio, of course, doesn't hurt either, especially in a genre built on the fetishization of guns and their skilled use. Chigurh does indeed have the biggest gun.

Of course the Coens (and Cormac McCarthy before them) delight in surprising us with the moment when Chigurh's will is simply not sufficient, when he can't keep everything in front of him. As he drives away from presumably killing Carla Jean—implied in the film by a shot of Chigurh fastidiously checking his boots for blood after exiting her house—his car is unexpectedly slammed by another car running a red light. We see him checking his rearview mirror to monitor the position of two boys on bicycles as he proceeds through an intersection with a green light. The camera shoots Chigurh in profile from the right, and so when the other car smashes into his passenger side, the viewer is as surprised as Chigurh. No one sees it coming. Chigurh is clearly shaken as he exits the vehicle, and must negotiate with those same two boys for a shirt to conceal his (very) broken arm. He offers money, just as Moss offered money for a jacket on the U.S.-Mexico bridge, because he seems to have run out of options. Though Chigurh limps away from the scene, down the sidewalk and into an uncertain future, he has been reduced to the object, rather than the subject, of violent action. The boys comment no less than three times on the bone sticking out of his arm. "Look at that fuckin' bone," one of them marvels, awestruck at the pitiable spectacle that is Chigurh, bleeding on the sidewalk. Even Anton Chigurh, whose masculine will to power is so formidable, is vulnerable in this world, and even the staunchest will is no guarantee of lasting mastery.

The third male character, Sheriff Bell, is also the most complicated. He is played by Tommy Lee Jones, a native Texan who fairly oozes Western masculine presence. His role as the laconic, steadfast, and long-suffering Woodrow Call in the television series *Lonesome Dove* (1989) is the best example of the kind of characters viewers associate with Jones, though his parts in films like *The Fugitive* (1993) and *Men in Black* (1997) clearly traffic in that reputation of a rough man with deep but hidden feelings. More recently, his roles in *The Three Burials of Melquiades Estrada* (2005), which he also directed, and *In the Valley of Elah* show Jones portraying men steeped in masculine traditions—ranching in *Burials* and the military in *Elah*.

Jones brings to the screen immediate associations with Texas and the Western, the idea of tradition and a long-standing method for accomplishing goals, the aura of leadership, and the qualities of a paternal figure. In *No Country*, however, he proceeds to ironize these associations by playfully making reference to them on-screen. While preparing to take two horses to investigate the scene of the drug deal, Bell and his wife, Loretta, exchange what seems to be an oft-repeated bit of conversation. "Be careful," she says. "Always am," he replies. "Don't get hurt," she adds. "Never do." And finally, "Don't hurt no one," she insists. Bell appears amused and responds, "Well. If you say so." He mocks the very idea that he could be dangerous, much less lethal. Only if Loretta verbally forbids him, he jokes, will he refrain from actions better suited to a cowboy, a gangster, an action hero.

Nor does he echo Wendell's language as they explore the scene of the crime. They begin at a burning car, and Bell explains to Wendell how Chigurh stole and traded a series of vehicles. "That's very linear, Sheriff," Wendell compliments him. Speaking of the scene of the drug deal proper that they are yet to see, he adds, "OK Corrall's just yonder." As they examine the circle of cars and bodies, Wendell characterizes one set of killings as an execution, and the other as Wild West. Bell will only acknowledge that if it's not a mess, "it'll do till the mess gets here." The scene, in his language, is sufficient, but he is reluctant at this early stage to allow for its excess. He certainly refuses to associate it with anything like a romantic or nostalgic Western atmosphere. When they later arrive at Moss's trailer and see that the lock has been blown out, Wendell gets excited. "We goin' in?" he asks, and Bell answers in the affirmative: "Gun out and up." Wendell complies, but seems confused by Bell's amused refusal to follow suit. "I'm hiding behind you," Bell whispers. Here, Bell's reference is a phallic one—that they should enter primed to do damage, "guns" out and up—but his attitude toward that reference is dismissive. Bell mocks the very masculine codes that his character summons up as a Texas lawman.

And yet as the film continues, that attitude toward his own role as a sheriff, a citizen, and a man slides from gentle self-mockery and amusement to real regret, even grief as the killings escalate beyond his ability to curtail them. Those dead bodies eventually include Moss and Carla Jean, though Bell also laments the state of the world generally, as evidenced by young people's general lack of respect for their elders; he sees this in the abandonment of common conversational terms of courtesy, and, in more extreme fashion, in news items about serial killers preying on the elderly for their Social Security checks. Bell's sense of failure is most prominently emphasized in the film's denouement. After deciding to retire from law enforcement, Bell goes to visit his Uncle Ellis and comments to the older man that he feels "overmatched." He regrets, he says, that God never came into his life as he got older. "I don't blame him," he adds. "If I was him I'd have the same opinion of me that he does." Here, Bell's self-assessment is openly damning, leading Ellis to chide him that "you don't know what he [God] thinks." In the screenplay and the finished film, the Coens elect to cut a significant exchange that occurs between Bell and Ellis in McCarthy's novel. In it, Bell tells a story about his past that further emphasizes his sense of failure and his regret at not living up to his potential as a sheriff, a citizen, a man, and in the excised anecdote, a soldier.

In the novel, Bell introduces the topic with a question to Ellis: "Did you ever do anything you was ashamed of to the point where you never would tell nobody?" (*No Country*, 272). He talks about receiving the Bronze Star for fighting off a group of German soldiers in World War II. He adds, however, that after repelling their initial attack, he waited until dark and then ran away, leaving behind a group of wounded fellow soldiers. Although he notes that he almost certainly couldn't have helped them and further that if he had stayed he almost certainly would have been killed himself—and even further that he attempted to refuse the commendation—he still feels that his flight has tainted his entire life:

> If I was supposed to die over there doin what I'd give my word to do then that's what I should of done. You can tell it any way you want but that's the way it is. I should of done it and I didnt. And some part of me has never quit wishin I could go back. And I cant. I didnt know you could steal your own life. And I didnt know that it would bring you no more benefit than about anything else you might steal. I think I done the best with it I knew how but it still wasnt mine. It never has been. (278)

He and Ellis agree that Bell's father would have stayed at the scene, and Bell says that he thinks that makes his father the "better man." Ellis doubts that notion, but it does little to comfort Bell. McCarthy's novel takes pains to couch Bell's failure to catch Chigurh and prevent Moss's death within a much longer history of personal failure and loss. Bell interprets this earlier inability to prevent the deaths of his comrades as a failure of his life as a whole—or, at the very least, as the rendering of his life as inauthentic. He codes his own wartime survival as the ultimate theft, a crime that is no more beneficial than any other kind of wrongdoing. McCarthy's Bell sees the more recent events as a reinforcement and reminder of his

ongoing weakness and inauthenticity. In the film, however, we are en-
couraged to read Bell's weary posture and expression as primarily reflecting the burden of Moss's death alone. (In an additional departure from
the novel, the Coens place Bell's conversation with Ellis before, rather
than after, the scene between Chigurh and Carla Jean, and so presumably
Bell is unaware of her impending murder.) Here, the death of one man
is presented as more than enough to rouse feelings of inadequacy and to
knock the wind and the spirit out of Bell, perhaps permanently.

The film ends with Bell in his sunny kitchen on one of the first mornings
of his retirement, and this final scene provides an opportunity to consider
the damage Bell's spirit has suffered. He tells his wife about two dreams
he had the night before, both of which also reflect a feeling of regret and
loss. In the first dream, he meets his father in town. His father gives him
money, which he loses. In the second, he and his father are on horseback
at night, in the cold and the snow, riding through a pass in the mountains,
like in "older times." His father rides by him, carrying fire in a horn "the
way people used to do." Bell says that in the dream he knew that his father was going on up ahead to make a fire, "in all that dark and all that
cold," and would be waiting for Bell when he arrived. "Then I woke up,"
he finishes. The scene lingers on Bell and Loretta's faces for another moment, and then fades to black, the quiet sound of a ticking clock easing
slowly into the music that will run over the credits. In both dreams, his
father is still the "better man." In the world of the city, his father manages
money successfully where Bell does not, and in the world of the country,
the wilderness, his father is the one to "manage," or carry, the fire. Both
are currencies of sorts, and in both realms, Bell's father is equipped, while
Bell can only follow behind. Of course, having such a father is comforting,
but like the story of the film proper, it doesn't much help the fact that Bell
will always arrive second, a little too late.

Noticeably lacking from the film is the climax we might expect from a
story set in the West and employing the chase as a central element of the
plot. There is no showdown between any of these men. Moss is killed by
auxiliary drug employees, Chigurh's plans are thwarted by an anonymous driver, and Bell is either not quick enough or not motivated enough
to keep himself in the game at all. Earlier in the film, Moss and Chigurh
do engage in the destructive gun battle in Eagle Pass, but the two men
never face off, never speak to one another in person, and neither kills the
other. In fact, except for one brief shot in which the camera looks over
Moss's shoulder at Chigurh diving behind a car, the two men never even
appear in the same frame. If this can be considered a showdown of sorts,
it is both unsatisfying and incomplete.

In fact, perhaps the most impressive showdown of the film occurs not
between any of the male characters but between Chigurh and Carla Jean.

In a film largely faithful to McCarthy's source text, this scene marks the most notable change from the novel. There, Carla Jean initially resists calling the coin toss that Chigurh offers as a chance at staying alive. "God would not want me to do that," she says, but when Chigurh insists, "This is your last chance," she submits. "Heads" (*No Country*, 258). The coin is tails, and so she loses. She tries to argue, however, that it isn't the coin that makes the decision, that in fact Chigurh is the mover, "the one" here. Chigurh counters, however, and in a long explanation, argues that in fact Carla Jean's death is both necessary and, in its own way and under Chigurh's principles, just. "You can say that things could have turned out differently," he says, "That they could have been some other way. But what does that mean? They are not some other way. They are this way. You're asking that I second say the world. Do you see?" (260). And, as the scene ends, Carla Jean answers in the affirmative. "Yes," she said, sobbing. "I do. I truly do." "Good," Chigurh responds, and shoots her (260).

In the book, Carla Jean is convinced by Chigurh's argument—she says that she understands. She assents to those principles that demand her death. But the Carla Jean we see in the film has quite a different reaction to her impending murder. She enters the bedroom where Chigurh is waiting, and the two are briefly framed in the same shot. Like the shot that framed Moss and Chigurh together, if only for a moment, this one looks over Carla Jean's shoulder at Chigurh. But unlike that earlier scene, no one runs away. They both sit and calmly discuss the situation. "You got no cause to hurt me," Carla Jean asserts. "No, but I gave my word," Chigurh responds. "That don't make sense," Carla Jean tells him, taking the rhetorical position more often held by Chigurh. Chigurh explains the necessity of killing her, but offers a coin toss as a chance to defy death. "This is the best I can do," he tells her. "Call it." Carla Jean once again responds by identifying what she sees as his fundamental irrationality: "I knowed you was crazy when I saw you sitting there. I knowed exactly what was in store for me." "Call it," Chigurh insists. "No. I ain't gonna call it," she counters. "Call it," Chigurh says, for the third time. But Carla Jean refuses and sticks to her guns, so to speak. "The coin don't have no say. It's just you." Though Carla Jean dies, she admits no assent. She may be penetrated by Chigurh's bullet but she remains unpenetrated, as it were, by his assertions of principle. This female character, then, may be the best "man" of the movie.

Chigurh consistently proves formidably intimidating to the men he encounters. Even Carson Wells, who was somewhat flippant about their association and Chigurh's character, reveals real fear when Chigurh finds him in the Eagle Pass hotel. Carla Jean, however, refuses to wilt, as does another woman in the film—the large, festively bouffanted woman working in the office of Moss's trailer park. When Chigurh comes looking for

Moss, he hits what appears to be a literal and figurative brick wall. "Did you not hear me?" she asks in irritation. "We can't give out no information." When Chigurh pauses, considering the sound of a toilet flushing and thus the possibility of a witness, the woman watches him in consternation that threatens to escalate into physical action. For all Chigurh's skills at intimidation, they don't seem to work on these two women.

The real message of the story is perhaps provided by another young woman as well as an old, wheelchair-bound man, who are certainly nothing like traditional figures of phallic mastery. Near the end of the film, Moss waits for his wife at a motel in El Paso, and a girl by the pool tries to charm him into sharing a few beers. Does he keep looking out the window, she asks, because he's watching for that wife of his? "Lookin' for what's comin'," he replies. "Yeah, but no one ever sees that," she playfully chides him. Ellis echoes her a few minutes later when he talks to Bell, in a repetition that mirrors the two imperatives to "hold still" at the beginning of the film. When Bell comments that he feels overmatched by the things he's up against, Ellis responds, "You can't stop what's comin." He further adds that to think you are in control of events in the world is not only incorrect, but relies on the false assumption that you are more important than you actually are. "It ain't all waitin' on you," he says. "That's vanity." Instead, Ellis suggests that the proper course is to recognize the formidable forces that are beyond your power to shape, and that in fact are "nothin' new" after all. "All the time you spend trying to get back what's been took from you more's going out the door. After a while you just have to try and put a tourniquet on it." Phallic mastery, he intimates, is not only an illusion but a dangerous one at that. In trying to hold on to some things, you lose others. As Bell sits at his breakfast table relating his dreams of the night before to his wife, it's not clear how much of Ellis's advice he has internalized. Bell may very well have managed to "put a tourniquet" on his losses, as his beloved wife is still alive and his marriage intact. How much difference that makes to him, however, is unclear, and the ticking clock that closes the film indicates that perhaps only time will tell.

No Country for Old Men reveals a particularly masculine dread—that you can't always keep things in front of you and under your control. Things won't hold still, waiting for the assertion of mastery. Danger approaches from all directions—in Chigurh's case, it comes from the side, and in a split second transforms a confident assassin into something like roadkill. You can't see it, and you can't stop it. Masculine doggedness will just get you into trouble. The film seems hostile to masculinity in animal forms as well, as no fewer than three rough, tough pooches all get shot before the narrative has progressed very far. Moss sees one wounded pit bull as he approaches the site of the drug deal, another lies dead at the scene, and the third—and most memorable—gives chase when Moss returns that night only to find himself with unexpected company. After a short, very high-energy pursuit over land and through water, Moss manages to dry out his gun cartridge and plug the dog in mid-pounce, clearly without a split-second to spare. Despite this—well, this *doggedness*—all these animals suffer. The *cats* in the film, animals generally associated with feminine qualities rather than masculine, fare much better. A number of them swarm over and around Ellis, who is arguably the moral center of the film, and seem to have the run of his small shack. Perhaps more notably, in Eagle Pass, just about the time that Moss is figuring out what kind of trouble he's really in, he returns to the hotel lobby and sees that the man at the hotel desk has been killed. In front of the desk, a small cat happily laps at the milk that has spilled from its dish, presumably as a result of all this fracas, as Wendell might have put it. But the cat—the feminine—makes a nice meal out of that spilled milk, no tears of regret in sight. In the end, the Coens' Western emphasizes the renunciation of attempts to achieve and maintain masculine control. *No Country for Old Men* takes us from opening shots of wide open spaces to a final, close-up portrait of loss. The camera lingers on Bell's face, and invites us to consider a story that moves beyond myth and into a more constricted and personal space, one that is populated by the ghosts of what we might have wished to be.

REFERENCES

Before Night Falls. 2000. Dir. Julian Schnabel. El Mar Pictures.
Cawelti, John. 1984. *The Six-Gun Mystique*. Bowling Green: Bowling Green University Popular Press.
A Fistful of Dollars. 1964. Dir. Sergio Leone. Constantin Film Produktion.
The Fugitive. 1993. Dir. Andrew Davis. Warner Bros. Pictures.
The Good, the Bad, and the Ugly. 1967. Dir. Sergio Leone. Arturo González Producciones Cinematográficas.
In the Valley of Elah. 2007. Dir. Paul Haggis. Blackfriars Bridge Films.
Lethal Weapon. 1987. Dir. Richard Donner. Silver Pictures.
Lonesome Dove. 1989. Dir. Simon Wincer. Motown Productions.
Mar adentro (The Sea Inside). 2004. Dir. Alejandro Amenábar. Sogepaq.
McCarthy, Cormac. 2005. *No Country for Old Men*. New York: Alfred A. Knopf.
Men in Black. 1997. Dir. Barry Sonnenfeld. Amblin Entertainment.
Neale, Steve. 1993. "Prologue: Masculinity as Spectacle: Reflections on Men and Mainstream Cinema." In *Screening the Male: Exploring Masculinities in Hollywood Cinema*, ed. Steven Cohan and Ina Rae Hark, 9–20. London: Routledge.
No Country for Old Men. 2007. Dir. Joel Coen and Ethan Coen. Miramax Films.

Peek, Wendy Chapman. 2003. "The Romance of Competence: Rethinking Mascu-
   linity in the Western." *Journal of Popular Film and Television* 30, no. 4: 206–19.
Pumphrey, Martin. 1988. "Masculinity." In *The BFI Companion to the Western*, ed.
   Edward Buscombe, 181–83. London: BFI, 1988.
Shane. 1953. Dir. George Stevens. Paramount Pictures.
The Three Burials of Melquiades Estrada. 2005. Dir. Tommy Lee Jones. Europa.
Wright, Will. 1975. *Six Guns and Society: A Structural Study of the Western*. Berkeley:
   University of California Press.

12

✝

A Flip of the Coin:
Gender Systems and
Female Resistance in the
Coen Brothers'
No Country for Old Men

Erin K. Johns

No Country for Old Men depicts more than the murderous rampage of a psychopathic hit man; it critiques the complicated gender systems that exist as a result of patriarchal systems like the law. As the sheriff, Ed Tom Bell represents the actual, physical law as he works to enforce it. Llewelyn Moss fulfills the role of hunter, which associates him with a natural code that is tied to the earth even though that code is at odds with the curiously questioning persona of his wife, Carla Jean Moss. First portrayed as an obedient and subservient wife, Carla Jean gains agency as the film progresses; she becomes a woman at odds not only with her husband, Llewelyn, but also with Anton Chigurh, the systematic and cold psychopathic killer who relies on the system of fate. In this chapter, I explore how each of these male characters, Ed Tom, Llewelyn, and Chigurh, fulfill traditional systems—especially involving the law and gender categorization. The male characters cope with a vastly changing gendered landscape: one where men are lost to the traditional roles of the law and women resist those masculine systems and laws. Therefore, the men are constantly creating their own personal laws or codes in order to make up for the lack of symbolic order, which represents the disintegration of what Jacques Lacan (1993) refers to as the "Law-of-the-Father." Carla Jean Moss and Loretta Bell, Ed Tom's wife, recognize and work with and against all of the different and constantly adapting masculine systems. The two major women in the film offer the only places of resistance to the ultimate masculine system: the justified fate that Chigurh inflicts through death. Carla Jean and Loretta recognize these male systems and will no longer be complicit in them—especially if they lead to the further demise of human kind. The women, unlike the men, realize that they have a choice, which the men fail to acknowledge by continually adapting masculine power systems to suit their own needs rather than simply resisting those laws and that tradition. I argue that the Coen brothers' *No Country for Old Men* (2007) uses female characters as the only places of resistance to the social order, that is, the law of the father and the masculine systems that surround and doom all of the male characters throughout the movie.

The three main male characters, Ed Tom, Llewelyn, and Chigurh, all represent three very different systems—although each system relies on a particular code that is essential to the construction of patriarchal control. Separately, each man seems lost in a rapidly changing modern world—one where patriarchal power is slowly losing its grasp on one of its subjects, the woman. This new social landscape is one that has altered significantly in the United States as a result of the equal rights movement—a movement that exposed many of the masculine, patriarchal systems as not only no longer necessary, but belonging to the past. Regardless, the male subject must confront his altered social position as one who is no longer the sole possessor of power, exposing his impotence by adhering to an outdated and outmoded social system. Each of the male characters rely on systems and codes that belong to another era—one that has suddenly been disrupted by female resistance during the time period of the film (the 1980s). *No Country for Old Men* is a film that exposes the masculine confrontation with the Other as both the woman and the rather foreign sounding and looking Chigurh. Although he is in many ways exoticized, Chigurh adheres to a specific code and faith that subversively aligns him with the masculine—a confirmation that also results from his association with violence.[1] Thus, together, each man represents three different components of an outdated patriarchal system: Ed Tom, as a police officer, is the literal law; Llewelyn, as a hunter, represents a law of domination at the expense of others; and Chigurh, as a hit man, represents a higher code or law—fate—that associates his character with Jean-Pierre Melville's Jef in *Le Samourai* (1967). Separately, each of these men face their domination by female resistance in a country that is not only "no country for old men," but perhaps, no country for any man. Ultimately, *No Country for Old Men* is a film that conforms to a larger gender project that exists in many of the Coen brothers' films—a project that exposes the faulty nature of male codes/systems in the face of female resistance.

For Jacques Lacan (1993), the issue of sexual difference is part of a much larger patriarchal ideological system that relies on the feminine as subject to the masculine. This identification with the feminine subject position results from what Lacan defines as the Name-of-the-Father: a process whereby the subject conforms to a specific role in the symbolic order, which Lacan terms as the law. Lacan writes in *The Seminar of Jacques Lacan: The Psychoses: 1955–1956,*

> In order for the human being to be able to establish the most natural of relations, that between male and female, a third party has to intervene, one that is the image of something successful, the model of some harmony. This does not go far enough—there has to be a law, a chain, a symbolic order, the intervention of the order of speech, that is, of the father. Not the natural father, but what is called the father. The order that prevents the collision and explosion of the situation as a whole is founded on the existence of this name of the father. (1993, 96)

The order that results from the name of the father is that of the law or more generally, of codes and systems that allow the symbolic order to create a binary of male and female. More importantly, this symbolic order is also what allows for the feminine to assume a subject position, which is the very position that the Coen brothers attempt to challenge through the female characters in the film. In *No Country for Old Men*, the Coen brothers expose rather than conceal ideological apparatuses like the symbolic order resulting from interactions between gender and the law. The Coens' exposure of the problematic traditional female subject position results in a postmodern film that is conscious of its own position in representing, challenging, and subverting ideological apparatuses concerning gender. Thus, *No Country for Old Men* represents a traditional gender structure that is in distress—a representation of rapidly changing gender positions during the last twenty years of the twentieth century.

The opening of *No Country for Old Men* establishes that the disintegration of the law (and by extension patriarchy) is a major theme of the movie. As a montage of images of the Western landscape appears on the screen, each image dissolves into another image—locating the instability of not only the image but cultural associations with images of the West.[2] Already, the Coen brothers signal their postmodern generic intents— emptying the Western of its genre conventions and its strict adherence to a masculine code. Additionally, as Joan Mellen asserts in "Spiraling Downward: America in *Days of Heaven, In the Valley of Elah,* and *No Country for Old Men*," "*No Country for Old Men* is set on a flatter landscape of West Texas desolation where nature can no longer be listed even ironically as a metaphor of transcendence. . . . The level of urgency has risen, even as the Coens . . . depict a society devoid of safety, tranquility, or solace" (2008, 28). Mellen also identifies the generic instability that is often a staple of the Coen brothers' films.[3] Ed Tom's voice-over further marks the collapse of the law in a foreign, yet modern landscape; his very first remark situates the masculinity of the law by remarking on his grand-father and father. Ed Tom says, "I was sheriff of this county when I was twenty-five. Hard to believe. Grandfather was a lawman. Father too. Me and him was sheriff at the same time, him in Plano and me here. I think he was pretty proud of that. I know I was." As the voice-over continues, Ed Tom relates the story of a boy who killed a fourteen-year-old girl and wonders at this new form of violence in society; he says, "You can say it's my job to fight it [the something he doesn't understand] but I don't know what it is anymore." Although it seems as if he is describing this some-thing as a new form of violence that makes up the modern age, I assert that Ed Tom is in fact remarking on the "it" as a society that has created a new code and system despite that code's incompatibility with the tra-ditional law. In essence, *No Country for Old Men* depicts a society whose sense of the masculine has lapsed; the male figure must confront his in-ability to function in this other and new world. When he describes the murderer in the opening voice-over, Ed Tom describes both the society's and the murderer's different justifications for the crime itself: "Papers said it was a crime of passion but he told me there wasn't any passion to it. Told me that he'd been planning to kill somebody for about as long as he could remember. Said that if they turned him out he'd do it again. Said he knew he was going to hell. Be there in about fifteen minutes. I don't know what to make of that. I surely don't." Ed Tom does not understand how a masculine character can act without an internal or social code. Thus, resis-tance by female characters to both the new and old code/system exposes the ineffectual nature of all codes and systems, because they are part of a masculine project that relies on the female maintaining her subject posi-tion. It is the breakdown of the patriarchal and masculine law that is at stake in *No Country for Old Men*—exposing the reliance of the masculine, whether old-fashioned (Llewelyn and Ed Tom) or modern (Chigurh), on systems (laws) that are continually defied by the feminine.

Although the film opens with Ed Tom's voice-over, the viewer does not become familiar with any images of him until almost a quarter of the way through the movie. Ed Tom's first appearance is in his sheriff's out-fit, loading a horse onto a trailer, and discussing a crime with his wife. In the scenes involving Ed Tom and Loretta, Loretta always functions as the voice of reason and common sense; her attitude is one of great confidence and mockery in her position as responsible wife and homemaker. As Ed Tom loads the horse and attempts to placate his wife, Loretta responds by laying out the "law" he should be following at work:

Ed Tom: I love you more and more every day.
Loretta: That's very nice. Be careful.
Ed Tom: Always am.

Loretta: Don't get hurt.
Ed Tom: Never do.
Loretta: Don't hurt no one.
Ed Tom: If you say so.

From the first scene involving Ed Tom, the narrative displaces him as a figure of authority—a reading that aligns with his outdated position as an Old West sheriff. Instead, Loretta appears as the figure who imposes the law—a reversal of heteronormative, patriarchal gender relationships. This scene also offers the first sign that there is something amiss with masculine systems and codes, because the woman, instead of the sheriff (and the physical extension of the symbolic law), offers the law that the sheriff should follow. In this first scene between the two, it becomes apparent that all Ed Tom exposed in the opening voice-over is true—the masculine system of the law is under attack by the Other's resistance, whether the psychopathic teenage boy killer of the voice-over or the wife, Loretta.

As a figure, Ed Tom is submitting to slow extinction; he is old and about to retire. By the end of the movie, Ed Tom fulfills that extinction narrative by retiring from the law in response to the modern, psychopathic violence of the contemporary landscape. In essence, Chigurh, as a psychopathic figure, never fulfills his mission of extinguishing the life of Llewelyn; Chigurh's ultimate hit is that of the traditional law—extinguishing Ed Tom's career and belief system. In *No Country for Old Men*, Chigurh is the most threatening to the symbolic system that is rapidly deconstructing throughout the film rather than through his actual acts of physical violence. In the film, as in Cormac McCarthy's novel, the real victim is Ed Tom and the old order that is being rapidly replaced by a new, modern system—a system that functions through the resistance of the Other. Loretta, like Chigurh, functions as this Other by imposing the rules and remaining a part of this new system—abandoning the home in favor of a job. By the end of the movie, Ed Tom is depicted at a lonely breakfast table, and it is here that the viewer realizes that Ed Tom (and by extension the law) has retired—slowly dissolving from not only physical but also symbolic existence. When Ed Tom asks Loretta to go riding with him during the day, Loretta responds, "Lord no. I'm not retired." Shortly after, Ed Tom discusses his dream from the previous night. This particular emphasis on the dream exposes the law as a part of the symbolic order that has no real connection to the modern landscape. Ed Tom says of his dream, "All right. Two of them [dreams], both had my father in them. It's peculiar. I'm older now than he ever was by twenty years. So, in a sense, he's the younger man. . . . The second one it was like we was both back in the older times. . . . And in the dream I knew that he was going on ahead.

. . . And I knew that whenever I'd got there, I knew that he'd be there. And then I woke up." In reality, Ed Tom never really wakes up, because the masculine system, the law (of "olden times") becomes nothing other than a symbolic representation of a system of beliefs that is outdated and retired. After Ed Tom discusses his dream, the camera cuts quickly to Loretta as the sound of the clock ticking permeates the room. Just as quickly, like a dream, the screen goes black—metaphorically representing that the viewer, like Ed Tom, wakes up. Ironically, unlike Ed Tom, the viewer never actually wakes up, because the viewer is already a part of that modern system to which Ed Tom succumbs.[4] Ed Tom must wake up because he is a part of an old system that has rapidly disintegrated in the modern landscape. This system, which relies on the "law" and patriarchal control, has always been a dream, much like Ed Tom's father (exposing what Lacan [1993] terms the Law-of-the-Father). In reality, Ed Tom belongs to the world of the dream, with his father, with a system that no longer exists. Although he may be alive, Ed Tom is symbolically killed by his retirement from his position as sheriff—making his retirement a death that exposes the already symbolic position of the law.

Outside of his final retirement, Ed Tom has his antiquated belief system exposed during a diner conversation with another sheriff of a similar age to Ed Tom. The two sheriffs expose the beliefs of a 1950s patriarchal system—commenting on children with "green hair and bones in their noses" as well as the slow retirement of the terms *sir* and *ma'am*. Additionally, these two sheriffs discuss the modern social changes in biblical language that includes "the dismal tide" and "signs and wonders." The language further displaces Ed Tom from an understanding of contemporary society. Thus, the law of the symbolic system is tied not only to the patriarchy, but to a white, male, Christian patriarchy. In order to subvert the power structure that depends upon patriarchal control, *No Country for Old Men* is a movie filled with Others—the other sex, another race, and another generation (or country). Ed Tom functions as the normative standard to which the Other is measured—emphasizing the dislocation of the masculine/feminine gender binary.

Like the complicated nature of gender, *No Country for Old Men* also disrupts narrative expectation by making Ed Tom the focal point of the narrative rather than Llewelyn Moss. This disruption also influences the function of the Western genre of the film, because Ed Tom (the sheriff) is still the hero the viewer expects of the genre, even though Llewelyn is the implied hero of the tale. If Ed Tom is supposed to be the "good guy" and Chigurh the "bad guy," Llewelyn is a man caught in between—one who attempts to straddle the old and new worlds. Regardless of his straddling position, Llewelyn also relies on a system in much the same way that Ed Tom attempts to conform to an outdated law. Like Ed Tom's betrayal of

the system through retirement, Llewelyn betrays the system by succumb-
ing to greed. When he first appears in the movie, the viewer does not see
him, but instead, the viewer focuses on what Llewelyn is seeing through
a point-of-view shot; this shot is that of the scope of a rifle focused on a
single antelope in a pack of roaming antelope in an empty Western plain.
Llewelyn meticulously adjusts the scope and focus on his rifle. Llewelyn
calmly waits to take the best shot possible, and he slowly pulls the trigger.
The shot injures the antelope, but does not kill it; Llewelyn's reaction is
one of obvious disappointment at the wasted shot. Llewelyn bends down
and picks up the shell casing from the ground and places it in his pocket—
showing that Llewelyn is a man who respects the environment and does
not indulge in waste. When he stands up, Llewelyn's simple clothing (a
white and brown flannel shirt and jeans) blends into the Western landscape. From this initial scene, Llewelyn represents a natural code—one
that is often associated with the hunter. Like Ed Tom, Llewelyn also relies
on a particular system—one that overlaps the oldest world (that of the
hunter and gatherer) and that of the new (the Vietnam veteran). Llewelyn
ultimately meets his death because he betrayed his system for greed—
taking the money from the drug deal in an attempt to enter the capitalist
system. This system is completely incompatible with the hunter and gatherer code that relies on usefulness and reducing waste. Instead, capitalism
is a system that ties a person to conspicuous consumption—a system that
depends completely on excess and waste rather than minimalism. Llewelyn must enter the capitalist system in order for him to be a viable target
for Chigurh; his life, like the money, is an excess that becomes expendable
in a society that is set on consumption.

The epitome of excessive consumption is in fact Chigurh—a figure
that consumes life rather than money as an expendable object. Ironically,
Chigurh endows money with specific faith properties by associating the
coin toss with fate—a cosmic order that justifies Chigurh's actions. Chigurh is unique in that his reasons for being a hit man are far outside of the
capitalist system; he kills because he enjoys it (like the young boy from Ed
Tom's voice-over at the beginning of the film). Traditionally, the hit man
character is a cold, calculated killer, but one who follows some sort-of
code system. This film tradition stems from Melville's Jef in *Le Samourai*
to recent incarnations of the hit man in Jim Jarmusch's *Ghost Dog* (1999).
These are all men who follow a particular code of honor that also includes
loyalty to a particular boss or job. Unlike Chigurh, these hit men do not
necessarily look like they enjoy killing, but enjoy the regimented structure
of the code or law. In *No Country for Old Men*, the character that actually
fulfills the stereotypical conduct of the hit man is Carson Wells. Wells
imposes a rigid structure to his interactions with his line of work and
with Chigurh, who does not follow the laws of etiquette related to being

a hit man. By declaring Chigurh a psychopath, Wells acknowledges the code of the hit man by openly defying Chigurh's lack of respect for that code. Carson responds to the Texas boss's question about how dangerous Chigurh is with a quick, sarcastic reply: "Compared to what, the bubonic plague. He's bad enough you called me. Yeah. He's a psychopathic killer, but so what? There's plenty of them around." From the moment that Carson enters the film, the viewer is aware that Carson is the hit man that Chigurh should be. Because he is logical and business-like, Wells fulfills the generic expectations of the role of the cinematic hit man—a character types that the film openly anticipates and deconstructs through Chigurh. Chigurh's lack of conformity with this system is what makes him an unnerving "bad guy" to the viewing audience. When Chigurh goes to Mexico to kill Carson, Carson questions Chigurh's free will, which is antithetical to Chigurh's system of fate:

> Chigurh: And you know what's going to happen now, Carson? You should admit your situation. There would be more dignity in it.
> Carson: You go to hell.
> Chigurh: All right. Let me ask you something. If the rule you followed brought you to this, of what use was the rule?
> Carson: Do you have any idea how crazy you are?
> Chigurh: You mean the nature of this conversation.
> Carson: I mean the nature of you. You . . . you . . . can have the money, Anton.

Chigurh is able to point out to Carson the complete ineffectuality of his code, or his "rule," in the face of a man who does not follow that same code. This code, even though it belongs to a hit man, is meant to mimic that of the law, of a patriarchal rule. In this manner, it would be easy to discuss Chigurh as yet another character who is Other and resists patriarchal control. The problem with reading Chigurh as an Other is his own insistence on a code. It may be a different code than that of Carson, but it is a code nonetheless—the coin toss.

Carson's code accepts some amount of free will, because he asks for his life even though it is a futile attempt; he reminds Chigurh that he does not need to do this. Chigurh does not accept his own ability at invoking free will, because he has created a rule of his own through his use of the coin toss. Conversely, in an earlier scene, Chigurh also uses the coin toss to determine the fate of a gas station attendant—offering his own interpretation of money, life, and the system of fate that is tied to a simple coin. In this scene, Chigurh openly scoffs at the fact that the attendant has "married into" his business—a scoff that is meant to emasculate the attendant for not fulfilling his own masculine, social role. As the conversation between the attendant and Chigurh continues, Chigurh asks the attendant to call the coin toss and offers a rather existential reading of the coin (or fate):

Chigurh: What's the most you ever lost in a coin toss?
Attendant: Sir?
Chigurh: The most you ever lost in a coin toss?
Attendant: Oh I don't know. Couldn't say.
Chigurh: Call it.
Attendant: Call it? For what?
Chigurh: Just call it.
Attendant: Well we need to know what we're calling it for here.
Chigurh: You need to call it. I can't call it for you. It wouldn't be fair.
Attendant: I didn't put nothing up.
Chigurh: Yes you did. You've been putting it up your whole life. You just didn't know it. You know what date is on this coin?
Attendant: No.
Chigurh: 1958. It's been traveling twenty-two years to get here. Now it's here and it's heads or tails. Now you have to call it.
Attendant: Now, I need to know what I stand to win.
Chigurh: Everything. You stand to win everything. Call it.

The attendant proceeds to call the coin toss and wins, but even Chigurh cannot give the man the satisfaction of that win; he must instruct the attendant about where to put the coin:

Chigurh: Don't put it in your pocket. It's your lucky quarter.
Attendant: Where do you want me to put it?
Chigurh: Anywhere not in your pocket—where it will get mixed in with the others and will become just a coin . . . which it is.

Although the attendant is unaware, Chigurh instructs him in the code of the coin toss and the insignificance of the monetary unit. Chigurh exposes the ironies surrounding traditional forms of masculinity and patriarchy, and in some ways, he could openly challenge those systems. Additionally, Chigurh exposes the symbolic nature of his system of fate to the viewer by acknowledging that the coin is really nothing other than a coin: humans give the coin its symbolic significance. Despite the potential structure he exposes, Chigurh must find a new code and his own law of "fate" to justify his actions, which prevents him from resisting or challenging the patriarchal systems in the ways that he imagines. Instead, Chigurh simply replaces one law with a new law, because he retreats into an ultimately masculine position and role. The sheriff, the hit man, and the natural man may all have codes that they honor and fulfill, but Chigurh creates yet another code that must be fulfilled as well. The fact that Chigurh creates a code to justify his actions prevents him from resisting the law. By violating the physical law, Chigurh recognizes those systems (like the law), but he cannot escape them. Although Chigurh does not comply with the law of Ed Tom, his insistence on a reactionary law still assumes the necessity of a guiding principle to the symbolic order he realizes through serial murders.

Thus, it would be easy to read Chigurh as a complete Other, except for the fact that he creates his own law—the law of fate, the law of the coin toss. In many ways, Chigurh represents what happens to masculinity and patriarchy when the law has already been confronted by the Other and must find a new law. Interestingly, unlike the female characters, Chigurh never really resists the law because he creates a new law, a new rule, and a new code to justify his own actions—even if he displaces those actions onto the coin toss of fate. Chigurh represents a rapidly changing masculine landscape, one that must continue to function despite the breakdown of patriarchal control from female resistance. To feminine characters, the original code, which reflects the law, patriarchy, and the creation of subject positions, is perhaps just as psychopathic as the new code that Chigurh represents, because they are both employed as a way to create a balanced, masculine, system of morals. Codes, whether original or new, are thus inscribed in the masculine gender throughout *No Country for Old Men* regardless of whether Chigurh is a psychopath or not. The real psychopathic system is the law, the patriarchal system that demanded subjects, objects, and no resistance—a system that both Loretta and Carla Jean recognize and attempt to resist in different ways.

Although Loretta is a rather peripheral character, her relationship with Ed Tom is one of middle-aged comfort, offering Loretta the opportunity to voice her opinion and subtly resist Ed Tom's interaction with the law. In her first scene, Loretta appears on the screen as a stereotypical western woman—opinionated, vocal, and a little bit sassy. Loretta is aware of the systems inherent in the law, but her position as wife offers her an outsider position that enables her criticism of the systems and laws around her. As Ed Tom loads a horse onto the trailer, Loretta immediately comments on the financial costs of maintaining a horse. Loretta often confronts Ed Tom about the illogicality of the systems in which he is so heavily invested. Loretta's brief comments endow her with a certain amount of agency, a voice that constantly mocks and defies masculine codes/systems. In that introductory scene, Loretta becomes the giver of the law (as I discussed earlier), which ultimately subverts Ed Tom's power as not only a sheriff, but as a husband and even as a patriarchal figure in general. The two brief scenes that include Loretta show Ed Tom as a man who is powerless— unimportant compared to his quick-to-comment wife. Loretta frequently exposes the arbitrary nature of the law through her brief remarks, which gives her the authority to subvert the masculine power structure in favor of something a little more forgiving and cynical. Unlike Ed Tom, Loretta's response to the changing modern landscape is not that of incomprehension, but cynicism—a humor that works because it exposes the instability of the very structures that Ed Tom attempts to maintain. Unlike Ed Tom, Loretta can never retire, because she does not rely on the same law. Loretta knows that retirement is not an option because she will eventually have to fulfill the codependent needs of her husband. It is this same codependent need that prompts Ed Tom, in the final scene, to ask his wife to go riding with him even though she has to go to work. Whether there is a real job for her to go to or not, Loretta, as wife, is the outsider, one who is always outside the system, and one who cannot conform to the law. Instead, Loretta does not have to struggle with the idea of retirement, because even in retirement, Loretta will still be responsible for helping her husband mask the fact that he has outlived his usefulness since he has outlived the law.

Unlike Loretta, Carla Jean falls into the more traditional role of wife—constantly following all of Llewelyn's instructions. Despite this loyalty, Carla Jean is slowly moving away from her role as obedient wife—a movement that is exhibited by her need to question everything. Carla Jean may ultimately follow Llewelyn's instructions, but she does not do it without a series of questions regarding his plans. Carla Jean is first introduced silently watching television on the couch of a trailer—waiting for Llewelyn to come home. As soon as Llewelyn enters the trailer, Carla Jean immediately bombards Llewelyn with a stream of questions concerning where he has been and what he has been doing all day. Eventually, Llewelyn sits down on the couch beside Carla Jean in an awkward medium shot that exposes a simplicity and playfulness in their relationship. Like Loretta, Carla Jean also resorts to a humorous and cynical response to her husband, exposing the emptiness of the masculine threats that Llewelyn is attempting to lodge at her. Llewelyn responds to Carla Jean's questioning: "Keep running that mouth of yours. I'm going to take you in the back and screw you." Carla Jean quickly responds, "Big talk." Llewelyn then remarks, "Keep it up." This initial scene creates an awkward gender dynamic that shows Llewelyn as the dominant force in the household at the same time that Carla Jean openly tests the boundaries of that power or law. Carla Jean's confrontation with Llewelyn's masculine, hunter code exposes its impotence. As the movie progresses, Carla Jean slowly crosses the boundary between submissive wife and resistant woman—exposing her as the only character who resists not only Llewelyn's code but Chigurh's as well. The only system to which Carla Jean submits is that of the already old and decayed code of Ed Tom; this submission is the very moment in the film when Carla Jean realizes her own agency and her ability to resist the masculine codes and systems that have constantly repressed her.

Unlike Llewelyn, Carla Jean eventually recognizes the incompatibility of money with Llewelyn's hunter/gatherer code. Additionally, Carla Jean realizes that Llewelyn is in a situation that is beyond his power even though he is too stubborn to appreciate it. Instead of remaining the passive wife, Carla Jean decides to act and ask Ed Tom to help Llewelyn. By contacting Ed Tom, Carla Jean exhibits her first moment of agency in the film, and the viewer suddenly becomes aware of the fact that Carla Jean is not nearly so clueless as she appears to be. Despite all of her questioning, Carla Jean is able to recognize the fact that Llewelyn's way is not compatible with the drug cartel, the hit man, or the capitalist system in general. When she calls Ed Tom, Carla Jean exposes knowledge of Llewelyn that seems to directly contradict all of her questioning throughout the beginning of the film; she says, "Llewelyn would never ask for help. He never thinks he needs any." To this, Ed Tom replies, "Carla Jean, I will not harm your man. And he needs help whether he knows it or not." Carla Jean recognizes the incongruity between Llewelyn's ways and the capitalist system, but she does not realize at this juncture that turning to another masculine system will still lead to Llewelyn's ruin. Instead of finding another way to approach the situation, Carla Jean resorts to a masculine system and code, a law that is already decaying and about to retire. The impotence of the traditional law is finally exposed when Ed Tom is unable to reach Llewelyn in time to help or protect him. Fortunately, Carla Jean will not rely on any masculine system in order to save herself or anyone else again.

In one of the final scenes of *No Country for Old Men*, Carla Jean had to bury not only her husband but her mother as well. At her mother's house, Carla Jean quietly enters into the emptiness of both the house and her life after the death of her husband and her mother. In a short shot, Carla Jean sits at the kitchen table—taking in the eerie atmosphere of the empty house. Carla Jean then moves to enter into the bedroom, which is where Chigurh is quietly sitting. Carla Jean and Chigurh have the following long conversation:

> Carla Jean: I knew this wasn't done with. I ain't got the money. What little I had is long gone and there is bills aplenty to pay yet. I buried my mother today. Ain't paid for that neither.
> Chigurh: I wouldn't worry about it.
> Carla Jean: I need to sit down. You got no cause to hurt me.
> Chigurh: No. But I gave my word.
> Carla Jean: You gave your word?
> Chigurh: To your husband.

Carla Jean: That don't make sense. You gave your word to my husband to kill me?
Chigurh: Your husband had the opportunity to save you. Instead, he used you to try to save himself.
Carla Jean: Not like that. Not like you say. You don't have to do this.
Chigurh: People always say the same thing.
Carla Jean: What do they say?
Chigurh: They say, "You don't have to do this."
Carla Jean: You don't.
Chigurh: Ok. [He flips a coin.] This is the best I can do. Call it.
Carla Jean: I knowed you was crazy when I saw you sitting there. I knowed exactly what was in store for me.
Chigurh: Call it.
Carla Jean: No. I ain't going to call it.
Chigurh: Call it.
Carla Jean: The coin don't have no say. It's just you.
Chigurh: Well I got here the same way the coin did.

After this line, the camera cuts to the front of the house as Chigurh exits and carefully wipes his boots on the front steps. Despite her refusal to call the coin toss, Chigurh still kills Carla Jean. Carla Jean's final act of agency exposes the insubstantial nature of Chigurh's coin toss code and of fate more generally. By refusing to call the coin toss, Carla Jean proves that the coin really has no say and that in the end it is just Chigurh; she exposes the insignificance of the code that Chigurh lives by because she realizes that it is yet another masculine code. The coin toss code is the same as Llewelyn's hunter code and Ed Tom's law.

At first glance, Carla Jean may seem like a peripheral character, but in reality, she is the only character that offers a true moment of resistance. Carla Jean's futile attempts to avoid her fate expose how ineffectual masculine codes and systems truly are. Thus, Carla Jean refuses to call the coin toss because it is yet another useless, masculine code that disguises the "real." Throughout the film, the masculine characters are either unable to confront or completely unaware of the strict boundaries that their codes and systems set for them. Often discussed as the subject of masculine and patriarchal structures, the feminine characters are able to observe and resist these codes because of a changing subject position—one that is no longer eager to accept a submissive role. In this final scene, Carla Jean exposes a gender struggle that exists throughout the entire movie—between a code and individual agency.

Overall, the gender structures of *No Country for Old Men* function in a similar manner to other Coen brothers' movies. Men are often depicted as relying on codes and systems that have been displaced in the modern landscape.[5] The women are usually successful and resistant—ushering in

a new type of woman that attempts to resist the law by her own awareness of her own subject position in that law.[6] Although set in the 1980s,
No Country for Old Men exposes the rapidly changing gender structure
of the twenty-first century: one where stereotypical and traditional male
roles are constantly being resisted and replaced by roles that have traditionally been termed feminine. By refusing to call the coin toss, Carla Jean
recognizes the necessary female resistance required to displace these masculine codes and systems. *No Country for Old Men* exposes a much larger
twenty-first-century gender struggle than is completely apparent in the
film's structure: What does it mean to be a man in a world where the
masculine code/system is constantly being resisted? What can a man do
when he simply performs a code or system and thus a gender? Perhaps,
as the end of the movie suggests, a man can either wither away quietly
into retirement or fashion himself a sling for his broken body—still disappearing from the scene like a ghost. In either case, *No Country for Old Men*
shows that a ghost is all that is left of masculine or patriarchal systems
and codes.

NOTES

1. Although an argument could be made for Chigurh as Other and thus feminine, I feel that his association with violence and a strict adherence to a violent
code actually aligns him as another impotent, masculine figure. Chigurh may
appear at surface level to be Other, but in fact, he represents yet another code/
system that makes up the construction of the patriarchy.

2. For a further discussion of the use of the Western landscape in *No Country
for Old Men*, see "Gone Tomorrow: The echoing spaces of Joel and Ethan Coen's
No Country for Old Men" by Geoffrey O'Brien. Particularly, O'Brien comments on
the subversive use of the landscape as what "feels, for a few opening moments
at least, like a paradise of spaciousness—except that the desert is littered with
wrecked cars and rotting corpses, and the rest of the wide-open spaces have been
layered over with highways and motels and all sorts of other precisely observed
junk" (2007, 31).

3. Mellen also remarks in "Spiraling Downward" that "any connection to the
Western, however, is tenuous. Given that what is at stake is a monstrous distor-
tion of the human, these films [*Days of Heaven, In the Valley of Elah*, and *No Country
for Old Men*] have more in common with science fiction" (2008, 24). I agree with
Mellen in her reading of the Western in *No Country for Old Men*—for the film
inadequately fulfills the repeated components of the Western genre. Instead, *No
Country for Old Men* relies on multiple genres that undermine a strictly Western
generic reading of the films plot and cinematography. Mellen, though, is more
concerned with arguing for a political reading of *Days of Heaven, In the Valley of
Elah*, and *No Country for Old Men* based on their inclusion of the Vietnam War/
veteran as a reading of imperial politics.

4. In "Spiraling Downward," Mellen (2008) makes this point about encouraging the audience to wake up in the same way that Ed Tom says he does. Ironically, though, I would assert that the Coen brothers are actually exposing the viewer to that fact that he is already awake. There is no need for the viewer to wake up from the dream, because the modern audience is already a part of the modern structure of which Loretta and Carla Jean are a part.

5. In "The Privileged White Male Meets the Other(s): Images of Power in the Postmodern Films of the Coen brothers," Charles Soukup focuses on the outsider status of what he terms the "Fool Antihero" (2006, 316). Although Soukup's overall argument is to discuss the privileged outsider status that the Coen brothers ultimately share with their Fool Antiheroes, his discussion of the merger of the comedic with the serious through genre blurring is particularly interesting in its usage of the privileged male as obtaining an outsider status (316). I agree with much of what Soukup discusses in regard to Coen brothers' movies in general, but I do not feel that his argument extends so readily to *No Country for Old Men*. Regardless, I assert that the Coen brothers are attempting to represent a sort-of outsider or other status of the white male that reflects a more contemporary reading of the modern gender landscape. This, though, is a subject that is outside the scope of this chapter.

6. Other Coen brothers' movies that have a similar gender dynamic include *Fargo* (1996), *Raising Arizona* (1987), *Barton Fink* (1991), and *The Big Lebowski* (1998). In these films, women are depicted as successful whereas men concoct expansive schemes that rely on a more traditional masculine and feminine gender roles. In essence, these Coen brothers films, like *No Country for Old Men*, expose the rapidly changing gender structure since the Equal Rights Movement. These films also expose the displacement of traditional masculine roles that result in male characters that cannot succeed in a world that no longer relies on the feminine assuming a subject position.

REFERENCES

Barton Fink. 1991. Dir. Joel Coen and Ethan Coen. Circle Films.

The Big Lebowski. 1998. Dir. Joel Coen and Ethan Coen. PolyGram Filmed Entertainment.

Fargo. 1996. Dir. Joel Coen and Ethan Coen. PolyGram Filmed Entertainment.

Ghost Dog: The Way of the Samurai. 1999. Dir. Jim Jarmusch. Pandora Filmproduktion.

Lacan, Jacques. 1993. *The Seminar of Jacques Lacan: Book III: The Psychoses, 1955–1956*. Trans. Russell Grigg. New York: W.W. Norton.

Mellen, Joan. 2008. "Spiraling Downward: America in *Days of Heaven, In the Valley of Elah*, and *No Country for Old Men*." *Film Quarterly* 61: 24-31.

No Country for Old Men. 2008. DVD. Dir. Ethan Coen and Joel Coen. Buena Vista Home Entertainment, Inc., and Paramount Vantage.

O'Brien, Geoffrey. 2007. "Gone Tomorrow: The Echoing Spaces of Joel and Ethan Coen's *No Country for Old Men*." *Film Comment* 43: 28–31.

Raising Arizona. 1987. Dir. Joel Coen and Ethan Coen. Circle Films.
Le Samourai. 1967. Dir. Jean-Pierre Melville. Compagnie Industrielle et Commerciale Cinématographique.
Soukup, Charles. 2006. "The Privileged White Male Meets the Other(s): Images of Power in the Postmodern Films of the Coen Brothers." In the Image of Power in Literature: Selected Papers [of the] 2006 Conference, Society for the Interdisciplinary Study of Social Imagery, 315–22.

13

✝

Grace and Moss's End in
No Country for Old Men

Dennis Cutchins

It's difficult to know when you should take the Coen brothers seriously. They are notoriously flippant in interviews. Nevertheless, I am prone to take Joel Coen's 1998 observation that he would like to make a Western seriously, at least in retrospect (Lowe 2006, 99). Their 2007 adaptation of Cormac McCarthy's *No Country for Old Men* certainly fits the description of a Western, although it is set in 1980 rather than 1880. But there are westerns and there are westerns. Film adaptations of novels are always interpretations of the literary texts upon which they are based, and interpretations usually show the fingerprint of the interpreter. In the case of *No Country for Old Men*, the Coen brothers offer a particularly strong and interesting interpretation of Cormac McCarthy's Western novel, but it is one that seems to owe at least as much in some ways to what might be called the Coen style as it does to generic Westerns, to McCarthy's *No Country for Old Men* (2005), or to McCarthy's earlier western novels.

The Coens' *No Country for Old Men* is certainly not typical Hollywood fare. Narrative gaps, for instance, are not unusual in McCarthy's novels, but a willingness to leave narrative gaps in place is somewhat unusual for big-budget Hollywood film adaptations. Many, perhaps even most adaptators can't resist the urge to show the events and explain the details that the novelist leaves out. In McCarthy's *All the Pretty Horses* (1993), for instance, the abduction of the captain by the *hombres del país*, the "men of the country," near the end of the novel mystifies both readers and, apparently, John Grady himself. John Grady wakes to find the men standing over him. They take the captain without explanation, but leave John Grady his horses, and in a gesture reminiscent of Luke 3:11,[1] even give him a serape. In the film adaptation of this event (2000), however, Billy Bob Thornton and Ted Tally can't resist making this event both more explicable and more narratively satisfying by having Orlando be part of the group that abducts the captain. This old man has been held in jail by the captain for several months for no reason he can name. John Grady had earlier released the old man during his kidnapping of the captain, so Orlando has both a reason to hate the captain and a reason to do John Grady a favor. Thus the captain's abduction in Thornton's adaptation *makes more sense* than it does in the novel.

Generally speaking, this is not the case in the Coens' *No Country*. They make sure that their film retains the kinds of narrative gaps that require audiences to invest themselves in the text. One of those gaps is certainly the film's depiction of Moss's death. Judging from the conversations I overheard while walking out of the theater after watching the film for the first time, these gaps may have been a little too broad for the average viewer. Many of the other filmgoers had not read the novel, and Moss's off-camera death came as nasty surprise to them. I was not surprised by his death, but I must admit that still I was somewhat disappointed as I left the theater. I had read the novel and knew, more or less, what was coming, but Moss's end still felt a little flat to me. I've come to believe that my own disappointment stems not from Moss's death, nor even from the film's ending. Rather I found myself disappointed by the film's insistent portrayal of the world as a meaningless place in which the lives of human beings are dictated solely by fate or happenstance. This worldview, arguably the film's central feature, is quite different from that found in McCarthy's novel, and the difference between the two texts is nowhere more apparent than in the scenes leading up to and including Moss's death.

In some ways the two texts are similar in their portrayal of the death, and it might appear to be only morbid curiosity that would drive me to explore the details of the murder. Moss certainly dies in both the film and the novel. And in both cases he is apparently assassinated by the Mexican drug gang that has pursued him,[2] along with Chigurh, since they discovered him at the scene of the failed drug deal. In both texts his death is a bit mysterious since it is not narrated in the novel, and it takes place off camera in the film. It is, nevertheless, in the details of the assassination that the two texts differ, and I would argue that my desire to understand these differences is not simply a gruesome fascination or a desire to see blood. Rather it represents the same engine that drives Greek tragedy. That, in short, is a desire to understand how the world works: to see what happens to a character who may be superior to me in many ways, but who still finds himself subject to a world full of bad luck, illness, and defeat. I want to know how Moss faced that last defeat.

In some ways the novelist's and the filmmakers' refusal to show the death is curious. Certainly both McCarthy and the Coens have no compunction about describing and depicting plenty of other deaths in the novel and in the film,[3] but both refuse to gratify viewers in this case. Perhaps in refusing to "show" the murder both McCarthy and the Coens hope to turn our attention away from the actual events, the narrative of the death, and force us to view Moss's death, as they say, philosophically. In other words, both readers and viewers may be forced to ignore the "what," the immediate causes of Moss's demise, at least temporarily, and to focus their attention instead on the why, the deep reasons for the death. But as with most tragedies, both literary and otherwise, those seeking closure and meaning in the film and the novel will likely feel the need to understand the details of Moss's last moments; they will want to know what *really* happened. As a student recently said to me, in the face of a tragedy our only comfort lies in the details. We want to know if Moss's death, even at the last moment, was preventable. Was it the result of choices Moss himself made? Was it simply the result of fate or of bad luck? Ultimately, the novel provides answers to some of these questions that the film explicitly denies.

Moss's death scene in the film begins with a shot of the Desert Sands Motor Hotel in El Paso from the front seat of Sheriff Ed Bell's police cruiser. Earlier scenes have established this as Moss's location. Throughout this scene viewers are more or less limited to shots of what Bell can see. He is clearly the focal character for this scene, and we know only what he knows. In the first shot of the hotel we can hear a popping, rattling noise, though it is not loud. That first shot is followed by a reaction shot of Bell driving. He looks confused and a bit concerned, but not really worried. The third shot is again through the windshield of Bell's cruiser, though this is plainly a point-of-view shot now. We see the gang of killers speed out of the motel parking lot in a dark Ford pickup. A second reaction shot of Bell shows that he is now worried. He grips the steering wheel. A brief third-person shot in front of the hotel shows the killers speeding away and Bell pulling into the parking lot. This is followed by a series of point-of-view and eyeline-match shots as Bell quickly walks through the parking lot. The camera, as it traces what Bell apparently sees, pauses on the spent shell casings, the dead woman in the pool, the wounded killer, and finally on Moss's bloody body. The shot of Moss is somewhat oblique, and were it not for his familiar shirt and hat we might not know that it was him. The scene closes as Bell asks a family, in English and Spanish, to call the police.

Like the film, the novel is not completely clear about how Moss dies since the attack is not narrated. All readers have is the second-hand report of an eyewitness.[4] According to the Culberson County sheriff (in the novel the killing takes place in the tiny town of Van Horn), the killer (in the novel there is only one) grabs a hitchhiker, a young woman whom Moss has befriended, and drags her out of her room. Moss leaves his room and faces the man, gun in hand, but relinquishes his gun when the man threatens to kill the hitchhiker. As soon as Moss lays his gun down the assassin kills the girl and shoots Moss. Despite his mortal wounds Moss retrieves his gun and shoots the assassin.

On the face of things, the two death scenes seem quite similar, apart from a few surface differences like the number of assassins. And the ultimate result is the same—Moss ends up dead in both cases. If we accept the viewpoint of Anton Chigurh, the assassin sent to retrieve the lost money, this is what counts. He insists that Moss's death is an inevitability, a simple result of the causes earlier set in motion. Several times in both the novel and film Anton Chigurh explains this notion of why things happen. He describes a world in which all actions are dictated by fate, one in which human decisions play little or no role. Moss was dead, he argues, the moment he picked up the money (*No Country*, 184). The details of his death are irrelevant. We must note, however, that Chigurh's explanations are not disinterested. In both the novel and the film Chigurh uses this reasoning to excuse his murder or near murder of several characters as being out of his control. The most striking of these episodes are the coin flips he occasionally offers his victims.

Near the beginning of both the novel and the film Chigurh stops at a small gas station. In conversation with the proprietor Chigurh seems to grow annoyed and suddenly asks the man, "What's the most you ever lost on a coin toss?" He proceeds to flip a quarter and demands that the storeowner call it. The man hesitates and Chigurh says, "I cant call it for you. It wouldnt be fair. It wouldnt even be right." When the man complains that he doesn't know what is at stake, that he "didnt put nothin up," Chigurh argues, "Yes you did. You've been putting it up your whole life. You just didnt know it" (*No Country*, 55–56). After the violence we have seen Chigurh commit already, the implications of this conversation are chilling. The hapless storeowner is staking nothing less than his life on the flip of a coin. Chigurh's "explanation" for his actions, though, is even more chilling. He apparently is prepared to kill the man for no other reason than the fact that the two of them are standing together in the store. The coin, Chigurh says, has "been traveling twenty-two years to get here. And now it's here. And I'm here. And I've got my hand over it. And it's either heads or tails. And you have to say. Call it" (56). The implication in this reasoning is that the man's life or death is simply the result of fate. Chigurh allows him to make a choice, but it is a meaningless choice since the coin toss is utterly random. "Meaningless" is something of an odd word to use here since the man's life seems to hang on his decision to choose heads or tails. But what I hope to suggest by calling it meaningless is that it cannot be made by any reasonable *means*. When the man correctly guesses heads he is saved not by his will or by his cunning, or even by the grace of God, but by a random event.

This basic description of the world should be familiar to readers of McCarthy's other novels. Coin flips like Chigurh's are discussed by the *dueña* Alfonsa in *All the Pretty Horses*. She notes that her father believed that "the responsibility for a decision could never be abandoned to a blind agency but could only be relegated to human decisions more and more removed from their consequences" (230). The example she gives is of a coin toss that was decided by the coiner who fashioned the coin with a certain balance—thus dictating the way it would fall in a coin toss years later. Again, the result of the coin toss may have been dictated by human choices, but those choices are so far removed from the consequences as to be utterly meaningless. In that same novel the prisoner Pérez attempts to extort protection money from John Grady Cole and Lacey Rawlins. He threatens them obliquely by describing the dangerous and chaotic world of the prison, "a world of possibility that has no end" (*Pretty Horses*, 188–89). He later explains that any idea of control in the prison in which they all live, or in the world outside for that matter, is simply an illusion (195). Both of these characters are describing, more or less, the same worldview suggested by Anton Chigurh. But perhaps more importantly, they are also describing the world that is depicted in the Coens' adaptation of *No Country*. The Coens, in short, have apparently accepted Chigurh's explanation for the violence he commits as simply the result of a fatalistic or chaotic world.

Chigurh's world, in some ways, seems contradictory. The concept of a fate-driven world seems, at least on the surface, very different from that of a chaotic world. They are similar, however, in one important way: both conceptions of the world deny the efficacy of agency. The notion of a chaotic world suggests that individual decisions don't matter since the results of those decisions are arbitrary. And the idea of fate suggests that individual decisions don't matter because only the arbitrary will of God (or something like God) matters. Questions about agency become something of a theme in the novel, reinforced in several places. Most notable of these is the story Sheriff Bell tells about the actions that earned him a Bronze Star in World War II. The medal was awarded for an act he considers cowardly. Faced with the hopeless task of trying to save his men, who are wounded and may be dead, Sergeant Bell chooses, instead, to save himself. He abandons his men and returns to the American lines. He has lived his life, he explains to his uncle, in an attempt to "make up for" this act of cowardice (*No Country*, 274–78).[5]

The problem with the film's depiction of the world, and this is certainly true with Chigurh, is that it is largely based on the word of dishonest characters, Chigurh included. In *All the Pretty Horses* Pérez is almost certainly being dishonest. While his "warning" may be generally true, it is specifically a lie. The world *is* a dangerous place in which unexpected things do happen, but within hours of the boys' first meeting with Pérez, Rawlins is attacked, likely on Pérez's orders. The prisoner's warning had been, in reality, a threat made to coerce protection money from the boys, and his suggestion that the world of the prison was out of his control is thus disingenuous to say the least. Chigurh's descriptions of a chaotic world seem to serve the same sort of self-interested ends. Accidents do happen, of course, as Chigurh's car wreck shows, but most of the violence in the novel is the direct result of the decisions characters (usually Chigurh) make.

This is ultimately the problem I have with Moss's death. Because it happens off camera in the film and remains largely unknown to Bell and unknowable to us, Moss's death seems too much an inevitability—the result of fate. The Coens have accepted Chigurh's explanation that Moss was dead the moment he picked up the case of money. In the novel, at least, Llewelyn Moss's death is not dictated the moment he takes the money, nor is his death an inevitable result of fate. Rather he dies because of meaningful decisions he and others make. Because he is able to make decisions and exercise agency, the Moss of the novel lives in a meaningful world in which things happen for a reason. He cannot control all of his circumstances, or even the consequences of his decisions, but he does make meaningful decisions.[6]

There are several important differences about the way Moss dies in the novel. The most important of these differences is that Moss exercises agency throughout the novel. His death is not dictated by fate, at least not the kind of inevitable fate we typically mean when we say that word. With this in mind it is fair to say that the novel is qualitatively different from the film since the novel's Moss has a good deal more control over his own fate than the cinematic character has over his. Moss's decision in the novel, for instance, to put down his gun obviously plays a role in his death. Moreover, in the novel Moss is not killed because the assassin is more capable or skilled. As he had earlier with Chigurh, Moss has the assassin in his gun sights, but in this case he relinquishes his control of the situation in order to save the girl. Thus Moss dies because the assassin takes advantage of his humanity, his concern for others, his *charity*, if you will.

Moss's willingness to put down his gun in order to save the girl is an important event, and one that is completely missing from the film. As he has all along, McCarthy allows Moss a choice even at this extreme moment and permits him to exercise agency, in this case the intention to willingly sacrifice his own life in an effort to save the young girl. The fact that the assassin kills the girl anyway should not lessen or demean Moss's willingness to sacrifice himself. The same may not be said of the film's Moss. He dies, we are left to believe, either because he was not fast enough on the draw, or because he was simply outgunned (in the film there are at least four killers involved in Moss's death). The Coens, in short, do not allow Moss any agency in his death and certainly do not allow him the noble gesture of putting down his gun in order to save the girl. In fact, the Coens remove the girl almost entirely from their adaptation. She is replaced by the woman who flirts with Moss at the motel pool. The removal of this character may be the most significant narrative change the Coens make in their film. Moss's relationship with the hitchhiker is a very important one, and we need to understand it in order to understand both his death and the world of the novel.

In the novel Moss leaves the Mexican hospital and hires a taxi in Mexico to drive him to San Antonio. There he buys a truck and starts for El Paso and his rendezvous with Carla Jean and her mother. He drives fewer than twenty miles, however, before he stops to pick up a hitchhiker. This may not be the completely charitable act of a good Samaritan, but Moss's motives seem to be pure. He originally picks her up, apparently, so that he can rest on the drive. His plan is a failure, however. His pain and his worry keep him from sleeping in the truck, but he does not abandon the girl. Instead he begins to show some concern for her. He feeds her and provides a separate hotel room for her. At one point he asks her, "Does they anybody know where you're at?" (*No Country*, 225). The girl replies that Moss knows where she is. In a play on the Heisenberg uncertainty principle,[7] Moss answers, "I don't know where you're at because I don't know who you are" (225). Moss's suggestion, of course, is that knowing *where* the girl exists, is meaningless unless one also knows *who* she is. In short, one must care about her before her location makes a difference. Moss is somewhat disingenuous here, however, since he already seems to care about her. Eventually he learns that she is running away to California, and he gives her one thousand dollars "to go to California on" (223). Later he suggests that he has given the gift in order to protect her and to keep her from hitchhiking (235). Again, Moss could have been much more generous, but it is important to note that he performs this relatively small act of kindness in his moment of extreme need. He is being chased by men who have sworn to kill both him and his wife. In this light his kindnesses toward the girl seem more openhanded.

In perhaps their most important exchange, Moss and the girl discuss her planned trip to California and her attempt to start a new life. Moss suggests that the best way to get to California would be to arrive, "and not know how you got there" (*No Country*, 227). This statement seems cryptic, however, and a moment later he expounds, "It's not about knowin where you are. It's about thinking you got there without taking anything with you. Your notions about startin over. Or anybody's. You don't start over. That's what it's all about. Every step you take is forever. You cant make it go away. None of it. You understand what I'm sayin?" (227). It's not clear if the girl understands what Moss is saying, but readers may realize that he is suggesting that human nature and personality are more or less constant, as are our responsibilities toward those around us. We do not arrive anywhere, so to speak, without having traveled there.

Moss's concern for the girl and his feelings of responsibility toward her likely look familiar to those who have read McCarthy's other novels, particularly the third novel of the Border Trilogy, *Cities of the Plain* (1998). Edwin T. Arnold (2002) has suggested that McCarthy's fiction is highly intertextual and that images, events, and actions are often repeated throughout McCarthy's body of work. He lists and describes these repeated tropes in his article titled "The Mosaic of McCarthy's Fiction." I'd add one more item to Arnold's list. Soon after Moss meets the hitchhiker she describes herself as "a fellow traveler" (*No Country*, 219). In the epilogue of *Cities of the Plain* the term *traveler* is used to discuss the debt the living owe to those who have come before them. We are all, in the scheme outlined there, travelers on the Earth. People have traveled here before us, and people will travel here after us. In the last few pages of the novel Billy Parham meets a mysterious traveler whom he at first believes may be death personified. The man describes a dream in which a traveler stumbles upon a sacrificial alter and discovers a procession preparing for the sacrifice of a young girl. In the dream the traveler willingly offers to sacrifice himself in some kind of pagan ritual in order to save the appointed victim. After describing the dream the man explains to Billy the debt all human beings owe to those who have gone before: "Every man's death is a standing in for every other. And since death comes to all there is no way to abate the fear of it except to love the man who stands for us. We are not waiting for his history to be written. He passed here long ago. That man who is all men and who stands in the dock for us until our own time come and we must stand for him. Do you love him, that man? Will you honor the path he has taken? Will you listen to his tale?" (*Cities*, 288–89). This act of sacrifice is mirrored in McCarthy's *No Country*. Moss is clearly willing to stand in the dock for the young hitchhiker. This parallel between the two novels suggests the importance of this image for McCarthy and also makes its absence from the film all the more apparent. Moss's kindness toward the young hitchhiker, his willingness to sacrifice himself for her, and his ultimate faithfulness to Carla Jean[8] are all absent from the Coens' film.

Moss's relationship with the hitchhiker is replaced in the film by the short scene at the motel pool. But the woman's shabby flirting and Moss's reluctant agreement to have a beer with her clearly do not mean the same things as Moss's relationship with the hitchhiker, and her subsequent death. I would argue that these omissions are not simply an effort to streamline the story or limit the number of characters in an already complex film. Rather these changes represent the Coens' rejection of McCarthy's notions of grace as well as his portrayal of a meaningful world. In lieu of these novelistic elements the Coens have substituted their own rather fatalistic, amoral worldview.[9] Grace may be a central element in McCarthy's body of work, but it is not a quality normally associated with the films of the Coen brothers. As far as I know, the only person ever to claim that a Coen film dealt with grace was actor Jeff Bridges when he suggested that *The Big Lebowski* (1998) was about the need for grace (Susman 2006, 85). Because the Coens refuse to allow grace to exist in their adaptation of *No Country*, the world of the film exists as something quite separate from the world of the novel and closer to the worlds of previous Coen films.

Several elements of the Coens' *No Country for Old Men* will look familiar to fans of the filmmakers. The first, of course, is the setting. Both the novel and the film are set primarily in Texas, but the Texas of the Coen's *No Country* is closer to the Texas of *Blood Simple* (1984), their first feature film, than it is to the Texas of McCarthy's earlier works. In a 1987 interview that took place shortly after the release of *Raising Arizona* (1987), Joel Coen suggested that the setting of *Blood Simple* is not Texas as it exists, but as "something preserved in legend, a collection of histories and myths." A moment later he added that if you associate deadly passion "with a region of the USA, Texas is the most logical place" (Ciment and Niogret 2006a, 26). In the words of Loren Visser, the scheming and murderous detective in *Blood Simple*, in Texas, "you're on your own." Certainly Moss is faced with violent passions and finds himself largely "on his own" in *No Country*, but in the novel his associations with his wife and with the young hitchhiker make him much more of a social being than most of the Coens' characters.

There are other distinctive Coen elements in the adaptation. R. Barton Palmer observed back in 2004, before the production of *No Country*, that there are distinct patterns to be found in the films of the Coen brothers. He suggests, for instance, that their characters are often faced with the problem of "mastering a brute reality ruled by the principle of seemingly diabolical mischance" (Palmer 2004, 53). He goes on to suggest that "the typical Coenian narrative focuses either on pathetic losers whose attempts to make a 'big score' of some kind spectacularly misfire or on those of more virtue or purer heart who in their cunning or simplicity persevere

to transcendence of some kind" (53–54). In these terms *No Country* begins
to sound like a fairly typical Coen brothers film. Moss's attempt at a "big
score" definitely lands him in serious trouble and begins the chase scene that
will last for most of the rest of the film. This is also true of the novel, but the
novel, as I have suggested, seems to offer more than just the chase.

None of what I have written thus far should be understood to imply
that the world of McCarthy's novels is a nice one. Far from it. This novel
in particular portrays a dangerous world and horrifying evil, but in Mc-
Carthy's *No Country*, that evil is always at least somewhat balanced by the
rough and imperfect displays of grace and charity that exist along with
the novel's violence and destruction. Indeed it may be argued that the acts
of grace and charity in McCarthy's novel(s) are more meaningful because
they are performed not in a nice world, but in the face of violence and destruction. McCarthy consistently returns in his work to questions of evil
in his novels, and his image of evil is often associated with two central
traits—single-minded determination and utter independence. From the
murderous trio of *Outer Dark* (1968) to the judge of *Blood Meridian* (1985),
McCarthy's darkest characters share these traits. They seem to exist completely independent of society and to be unable to alter their course once
it has been set. Chigurh certainly fits this mold. He asks for help from no
one, even to the point of performing surgery on himself, and he pursues
Moss and the stolen money until Moss and everyone associated with the
failed drug deal is dead and the money is recovered.

Nevertheless, images of evil in McCarthy are always countered by
good, often religious elements. Religious discussions are, in fact, more or
less explicit throughout the novel. When Sheriff Bell, in some ways the
moral center of the novel, is asked if he believed in Satan, for instance,
he explains, "I guess as a boy I did. Come to the middle years my belief I
reckon had waned somewhat. Now I'm startin to lean back the other way.
He explains a lot of things that otherwise don't have no explanation. Or
not to me they dont" (*No Country*, 218). *No Country for Old Men* is, at least
in part, an attempt to understand or *comprehend* the evil in the world. I
like the word *comprehend* a little better in this case because it implies the
idea of inclusion or containment. Sheriff Bell in particular is working
throughout the novel to develop an understanding of the world that will
comprehend the kind of evil he is being forced to face. Like Bell, McCarthy
turns to notions of the sacred for explanations.

It may be McCarthy's desire to explore both the nature of evil as well as
the place of the sacred that makes him prone to include so much violence
in his novels. Edwin T. Arnold notes in his essay on "McCarthy and the
Sacred" that an understanding of Cormac McCarthy as "a writer of the
sacred should be beyond dispute" (2002, 215). Although he was discussing *The Crossing* (1994), Arnold might have been writing about *No Country*

for Old Men when he suggested that "the novel requires . . . a willingness to contemplate at no remove the mystical and the sacred. For an author who details so often and so explicitly the violence and despair and apparent randomness of life, the possibilities of grace, love, and charity in the world might seem remote, and yet these qualities appear repeatedly in his work" (2002, 216–17). As I have suggested in my brief analysis of Moss's death, notions of grace and charity are central to McCarthy's *No Country for Old Men.*

McCarthy has been fairly tight-lipped about his own religious feelings. In her June 2007 interview with McCarthy, Oprah Winfrey asked him pointedly about his belief in God. He answered, "It would depend on what day you asked me," but then quickly added "sometimes it's good to pray. I don't think you have to have a clear idea of who or what God is in order to pray. You can even be quite doubtful about the whole business" (McCarthy 2007). Though this is not a statement filled with evangelical zeal, it does seem to support Arnold's contention and suggest McCarthy's reverent attitude toward religious ideas.

Like McCarthy, the Coens have avoided saying much about religion, but what they have said reflects a markedly different attitude. Of his family's religious practices Joel Coen once flippantly remarked, "When Grandpa paid us a visit during the Sabbath, my mother used subterfuges to make him believe we were obeying the law and refusing to do all that was forbidden. That's how we learned about acting!" (Ciment and Niogret 2006b, 106). In a more serious mood, Ethan briefly discussed his own religious upbringing in an interview with Kristine McKenna. He noted that "Judaism was a central part of the house we grew up in. We had a religious upbringing. I went to Hebrew school every Saturday and had a bar mitzvah." Then he added, "But that just meant I got presents. I never took it seriously. Some part of it probably seeps in, but I think that's more of an ethnic than a religious thing" (McKenna 2006, 183). McKenna pursued the question of religion a bit more, however, and asked Joel point blank, "Do you believe in God?" His reply was, "Not in the Jewish sense. I don't believe in the angry God, Yahweh" (184). When she asked what he thought happened after death Joel replied, "You rot and decompose" (184).

Noting that McCarthy consistently creates and explores images of grace and that the Coens consistently reject them still leaves some thorny questions unanswered, however, because *grace* is somewhat difficult to define. Thomas F. O'Meara, in Mircea Eliade's sixteen-volume *Encyclopedia of Religion*, calls grace "the ultimate religious question and statement in any religion" and notes that many scholars consider it "the underlying reality of all religious enterprises" (1987, 87). Grace, in short, is the foundation that underpins practically every other religious idea. O'Meara suggests that grace is the result of the basic human "need for some divine assistance so that men and women might turn to God in faith and hope and to their neighbors in mercy and love" (1987, 85). This sentence suggests the close link between grace and charity, the "mercy and love" shown to neighbors. John Line, in Vergilius Ferm's 1945 *An Encyclopedia of Religion*, adds that grace is "the divine help continually afforded by which men are kept and sustained, and enabled to do what is otherwise beyond their power" (309). Encapsulated in this idea of grace is the notion that humans are fallible and, in fact, doomed to failure without divine help. Moreover, the need for grace teaches us to treat others with charity, kindness, and generosity in the light of our own weakness.

In it's most basic, and perhaps it's least religious form, grace is the simple understanding that human beings cannot get along without help, whether that help comes from God or from our neighbors. In Hemingway's *To Have and Have Not* (1937), the dying Harry Morgan puts it this way: "a man alone ain't got no bloody fucking chance" (225). This simple, earthy statement captures the secular essence of grace and identifies one of the central problems faced by several of McCarthy's protagonists, including Culla Holme, John Grady Cole, Billy Parham, Llewelyn Moss, and most recently the father in *The Road* (2006). Alone, these men have little or no chance to succeed. This lesson is not, however, an easy one to learn, particularly for McCarthy's cowboys, or an easy one to swallow for those of us who admire those cowboys. Of Harry Morgan's apparent revelation, Hemingway's omniscient narrator adds, "It had taken him a long time to get it out and it had taken him all his life to learn it" (Hemingway 1937, 225). Most of McCarthy's characters never learn this lesson, but Moss seems to be an exception. Throughout the novel we hear that Moss doesn't change his mind once it is made up, and that he doesn't need others. Carla Jean tells Sheriff Bell that Moss "can take care of hisself," and that he won't quit on what he has set out to accomplish, or at least "he never has" (*No Country*, 127). Perhaps surprisingly, Moss seems to share these characteristics in common with the ruthless Chigurh. Nevertheless, Moss does change his mind when he faces the assassin threatening the girl, and he quits when he lays down his gun. He apparently does learn lessons of grace and charity before his death.[10]

It should not be surprising that the Coens excise the elements of grace and charity along with the power of agency from Moss's character. To remove one from the narrative necessitates removing the others. In early Christianity the direct link between grace and agency was of central importance. O'Meara reports that much of the debate in the early Christian church was over the relationship between these two concepts (1987, 85–86). In simple terms the debate centered on questions of how much human actions count in this world. That debate is still fresh in

McCarthy's works. The writer seems almost obsessed with the role of agency in a postmodern world. John Grady Cole and Rawlins discuss the idea of agency early in *All the Pretty Horses*. Just before the boys attempt to recover Blevins' horse Rawlins questions the wisdom of what they are about to do. He explains, "Ever dumb I ever done in my life there was a decision I made before that got me into it. It was never the dumb thing. It was always some choice I'd made before it." John Grady asks, "Meanin what?" Rawlins answers, "Meanin this is it. This is our last chance. This is the time and there wont be another time and I guarantee it" (*Pretty Horses*, 79). Elements of this conversation are repeated near the end of *No Country* as Chigurh confronts and prepares to kill Carla Jean. As he did with the storeowner earlier, Chigurh offers Carla Jean a coin toss to save her life, but unlike the man, Carla Jean chooses incorrectly, at least in the novel.[11] Chigurh offers, "It could have gone either way," but unlike the lucky storekeeper, Carla Jean refuses to let the killer off the hook: "The coin didn't have no say. It was just you" (*No Country*, 258). Chigurh continues to deny his own culpability in the imminent murder. He insists, "I had no say in the matter. Every moment in your life is a turning and every one a choosing. Somewhere you made a choice. All followed to this. The accounting is scrupulous" (259). Although he insists on the fact that Carla Jean has made the choices that have led to this point, we must recognize that he is once again describing meaningless choices—so far removed from the consequences as to be absurd.

Chigurh's choices, on the other hand, are clear and explicit. He can kill Carla Jean, the storeowner or Wells, or he can allow them to live. He rejects this choice, however, insisting, "I had no say in the matter" (*No Country*, 259). This, however, is simply not true. Like Moss, the Chigurh in the novel has agency, but in denying that agency he also denies the grace and charity that accompany it. Thus he becomes profoundly independent. He becomes, at least until his car wreck, antisocial in the truest sense of that word; he has no concern for others or for the charity, the fabric of small kindnesses that binds society together. This is precisely what allows him to operate as he does. He is not swayed by personal or humane concerns and at least argues that he is only an instrument of fate. He does what he does because circumstances have dictated it. He claims no more decision-making power or agency than the coin flips he offers to Carla Jean and the storekeeper. Faced with their own imminent murders, both Wells and Carla Jean tell him, "You don't have to do this," implying that Chigurh has a choice in the matter, but his response to them suggests that this statement is a non sequitur. It doesn't even make sense to him. Chigurh, as Wells had earlier explained to Moss, is not motivated by people or things, but is, rather, a man of "principles" (153). Thus he must murder Carla Jean not because it serves any practical purpose, but because he had promised Moss he would do so. McCarthy implies in these passages that part of the nature of evil, perhaps the central part, is its denial of agency, especially its own.

   This notion of evil seems to mirror, at some level, the way the Coens have adapted the novel. They have certainly captured McCarthy's image of evil on the screen, but they have neglected the sacred elements of the novel. For McCarthy, Moss's trouble was never fated. His battle with Chigurh and the drug dealers did not begin when he took the case of money, for instance, but when he chose to return to the desert to bring water to the thirsty man. Moss's original decision to leave the dying drug dealer to his thirst and his fear of wolves was a pragmatic one. He did not have water to offer the man, and he couldn't carry him out. But his 2:00 am trip to the desert with a jug of water was an act of conscience and charity. Admittedly, it is not exactly the work of a good Samaritan, but Moss's attempt to bring water to the man was a decision to do a dangerous thing knowing full well what the consequences of that decision might be. He reasons with himself before descending to the scene of the drug deal, "For a Mexican dopedealer. Yeah. Well. Everbody is somethin" (*No Country*, 26). Moss's trip with the water is clearly an act of agency. In some ways it seems to mirror the pragmatic charity of Mark Twain's Huck Finn toward the murders and robbers he maroons on the storm-wrecked *Sir Walter Scott*. In his effort to explain his own intentions to save the men from the wreck so that "they can be hung when their time comes," Huck reasons, "There ain't no telling but I might come to be a murderer myself, yet, and then how would I like it?" (Twain 1995, 88). Huck's language is echoed by Moss's "Everbody is something." It is also reflected earlier in the novel when Sheriff Bell and two of his deputies find the body of one of Chigurh's victims in the trunk of a police cruiser. The deputies make a joke and Bell tells them to "dont be making light of the dead thataway." Wendell, his deputy answers, "You're right. I might be one myself some day" (*No Country*, 44). Moss's act of charity, as small as it might be, comes at a great personal cost, one that he more or less anticipated when he left his house

   Of course, this is not the first time that filmmakers creating an adaptation have struggled to deal with questions of grace, charity, and agency in the face of great evil. Please allow me to suggest an artistic analogy. George Stevens, the American filmmaker who directed *Shane* (1953), a Western that resonates with *No Country*, made a great many comedies and "light" films in the early part of his career. During World War II, however, Stevens volunteered, along with a lot of other Hollywood filmmakers, to work for the army signal corps making movies for the army.

Stevens filmed or supervised the filming of important event like the D-Day invasion and the liberation of Paris. But he also filmed the liberation of Dachau Prison Camp. Commenting on this experience, Stevens said that these concentration camps represented "the worst possible thing that has happened in centuries" (1984). It's likely that Stevens was not referring to the particular atrocities that were committed at the camps, but rather to the attitude, *the evil*, that made such atrocities possible. Stevens argued that there is nothing in the world like a concentration camp because "everything evil will be exposed in a day." Then he added, "It's deplorable because it undercuts one terribly." After returning home to postwar America Stevens found that his ideas about good and evil had became much more complex and problematic. After World War II the place of the spiritual in everyday life and in films became more tenuous, something that had to be consciously created, particularly for those who had experienced the war firsthand. As he was making one of his last major films, the monumental *The Greatest Story Ever Told* (1965), Stevens explained to a *Time* reporter that in making a film based on the Gospels, he intended to show the world "a new vision of Christ, a powerful man without the nursery kindness which Sunday schools perhaps tell you that he had" ("Forget the Incense" 1962, 34). This film, like most of Stevens's postwar films, struggled to give an accurate and detailed portrayal of evil alongside its depiction of good. One of the things he had apparently learned in the prison camp was that if you want to understand good, you must see it in the context of evil. Any notion of religion Stevens had after the war had to be able to *comprehend* the evil he had witnessed during the war. In the interview mentioned earlier Stevens put it this way, "If love wants to create justice, it can't be gentle, and I think that is the way of love this Christ really preached. Love is not sentimental" ("Forget the Incense" 1962, 34).

The same may be said of Cormac McCarthy's novels. *No Country for Old Men* may be a reverie on evil, but it is also an explanation for the necessity of grace and charity and the importance of agency. In art, O'Meara argues, "grace emerges from the dramatic reiteration of an active unseen presence that reveals 'the more' and it's opposite, the violent explosion of the holy, the beautiful, and the human" (1987, 87). For many Christian religions, O'Meara suggests, "grace is perceived as the axis along which the kingdom of God confronts institutionalized evil" (87). It is the way, he suggests, perhaps the only way evil might be confronted. Arguably, this is what McCarthy is portraying in *No Country for Old Men*. Any notion of grace that cannot comprehend the kind of evil Chigurh represents is ultimately worthless. In the final measure, it is precisely this grace that is lacking from the Coen brothers' film.

NOTES

1. Luke 3:11 says, "He answereth and saith unto them, He that hath two coats, let him impart to him that hath none; and he that hath meat, let him do likewise." Like many of the images in McCarthy's novels, this one is also repeated in other works, most notably in *No Country*. As the wounded Moss stumbles across the bridge into Mexico he asks some teenagers for a jacket to cover his bloodstains. The boys refuse to help until he offers to pay them five hundred dollars for the coat. Chigurh, too, is wounded late in the novel and offers to pay two young boys for a shirt to use as a bandage and sling. One of the boys responds that he can have the shirt for nothing, but Chigurh insists on paying.

2. Phil Snyder has argued that Chigurh actually assassinates Moss, but I'm willing, along with the Coens, to accept the word of the eyewitness (Snyder 2007).

3. McCarthy goes so far as to describe the brains of one victim, Wells, dripping down the wall behind him after he is shot with a 12 gauge.

4. In private conversations, McCarthy scholar Phil Snyder (2007) has suggested that this eyewitness might be Chigurh. I doubt that this is the case, however, since I find it unlikely that Chigurh would have left the assassin alive or allowed himself to be questioned by the police.

5. Faced with a similar choice by his memory of the dying Mexican drug dealer in the desert, Moss chooses to at least attempt to comfort the man.

6. It is worth noting here that a certain degree of agency is one of Aristotle's definitions of tragedy. In chapter 5 of *Aristotle's Poetics* he suggests that tragic figures must be, "*personal agents*, who necessarily possess certain distinctive qualities both of character and thought; for it is by these that we qualify actions themselves, and these—thought and character—are the two natural causes from which actions spring, and on actions again all success or failure depends" (1961, 62; emphasis mine).

7. Physicist Werner Heisenberg proved that it was impossible to know both the position and the momentum of a submolecular particle at the same time. Knowing one bit of information would necessarily preclude knowing the other. The years McCarthy has spent associating with physicists would suggest that he is familiar with this principle.

8. The girl invites Moss several times to sleep with her. He repeatedly turns her down, though not impolitely.

9. The Coens have consistently denied that their films have "morals." See Karen Jaehne's 1998 interview for an example of this (Jaehne 2006).

10. It might be argued that Moss does change his mind when he opts to take the water back to the wounded drug dealer, but giving the man water was not an option during his first trip to the site of the massacre.

11. It's unclear in the film if Carla Jean calls the coin toss or not. Chigurh insists that she call it, and she refuses. The camera then cuts to the outside of the house as Chigurh leaves by the front door, pausing to check the bottom of his boots before he walks away.

REFERENCES

All the Pretty Horses. 2000. Dir. Billy Bob Thronton. Columbia Pictures.

Aristotle's Poetics. 1961. Trans. S. H. Butcher. New York: Hill and Wang.

Arnold, Edwin T. 2002. "McCarthy and the Sacred: A Reading of *The Crossing.*" In *Cormac McCarthy: New Directions,* ed. James D. Lilley, 215–38. Albuquerque: University of New Mexico Press.

The Big Lebowski. 1998. Dir. Joel Coen and Ethan Coen. PolyGram Filmed Entertainment.

Blood Simple. 1984. Dir. Joel Coen. Foxton Entertainment.

Ciment, Michel and Hubert Niogret. 2006a. "Interview with Joel and Ethan Coen." In *The Coen Brothers: Interviews,* ed. William Rodney Allen, 25–35. Jackson: University Press of Mississippi.

———. 2006b. "The Logic of Soft Drugs." In *The Coen Brothers: Interviews,* ed. William Rodney Allen, 100–108. Jackson: University Press of Mississippi.

"Forget the Incense." 1962. *Time* 28 (December): 34–35.

The Greatest Story Ever Told. 1965. Dir. George Stevens. George Stevens Productions.

Hemingway, Ernest. 1937. *To Have and Have Not.* New York: Scribner.

Jaehne, Karen. 2006. "Ethan Coen, Joel Coen, and *The Big Lebowski.*" In *The Coen Brothers: Interviews,* ed. William Rodney Allen, 109–12. Jackson: University Press of Mississippi.

Line, John. 1945. "Grace." In *An Encyclopedia of Religion,* ed. Vergilius Ferm, 309–10. New York: The Philosophical Library.

Lowe, Andy. 2006. "The Brothers Grim." In *The Coen Brothers: Interviews,* ed. William Rodney Allen, 93–99. Jackson: University Press of Mississippi.

McCarthy, Cormac. 1968. *Outer Dark.* New York: Random House.

———. 1985. *Blood Meridian, or, The Evening Redness in the West.* New York: Random House.

———. 1993. *All the Pretty Horses.* New York: Vintage International.

———. 1994. *The Crossing.* New York: Vintage.

———. 1998. *Cities of the Plain.* New York: Vintage International.

———. 2005. *No Country for Old Men.* New York: Alfred A. Knopf.

———. 2006. *The Road.* New York: Alfred A. Knopf.

———. 2007. Interview. *The Oprah Winfrey Show.* Harpo Productions. ABC. June 5.

McKenna, Kristine. 2006. "Joel and Ethan Coen." In *The Coen Brothers: Interviews,* ed. William Rodney Allen, 163–87. Jackson: University Press of Mississippi.

No Country for Old Men. 2007. Dir. Ethan Coen and Joel Coen. Miramax Films.

O'Meara, Thomas F. 1987. "Grace." In *The Encyclopedia of Religion,* 16 vols., ed. Mircea Eliade, 84–88. New York: Macmillan.

Palmer, R. Barton. 2004. *Joel and Ethan Coen.* Urbana: University of Illinois Press.

Raising Arizona. 1987. Dir. Joel Coen and Ethan Coen. Circle Films.

Shane. 1953. Dir. George Stevens. Paramount Pictures.

Snyder, Phil. 2007. "Ethics in Cormac McCarthy's *No Country for Old Men*." American Literature Association Conference. Boston, May 24.

Stevens, George,w Jr. 1984. *George Stevens: A Filmmaker's Journey*. Dir. George Stevens Jr. Creative Film Center.

Susman, Gary. 2006. "Making It Clear: The Coen Brothers." In *The Coen Brothers: Interviews*, ed. William Rodney Allen, 93–99. Jackson: University Press of Mississippi.

Twain, Mark. 1995. *Adventures of Huckleberry Finn*. Ed. Gerald Graff and James Phelan. New York: Bedford Books.

14

Denial and Trepidation Awaiting What's Coming in the Coen Brothers' First Film Adaptation

Dennis Rothermel

Confrontation with death brings on not only recognition of the end of life but also contemplation of what life has meant. What has fate dispensed in this life one was allowed to live? What has one made of that life? What meaning has one created? These queries can come to mind even without the impetus of imminent demise. They are, however, disquieting questions. Not wanting to think about them until it's no longer possible to ignore them corroborates their immutability—the very last thing we forego thinking about is the one concern left over when all others have fallen away. Family, love, friends, career, success, accomplishments, faith, outlook, and convictions offer immediate and reassuring answers—but answers that overlook how deeply those questions penetrate.

There are those who turn away from the questions that death incites. There are those who are willing to turn toward death, not out of fixation with the end of life, but undeterred by the risk, finding in that confrontation the opportunity to forge a response. Finding a response entails nontrivial transformation—transformation out of how all those factors that have defined a life—family, career, and so on (Emerson 1926). Ralph Waldo Emerson exulted those moments of creation that necessitated setting aside the expectations of family, friends, and society, not because genius excuses one from all obligation and not because family, friends, and society aren't profoundly important, but because they aren't enough. Of all those ways of finding a response, none will be genuinely meaningful unless created and chosen, and not simply accepted as part of what is inherited from one's placement in the world. What is certain is that any easy answer must be phony, that there isn't any formulaic answer, and that there isn't ever any final certainty about an answer. As a corollary, it is not transformation to any predetermined outcome that can count as genuine. The more profoundly the transformation creates what one is, the more important it is that its genesis is authentic.

Socrates urged that the unexamined life is not worth living, which means that there is no meaning to life other than how life is invested with that meaning intentionally (Plato 1981, 38a). That meaning doesn't arise accidentally or unconsciously. Arthur Schopenhauer explains confronting the question of existence as leading away from the ephemeral worldly determinations of life. Further, Schopenhauer argues, all great works of art confront the meaning of life (1958, 406–10). Great art does this implicitly, whereas philosophy aims to work through these reflections explicitly. One may attribute Schopenhauer's insight into art to observation, and thence to some sort of empirical generalization. More properly, once this trajectory of artistic endeavor is perceived, it will become important to think through why it should be the case. Moreover, Schopenhauer's chosen exemplification was music. Thus it won't be from a work of art being explicitly didactic, narrative, or representational that it be great and philosophical in Schopenhauer's expectation. It will be in the construction of the aesthetic substance and soul of a work of art that it surpasses clichéd forms, attains greatness, and with that, proffers philosophical insight into the meaning of life.

Joel and Ethan Coen have filmed Cormac McCarthy's story of four hunters, and one philosopher: Llewelyn Moss, Carson Wells, Ed Tom Bell, Anton Chigurh, and Bell's uncle, Ellis. The hunters chase after the money, $2 million, which is sufficiently monumental to all but the extremely wealthy. Moss seizes it first. The other three chase him, though with different motivations. The four hunters launch upon the chase with all the woodsman's deep knowledge of the particulars of an environment's contingent details. The environmental terrain for the chase, though, has little to do with where a hunter naturally finds home. The hunters thus chase after an elusive but entirely artificial prize in a nonnatural terrain—like greyhounds racing around a track after a mechanical hare. For Moss, Wells, and Bell, the chase will transform into a confrontation with the meaning of life. Chigurh is the catalyst for that transformation, deliberately posing life-and-death confrontations to ponder the meaning of a person's life.

The Coens' realization of McCarthy's novel fills out the substance of these characters, preserving the personal confrontation with the issue of the meaning of life in strong relief against the background of the hunters chasing after the money. The genre trappings of the chase—suspense, caper, action, violence, and heroism—ultimately fall away as insignificant. Once the chase concludes, the final two reflective scenes exhibit the same unhurried rhythm that had pervaded the film throughout—an incongruous pace for the action-chase genre, but appropriate to the finality of those concluding scenes. The pertinent philosophical quest thus alone remains at the end and as having defined the entirety from the start. The story—in both the novel and the film—sheds standard genre form and thus approaches Arthur Schopenhauer's expectation of great art.

The Coens adapt Cormac McCarthy's novel as a thickly woven sequence of significant details and signs, thus placing the viewer—in place of McCarthy's reader—in a position of needing to read those signs, just in order to keep up with Moss, Wells, Bell, Chigurh, and, finally, Ellis. The viewer becomes one of the hunters, not from empathy with the fate of the action hero, but as a reader searching for what's important in the story. This further exemplifies what Schopenhauer expects of great art.

LLEWELYN MOSS, THE HUNTER

It is not immediately that Llewelyn Moss realizes that the blood splatters trailing off orthogonally from where he expected to see them occasions the redirection of his own fate. Peering through his binoculars in the direction where the odd blood trail points, Moss picks out a limping animal in the distance—a black pit bull, who pauses to turn back to look toward the man standing distant in the desert. The dog's look of recognition, distorted by the conflation of perspective through the binocular lenses and rippling in the heat waves from the desert floor, offers Moss an ominous apparition. He, too, will struggle to limp away to safety, to recuperate from mortal wounds, perhaps not to survive long.

Moss attends carefully to the minute signs that trace the presence of dangers and opportunities that the world presents. Inferring from what he observes in the aftermath of the desert shootout, he cautiously sniffs out the location of the money. Moss recognizes how the satchel of money represents the possibility for sudden transformation in his life. The money will be the means for liberating Carla Jean—and himself—from the spiritual oppression of working for wages. He is devoted to Carla Jean, which we understand from what he does and how he is in her presence. His warm but firm assurances to her affirm a love that isn't in need of effusive evocation. But the prize will be a burden that he won't be able to sustain, in spite of his persistent, enterprising will and his practiced hunter's wisdom. It will be Moss's inability to foresee *every* detail of what's coming that leads to his violent, sudden demise. Well beyond his imagination, Carla Jean, too, will be victimized by that failure.

Moss confronts imminent death physically in the accidental embrace with the lunging pit bull. He shoots and kills the dog just as it is on the verge of tearing out his throat. The dead dog falls on top of him, leaving Moss to lie under the weight of death's aborted deliverance. The unnaturalness of the embrace initiates Moss's separation from the normal order of the world. The dog's hell-bent ferocious pursuit extends that of the men in the truck who chase Moss across the dark landscape. The fury of the truck's banks of blaring lights and roar of its powerful engine give way to the animal's headlong dash after Moss into the river. Moss's limited ability to foresee continued threats of death affords him hope of remaining just ahead of deadly threats catching up with him. Moss's ingenuity in improvising plans and exploiting available objects as tools for the unique needs of the circumstances complement his intelligence about the details and forces of this world in which he is at home. Erasing his own trail, to become invisible forever with his burden and his love, will, however, lie beyond his reach, more absurdly so than he is able to conceive. It is in one of a series of unanticipated confrontations that he is felled.

Llewelyn ostensibly shares with Carla Jean contentment with modest expectations for material wealth and the unencumbered passions that a life without stress can nourish. He has the advantage of a vocation (welding) and an avocation (hunting) that reward his expertise and craft. Carla Jean speaks of her marginal job at a discount store as if it were prison sentence. She expresses her doubts and fears about Llewelyn's mysterious sudden disruption of their life. She asks him point blank whether he will return to her, accepts his simply stated promise that he will, and then accedes to his lead without resistance. She is deliberate but neither meek nor confrontational in her expression of doubts. She can hear in his voice over the phone that he's been hurt. The gentle tone with which she expresses these concerns is not very much different from her teasing queries about where he had been all day the day Llewelyn found the money, and where he got the pistol and the satchel. Llewelyn's non-answers to these queries would evoke angry reactions from a spouse not willing to accept evasive answers on trust. Llewelyn's quick anger shows in his reactions to Wells and Chigurh, but he shows no hint of that frustration toward Carla Jean. We see Carla Jean's morose resignation in response to Chigurh and her exasperation with her cantankerous mother, but there is no hint of either of those two emotional overtones when she expresses her worries to Llewelyn. Llewelyn's mysterious explanation of their need to leave home behind forever is delivered with no more urgency than if he were announcing plans for a necessary sojourn into town to do shopping, meet a medical appointment, and so forth. That Carla Jean's reactions to

Llewelyn's sudden mysterious doings register nothing of her mother's scathing complaints about Llewelyn and that neither she nor Llewelyn pays those remarks the slightest regard, confirm a strong unspoken trust that Carla Jean and Llewelyn have in each other. How Llewelyn's devotion to Carla Jean is the center of his purposes is obscure to Carla Jean's mother's blunt assessment, though that devotion is clearly understood by Carla Jean. We see in their brief scenes together a quiet but deep, loving rapport. This will be important to the story, since it is the love he has for Carla Jean that inspires Moss to take the risks he does. He will, however, put her happiness in life at risk, by putting his own life at risk, though he does not comprehend that he has done so. Chigurh's threat to kill Carla Jean only steels Moss's resolve. Ultimately that risk is realized, to encompass Carla Jean's assassination as well.

Moss's tactical responses to anticipated and visible threats show the practiced, calm calculation of a soldier. Upon realizing that his identity and address will be soon discovered, he arranges for Carla Jean and him to flee to an ultimate permanent destination yet to be determined, leaving everything behind forever. Upon finding the transponder, rather than discard it or flee again, Moss detects the presence of his adversary just on the other side of his hotel-room door, readies his weapon, and positions himself to open fire as soon as the intruder appears. He thus plays the situation as the means of drawing his pursuer into his sights, to prepare a counterattack and thus to seize that moment of his hunter's closing in as the moment to become the hunter himself. The counterattack stymies Chigurh only momentarily, at which point Moss does retreat. His further escape in the commandeered truck is unsuccessful. Moss then takes cover, but once again launches a counterattack at the exact opportune moment. Knowing his adversary is wounded, as is Moss, but in a secluded position, Moss then retires from the place of confrontation.

Moss's confidence in his ability to master his fate feeds on his skills in understanding the details and signs of his world, his past experience in combat, and his aspirations for a life for himself and Carla Jean that would be fulfilling for both of them. That confidence inspires a vision of mastery and freedom and also the one serious mistake that sealed his undoing—which can only seem foolhardy in retrospect. The biggest mistake in his actions was to return to the place of the shootout in the desert to take water to a dying man, a stranger who would easily have killed Moss without a thought if given the chance. The thought of having coldly left a man to die as part of his tactics to find the money that must be nearby would taint his transformation with the lingering misdeed of his future past.

Once having seized the satchel full of money and having begun his flight into obscurity, Moss displays motives and actions that puzzle the people he encounters: the dying man who asks for water, the cab driver, the boot salesman, the Del Rio motel manager, the sporting goods salesman, the INS border guard, the three young men on the border bridge, the driver who gives him a ride to Eagle Pass, the woman at the poolside who wants to seduce him, the pickup-truck driver, the Eagle Hotel night clerk, the mariachi band. That he is casual and taciturn only accentuates incomprehension in the people he meets and deepens the divide between him and the world that he otherwise had traversed previously without arousing puzzlement.

Moss's separation from the mundane world in which he was once at home finds him shedding possessions and clothing indifferently. Dressed in new shirt and pants, he emerges from the weeds where he has retrieved the satchel from where he had tossed it from the bridge. Momentarily bothered by the itching at the neck of the shirt, he pulls off the price tag that hung there. Along with every other possession, clothes too have become transitory, quickly acquired and discarded, devoid of fashion, reduced to pure temporary utility. There aren't any significant details to the world and life he's left behind than could be found in that path out of riparian weeds.

His last conversation—with the flirtatious woman sitting poolside at the motel in El Paso—concludes with his unknowingly portentous confession that he stands by his window looking out for what's coming. She warns that one never can see it in time, which he doesn't dispute. Moss is wide open to the possibilities for transcendent change and confident in his mastery of his own better purposes. His tolerance of risk—however well his actions are calculated—is that of a man whose verve for transformation unabashedly obscures the ever-looming incursion of merciless death in his world. There isn't much chance of Moss escaping his pursuers once they are hot on his trail. The only hope for him was for Bell to catch him first, and it would never have occurred to Moss that that was the case.

CARSON WELLS, THE TRACKER

It is with only subtle tones in his subdued conversational interactions that Wells registers his audacious confidence, his patronizing disdain for Moss and for the man in the high-rise office who hires him, and his frank assessment of Chigurh's ruthlessness. His pigeon-toed, moseying shuffle telegraphs his resistance to subservience, which he then demonstrates to his erstwhile employer by taking a seat before being bidden to do so. Wells taunts the man with circuitous responses about Chigurh. His lame joke about validating his parking ticket digs at the anomalous location of the headquarters of a drug-smuggling operation in a big-city high-rise office building. The lame joke in identifying the missing thirteenth floor reminds the man that he is living in a world governed much more by superstitious fear of bad luck that he would admit. That self-assured sardonic bravado is still with Wells when he shows up in Moss's hospital room holding flowers. Though he explains the ease with which he—or Chigurh—could find Moss, and how foreseeable was this outcome from the outset, Moss remains unimpressed. Chigurh also will underscore the inevitable outcome to Moss. Moss ignores that prediction, as stiffly as he ignores Wells's supplication of trust based upon common experience in the Vietnam War, and as stiffly as he refuses to acknowledge, against Wells's spare warnings, the danger that Chigurh poses to him and to Carla Jean.

Though he knows Chigurh, knows Chigurh's formidable skills, persistence, and ruthlessness, Wells has no reason to fear Chigurh until cornered, when he realizes that Chigurh has reason not to let him live. Wells bargains without begging and wheedles as best he can while trying not to seem undignified—since that alone would be sufficient annoyance to Chigurh. Wells then confesses that he doesn't belong in Chigurh's company—he isn't the hunter that Chigurh is, nor even Moss. Wells is the day-trader hunter—in it for diversion and profit, but not in it with his soul. Wells knows his adversary and element well enough to warn Moss that he's not cut out for what he's wandered into. Wells does not take his own advice.

Like Moss, Wells doesn't anticipate the worst outcome. Wells, though, lacks Moss's single-minded absorption with protecting his new-found fortune for the sake of the transformation of his life that it entails. Wells instead thrives within the sector of illegal enterprise that he understands professionally. Ultimately, he shies away from transgression of that carefully defined sphere that is established well enough to occupy downtown offices like any corporation. He has to understand his performance of the task he's hired to do in terms of what will sustain his trustworthiness for the sake of his on-going profession. Hence, his aim will be to return the money. By contrast, Moss's object in possessing the money aims beyond the life that he has known. Wells's perspective precludes both the confrontation with what a life could mean as defined by that profession and the need to come to terms with the advent of his own mortality.

ED TOM BELL, THE CATCHER

Like Wells and Chigurh, Bell chases after Moss, but for the sake of catching the man who does not fathom the danger bearing down on him from several angles. Like J. D. Salinger's Holden Caulfield, Bell finds defining purpose in looking out for the innocent who play innocently but oblivious of precipitous danger, and catching them at the moment just before they fall (Salinger 1945, 224–25). Though he muses about signs of cultural disintegration and the disuse of "sir" and "ma'am" among the young, Bell understands the overwhelming powers unleashed in the social economy by markets for illegal substances. The carnage in the desert is a result of that power, and it leaves an impression upon Bell. It is against this power that he confesses he is overmatched. That he guesses Chigurh will return to the crime scene in the motel room where Moss was killed and then proceeds there expecting to confront him shows that it is not the furiously murderous Chigurh that he feels overmatched against. The odd sociopath, such as the one described in his voice-over monologue that opens the film, or even Chigurh, pales in contrast to forces that he fears he can't fathom. Bell concludes that opening monologue by declaring his reticence to work in a world governed by what is beyond his comprehension. To accept that his job would require that he embark into that world, he would have to be okay with putting his soul in peril. The equanimity with which he utters how one could consent to that world betrays an understanding of that putative commitment; it betrays that it is something that he has thought about without apprehension, even though deciding against it.

Bell esteems the heritage of his profession. He is willingly resigned to the dangers it poses to life. He admires predecessors who abstained from carrying a sidearm. His sagacity in intuiting the story behind only a few significant observable clues alleviates his need to collaborate with representatives of broader jurisdiction of law enforcement than his—who substitute methodology for the abductive inference to most probable hypotheses. At the shootout crime scene in the desert, the only things Bell takes note of are the traces of dope in the bed of the pickup-truck, and the variety of spent shell casings. He won't be surprised later when it turns out the bullet-riddled trucks have phony registrations. The true identity of the dead men would also add nothing important to the compilation of evidence. When Bell and Wendell enter Moss's trailer, all Bell takes note of is the blown-out door lock, the impression it made on the woodwork opposite, and where it came to rest on the sofa below. He also notes the beads of sweat on the bottle of milk, and he infers that the intruder to the trailer had been there only shortly before and had drunk from that bottle. He needs to remind Wendell—who serves as the dramatic foil to Bell's sagacity—that all they know about that intruder is that he has recently drunk milk. There won't be any more purpose in looking for fingerprints on the bottle or elsewhere in the trailer, or for other clues, any more than it mattered who the trucks in the desert were registered to or who the dead men were.

Bell is unsettled about evil, about God, about his life. His two dreams that he relates to Loretta are about his life and about his death. His need to share them with her but, deflected by his own bemusement, betrays a barely suppressed recognition of their meaning. In his first dream, his father had given him money, which he squandered somehow in town. So Bell fears what he has done with his life, his career. In his second dream, his father rides by him over a mountain pass in a dark snowy winter night, hunkered in a blanket protecting the small warmth of embers preserved in a cow horn, heading for some campsite to wait in the cold, wet, dark landscape.[1] In spite of Bell's nominal Christian faith, the dream draws an atavistic picture of the afterlife that echoes how Homer depicted the netherworld populated with fleeting shades devoid of purpose or meaning (Homer 1963, bk. 11).

Bell has just one near encounter with Chigurh. Remembering that Chigurh does not hesitate to revisit a crime scene and knowing that the satchel of money hasn't been retrieved, Bell returns to the motel where Moss had been killed, expecting to find Chigurh there. He sees Chigurh's tell-tale sign—the blown-out door lock—which had not been there before. Now he knows that Chigurh has been there and could still be there. Unholstering his weapon, he is now at that isolated point in the terrain defined by his profession where he will confront a man knowing that each will have lethal intention for the other. All qualifications of motivation, justification, and legal authority fall away as insignificant at that moment. It means stepping into what he does not yet fathom that Bell describes as being ok with, consigning away not just one's life but one's soul. Bell is relieved to find tell-tale evidence of Chigurh's having been there and thus to falsely conclude that he isn't exposed to the danger that had stricken his approach with abject fear.

Bell won't have needed lessons to be drawn from what happens to the risk-tolerant Moss and Wells for his experiential wisdom to inform his emotions in the motel room. His fear congeals in the moment of recognition of the implications of the blown-out door lock and the glint of the reflection of light on the inner walls of the vacant cylinder. Aside from that glint, there is nothing but the surrounding darkness and what it could possibly conceal. On the other side of that glint stands Chigurh, waiting quietly and motionless, to the side of the door where he will remain unseen once Bell opens the door and slams it back against the heating/cooling unit next to Chigurh on the other side. Chigurh can see the colored reflection of Bell's uniform oozing across that glint in the empty lock cylinder as Bell approaches from outside. Chigurh won't venture to kill Bell for the sole reason that he has no reason to do so. Bell understands that Chigurh needs only the most frivolous reason for that evil to lash out at him—and beyond that he hasn't the slightest clue as to the identity of the man who could be his adversary.

Chigurh is the inchoate face of the seismic economic forces rippling through the world that Bell once thought he understood. The glint in the lock cylinder attracts intensive attention of both men for the moment, which will be all that ever connects Bell directly to the presence of those subterranean forces. The carnage in the desert provides overt evidence of their strength. It leaves an impression on Bell, and he cannot understand how it could do otherwise for Moss. Moss, though, has experience in warfare, where he would have seen carnage and learned to carry on in spite of it. That he survived that once will give Moss the expectation that he can again.

Bell's tribulation about his duty and career evolve with his ruminations about the warfare that has erupted in the pastoral land in which previously the worst he needed to confront was the rare occurrence of the remorseless murderer. After arranging for his office staff to call Loretta after he leaves, thus to avoid the explicit lie, Bell resolves ponderously to dedicate himself to truth and justice three times a day—a token renewal of duty to stave off his growing inclinations to step beyond how being an officer of the law constricts his actions. He meets with Carla Jean and concocts a tale for her sake, with the moral being that even in the contest of man and livestock the outcome isn't certain. This is a lesson corroborated in Moss's shot not felling the stationary antelope that he lines up in the telescope of his rifle. It is also a lesson nearly corroborated in the pit bull's pursuit of him down river. That Moss may not comprehend this lesson, which is what Carlo Jean tells Bell, is what puts Moss in peril. Bell ends his parable with mention of the pneumatic air gun used to euthanize beefs in meat processing plants to emphasize Moss's danger. That mention confirms that Bell understands Chigurh's method of forced entry and the other use he makes of that means. It also confirms that in Moss's contest with Chigurh, Bell foresees that Moss will be the one with the limited chances of the beast against the technical mastery of the butcher.

Bell's lingering thought of the presence of the assassin, Chigurh, propels him into the El Paso motel room where he suspects, correctly, that Chigurh will return, and suspects, again correctly, that he may still be there. This wouldn't be the studied procedure of the law man under those suppositions, but it is the circumstance contemplated when he avoids the conversation with Loretta, lest she inveigh upon him to reiterate his vow to be careful, not get hurt, and not hurt anyone. The sole purpose for Bell's returning alone to the motel room can only be to surprise and kill Chigurh. Having effectively lied to Loretta and Carla Jean about innocuous issues with possibly monumental implications, Bell seeks to exceed his office, his newly committed thrice-daily invocations to his secretary for the sake of truth and justice notwithstanding.

Chigurh is still on Bell's mind when he visits Ellis, which Ellis quickly surmises. Loretta's letter has given him enough hints on that score. Ellis's explication of the slim difference between those of his cats that are half wild and those that are outlaws, while pointedly keeping Bell's gaze, pinpoints what he says about the cats to exactly what torments Bell. Bell's compliance in holding that gaze acknowledges that he understands what Ellis means by that. Half of Bell's motivation for retiring is feeling over-matched. Half of it is an impulse to hunt down Chigurh unencumbered by the restraints of an officer of the law. Bell's tribulation is not over his fear, nor whether he can marshal his convictions in religious faith and cultural ideology to have the courage to hunt down Chigurh. Bell would have reason to believe that he could do this. He came within moments of catching up to Moss, and though he believed to have just missed Chigurh for the second time, in fact, he did catch up with him, too. Among the four hunters, Bell is the most economical and clearly reasoned in his movements. It is in Ellis's ripostes to Bell that we understand what Ellis perceives, that Bell's anguish concerns his yearning to exact revenge, contrary to the teachings of his faith, contrary to his professionalism, and contrary to his need to ensure that Loretta will not need to mourn his reckless loss, as had Carla Jean, or perhaps also to become victimized, as had Moss, Wells, and Carla Jean.

Bell's retreat from that world of precipitous loss leads him to visit Ellis to hear again stories of loss and death from before his time. The dusty hard-pan road leading to Ellis's remote home, the vaguely distinguishable domesticated and outlaw cats swarming about, and the clutter of the kitchen betray a life filled with idling memories and no remaining active purpose. Ellis consoles Bell to understand that it is a hard terrain upon which this hard life is placed. What Ellis calls "hard country" is not so much the geologic terrain as that borne of the human investment in a land never completely civilized. Taking it all on oneself to rectify evident evil is vanity. It is on this point that Ellis again pointedly holds Bell's gaze, and again Bell accedes to it, again to acknowledge that he understands Ellis's meaning.[2]

Ellis tells Ed Tom—because he asks about it—how long it took for Uncle Mac to die of a gunshot wound in the remote country, and how Aunt Ella had the anguished chore of digging a grave for him in the hard caliche the next morning. Ellis's point is that these horrifying folds in the fabric of the social world are not new, nor rare. The violent conflict of cultures in the Southwest in the nineteenth century exhibited the same rampant violence, which becomes most severe in those corners of the world most remote from the forces of social order. That the economic demands of this same social realm fuel the rule of violence is the paradox that Ellis understands well and that he is determined to impart to Bell. When in

John Ford's *The Searchers* (1956) Mrs. Jorgensen lifts the jug and gives it a swirl to judge by its heft how much Ethan and Lars have imbibed and then pronounces austerely that there wouldn't be a peace in the land until long after the bones of "us Texicans" are in the ground, it is this same hard *human* terrain that she addresses.[3]

Bell wonders about Ellis's feeling of vengeance for the man whose bullet crippled him. Ellis dismisses that desire as just more of the same bleeding that life extracts from a soul, for which the best one can do is "get a tourniquet on it." Bell's confession to Ellis that he feels God must have found his life wanting, and his needing to hear how a man died, are the lingering thoughts of the man who will have the two dreams he tells Loretta, which are about a squandered life and a cold death, respectively. Bell's life has been one spent within conscious view of its horizon, yet without the comfort of having forged meaning in its living that will counterbalance the inevitable.

ANTON CHIGURH—DEATH

Chigurh's first act is to transform shackles into weapons. Killing the deputy places him in an absurd full-body embrace with his victim, an image that Moss's embrace with the dog will recapitulate. With a slight grin and eyes wide open, Chigurh shows neither emotion nor exertion to interrupt his method of killing. The calculated encounter with the motorist on the highway relies upon his confidence to ask another calmly to stand still so that he can apply the instrument of slaughter. The calm, firm repetition of the request to step forward out of the car shows not a glimmer of emotion. That method of calm but firm instructions, repeated if necessary, to prod people nearly subliminally to do his bidding is one of his reliable tools. Chigurh's two carefully fashioned weapons show this same clear-headed calculation of—as he explains it—needing only one tool if you choose it correctly: the pneumatic air gun and the shotgun with silencer.

Chigurh's gait is steady and unhurried. His posture is unaffectedly erect. He is expressionless, except when he shows his transparently forced smile. His deep, slightly gravelly, as if electronically altered, voice retains the same tone, particularly when he repeats commands for what he needs. His clothes are tidy, dark and nondescript. His soup-bowl haircut signals a lack of concern with being attractive. He is passionless and methodical in killing. He is unflappable when faced with obstacles and undaunted regardless of setbacks. It would be easy to call him lunatic or psychopathic, were it not for his even temperament and inerratic thinking.

The small plastic wrapper for a package of cashews unfolds crinkling, after Chigurh leaves it crumbled up on the counter. This brief moment in Chigurh's tormenting the gas station owner is magnified by the detail shot that cathects the unspoken lethal meaning of the casual, unanimated conversation between proprietor and customer. All of time past and future evaporates in this momentary exchange between the two men on either side of the counter, on either side of the crinkling wrapper. All of the rest of the world falls away from the sole terrain of significance of that short expanse of the countertop defining the space between the two men. Chigurh imposes an excruciatingly frozen *here* and *now* that challenges the man into taking frank measure of his life. In the time that Chigurh's quarter has taken to traverse their world to this spot, how has this man given his life meaning, accomplished something that would make having lived that life worthwhile? That he is a hard-working man, content (like Llewelyn and Carla Jean) with modest means, a God-fearing man, considerate of others, a member of a community, a husband and a father—all this would conceivably suffice to prove his worth, and one could expect a proud defense of that lifetime's humble accomplishment. Chigurh's impertinent repetitions of the man's unassuming responses turns each one into an ironic statement of his life: that it hasn't meant anything, that there's everything wrong with everything, that there will be nothing else because there hasn't ever been anything else, that he closes his life's chances prematurely, that he doesn't know what he's talking about regarding his own life, and that calling the coin flip with nothing at risk is undistinguishable from having everything at risk. The quarter that he wins glorifies that equivalence. His own reticence to say what would vindicate him and his feigned obliviousness to Chigurh's imprecations confirm how deeply Chigurh's mocking impromptu existential trial has hit home.

Chigurh repeats the quarter stratagem with Carla Jean. In both instances the outcome is strategically indifferent to Chigurh. He reiterates for Carla Jean that he and the quarter arrived together, bearing her fate, as she repeats vainly to him Wells's pointing out that there isn't any purpose in it for Chigurh. We see a quarter a third time, on the second end of a conceptual match cut, as Chigurh feeds the car wash machine after presumably having killed the chicken farmer, whom he did need to eliminate and hence would not have offered his best deal.

That the man will have lived a life earnestly yet without ever having examined his own purpose will not be a piece of wisdom that loses any of its poignancy for being delivered by a man of profound evil rather than beneficence. It is what Chigurh thinks of the man in the gas station—that what meager property and accomplishment the man has he gained by having married into it. With an eerie impish smile that confirms for the man that indeed he was within an instant of annihilation, Chigurh's departure confirms that the coin flip was for him the appropriate judgment of a man whose life will not have gained or lost one iota of meaning for continuing past this moment or not. Chigurh repeats this same scrutiny of a life in the query he poses to Wells: "If the rule you followed led you to this, of what use was the rule?" It's not just his death that Chigurh thinks Wells ought to regret, but Wells's life such as led to this outcome, as it only could, sooner or later.[4] And wasn't that life ridiculous? The critique implicit in Chigurh's question isn't a consequentialist test of rule-governed behavior but a confrontation with the intrinsic worth of the rule. Now is the time for Wells to contemplate for what purpose he has lived his life.

It may be tempting to understand Chigurh's confrontations with his victims as the last proximate cause in a chain of deterministic events embedded in how people are placed in the world and live out their lives unaware of this fatalism. But this clearly isn't the meaning Chigurh imparts. That he wants to know what the gas station proprietor has done with his life, that he wants to challenge Wells with his own honest reflection upon his life, that both Wells and Carla Jean pose to him his freedom not to do this—these confrontations mean that the fact of the quarter having arrived at this time and place at the same time he has simply brings the terminus of life immediately close to the moment as life is lived, as the symbolic instigation for confrontation with its meaning. Was the life an accomplishment or pointless? Has this person created a life, or has life been a matter of the forces of the world flowing through the person and affecting every aspect of what is taken to be personal? These are more important questions than whether any given action can possibly be reconciled with an account of free will logically compatible with physicalism.

Chigurh's manner of killing is unmarked by emotional force—not anger, not vengeance, not fury, not bloodlust. Yet his conversation on the point of killing reveals empathy—he understands exactly what his cornered victim is thinking. It is that moment of thought that he wishes to probe. The killing is purely calculated, informed by his immediate needs, yet not strictly pragmatic. There wasn't any need to kill the gas station attendant, nor any risk. Killing Carla Jean followed from what he had promised Moss, a promise he intends to keep for himself. Shooting at the crow on the bridge, testing the weapon, testing his aim while moving, gives a measure to how casually Chigurh can kill, yet without remorse, even in *not* hitting the target. The black bird crying out and flying up in the air to the vertical boom-shot view offers the counterpart to an escaping soul—an escaping death. Chigurh opts not to confront Bell because there is no purpose in it, yet not insignificant risk. His efficiency relies upon that emotionless single-minded prioritizing of actions and purposes, yet also upon his cognizance of his own vulnerability. He is able to attend to his own serious wounds through a series of calculated actions to scrounge what he needs while not risking trace of his presence. His retreat from the encounter with Moss shows careful estimation of tactics that take his vulnerability into account.

Chigurh invokes the calm repetition of commands for the woman trailer court manager and would be within an instant of getting what he needs. As much as there is no hint of threat or terror in his voice, because he has no need to threaten, he has no reason—not even a whim—to eliminate this one more victim. One needn't have seen the encounter with the night clerk in the Eagle Hotel or the conclusion to the encounter with the chicken truck driver to know that in those instances there was a reason—though simply tactical.

Chigurh's last confrontation is with the two boys on bicycles. The fluttering noise of the playing cards fixed onto the bike frames with clothespins—to imitate the throbbing putter of a motorcycle, a bemusement all boys of a certain age learned to do—distracts Chigurh just long enough not to see the cross traffic speeding through the red light, which slams into his fate orthogonally, as had the unexpected blood trail for Moss in the desert.[5] That same boyish fascination with open-throated throbbing of the extravagantly powered, unmuffled truck engine is shared by the owners of the bullet-riddled trucks circling the victims of the desert shootout, by those who leave the motel in El Paso firing automatic weapons, and also by the armed men who chase Moss to the river. Chigurh, though, collects his wits, bargains with the boys, and attends to his injuries well enough to be able to walk away from this diversion on his path, whereas Moss followed the diversion. Seriously hurt, in severe pain, and partially disabled, but no more defeated than he had been after suffering the wound from Moss's shotgun, Chigurh once again gathers together what incidental objects he needs to effect his escape. Absurdly supplicant, and smiling wanly in recognition of that, he offers the boys astronomically inappropriate payment for a worthless article of clothing—just as had Moss bargained with the high school boys on the bridge spanning the border. It is precisely their contentment with the money for nothing, a real thrill greater than the imagined thrill of playing cards flapping in the spokes of their bikes, that he can rely upon. It is the modus operandi of the outrageously powerful to trump ordinary concerns with inconsequential inducements. He smiles because the boys implicitly affirm his existence and efficacy.

When Bell notices the beads of condensation on the glass of milk in Moss's trailer, he sits down to drink from it himself and stares ahead at his silhouette reflected in the blank TV screen opposite—just as we had seen Chigurh's when he sat there and drank. Looking for "someone who has recently drunk milk" will be all the identity Bell has of Chigurh and all he will ever get. It will be a descriptor that applies to Bell himself, which his evocation ironically declares. Chigurh's lack of attributes of the vicious criminal renders him invisible. There are other shadow, silhouette, and synecdochal images of Chigurh—in the back seat of the deputy's cruiser, in the doorway of Moss's trailer, through the translucent glass approaching the mobile home park manager's office door, and outside the Del Rio motel in his stocking feet. He questions whether he's visible to the accountant after killing the man who had hired Wells. Bell wonders to the El Paso sheriff whether Chigurh is a ghost, but it would apply just as well to Bell, who wonders about his effect upon the hard terrain during his presence on earth. When he suspects and unknowingly stands close to where Chigurh hides in the dark, Bell is captured—lit from behind—in that same ghostly silhouette image in the doorway to the motel room and again inside.

It is, however, with Moss that Chigurh matches traits more thoroughly—just as the two scarred men, Ethan Edwards and Cicatrice, are each other's double in *The Searchers*. Moss's invocation to the antelope to hold still is the same as Chigurh's request to the motorist. Each shows unrelenting persistence in his chosen goal. Each avails himself of the available incidental resources of the land or the hardware store to fill out a detailed improvised scheme for dealing calmly with a complex crisis. Each shows the perspicacious tactical expertise to understand attack and retreat, whereas others are motivated by instinctual fight or flight. Each manages medical attention after being wounded while protecting his location during treatment and recuperation. Each has his absurd full-body embrace with death. Moss's supplicant offers of sufficiently large bloody money to the young Americans on the bridge and to the mariachi band reiterate the logic of the power of violence to accompany the illegal market that Chigurh plays out with the boys. Moss and Chigurh will speak once by telephone—where Moss's spontaneous exhibition of anger differentiates him from the emotionless Chigurh. That quick sign of passion also pertains to their respective difference regarding the satchel full of money. We understand what it means to Moss—but we haven't a clue as to what it means to the man who drinks milk and kills wantonly, other than being the prize that others would kill or die for.

Unbeknownst to each other, they first come close enough for their paths to lie separated by the thin wall of the Del Rio motel room. In their eventual physical encounter in Eagle Pass, Moss and Chigurh are for just a moment but a few feet apart—and this time each is cognizant of the other's presence. They are now separated by a hotel room door easily penetrated by the weapons they both hold in their hands. In the ensuing action Chigurh wounds Moss and then follows the trail of blood to where he's hidden but pauses, cautiously, knowing the wounded man is dangerous. Moss advances, wounds Chigurh, and then follows his blood trail to where he's gone into hiding, but hesitates, cautiously, knowing how dangerous the wounded man is. This crossing of the blood trails recapitulates that moment in the desert when Moss comes across the first clue of an alteration of his fate, culminating the implications of Moss's initial choice in the desert.

Chigurh we must understand as a man, not a symbol, a cipher, an embodiment, or evil incarnate. It trivializes the significance of what he is and does to write it off to the quasi-metaphysics of vague symbols that mainstream Hollywood purveys. It works well in mainstream films to induce an audience to imagine hypostatized evil for which the projected story provides typifying representation. Much to the contrary of mainstream action drama, Chigurh is a villain who doesn't drool. There's nothing about him that can be coded as aberrant and hateful—other than his wanton killing. Yet he's the worst evil there is—namely, death. Not as symbol, or embodiment, or personification, but as genuinely *human*, a man who understands the logic of killing warranted by his found place in the world.

Chigurh's thinking and behavior are wholly within the realm of possibility for human nature. What leads him to that manner of behavior is fully informed by his cognitive and reasoning faculties, and not the upshot of dark passions cathected and amplified by a rare psychopathology, nor by an ethereal embodiment of the evil in the world, nor by the latent evil in human nature. He kills wantonly but without passion; his victims are chosen indiscriminately according to that logic, entirely without regard for their merit or virtue. He kills bystanders who happen by into his sights. He punitively kills those who have inconvenienced him and those immersed in the same illegal business. He kills Carla Jean as the logical result of Moss's refusal to accept his best offer. He calmly taunts his adversary, not as a psychological ploy but simply for the sake of stating what will happen before it does. Chigurh understands his place at the apex of forces greater than himself that are urgently violent because their absolute illegality entails that he *be* death, that he administer death as ruthlessly, indifferently, and arbitrarily as death itself. It is a role that he plays out consciously, more with curiosity than relish.

ELLIS, THE PHILOSOPHER

Ellis catches Bell's eye to enforce the warning that the difference between guardians and outlaws relies upon the exercise of conscience. It's not guaranteed by office, nor by character, nor by habit. He warns Bell of the spiritual degradation of gnawing vengeance. He assures him also that it is vanity to suppose that he personally can alter what's coming. He tells

Bell the story of the death and burial of Uncle Mac, which has the moral of this being a hard country, "hard on people, hard and crazy." This hasn't changed much since the initial colonization of the country. These are reflections of an old man, someone no longer having the responsibility for contributing to the vagaries of fate. The country remains ever rendering hard and crazy fates upon people. Escape from those damnations remains remote except as illusions promulgated by popular representations. These are the reflections that make this country difficult to endure in old age when sober reflections scrutinize the potential for redemption and saving grace. Hence, it is no country for old men.

Martin Heidegger explains how where the saving power reigns, there also lies danger (1977, 287–317). That danger mingling with the saving power arises from the artificial, which, as mere technical know-how, can embed what it reveals about being into what then covers it back over more opaquely. Or, creation can let what it reveals shine forth purely, which is poetic. The creations that Moss finds in the desert—the money and the narcotics—project opaquely into the complex nexus of the social world where money is funneled into the subterranean avenues of distribution of contraband into that world for those who beckon it. When he grasps the satchel of money, Moss has a pure vision of escape for him and Carla Jean from the entire expanse of that nexus. And so, as Heidegger attributes to the poet Hölderlin, from whom he has borrowed the association of danger with the saving power, we have this additional thought: "poetically dwells man on earth" (Heidegger 1977, 213). Moss, the welder, alloys a transformative fate onto the one that life has presented him, and in the instant it takes to surmise that the money must lie nearby.

What Heidegger has to say about anxiety, temptation, resoluteness, caring, and constancy will help separate the four hunters—Moss, Wells, Bell, and Chigurh (Dreyfus 1997, 304–28; Heidegger 1962, 304–58). Anxiety rises in the face of the meaninglessness of life, once the immutability of being-toward-death overshadows all concerns that human existence finds redemptive in life. In anxiety the assurances of meaning and purpose sustained by everyday concerns evaporate, and the familiar suddenly becomes alien. Chigurh deliberately poses this anxiety to the gasoline station proprietor, the mobile home park manager, the motorist whose car he will seize, and Carla Jean. As much as Wells pretends an independence from the everyday, he too is placed in anxiety by Chigurh's menacing interrogation. In the throes of anxiety, the appeal of escape back into the absorbing distraction of the everyday easily holds sway. Bell's inclination to find and confront Chigurh is this sort of temptation—one that will distract him from the being-toward-death that he has seen starkly confirmed for Llewelyn and Carla Jean, and, more importantly, for himself. Ellis will dissuade this easy escape, and not by urging upon Bell that he avoid the disquieting confrontation with mortality. Bell will remain immersed in that anxiety, as demonstrated by his dreams of his father.

Accepting meaninglessness offers liberation from anxiety, and with it a recognition that nothing that can be done or that happens has redeeming significance in life. Anxiety then loses its power to paralyze. Chigurh's unswerving clear-headed logic of the instrumentality of death and his assumed role as the interrogator of the anxious realize this manner of liberation. Chigurh's liberation, though, remains determined, unswerving, and acquiescent in the administration of death, which is still part of the everyday, however rarefied this function of the commercial activities of his chosen profession may be. Ultimately, Chigurh shares that with Wells, whether or not at the point of his own death he too will experience trepidation. A resoluteness to open possibilities finds in the moment of their acceptance the departure from the temptation to revert to the soft comfort of the everyday familiar world. Moss, when he comes across the crossed blood trails, finds that moment. Curiosity in transformation leads him to choose the trail other than the one that brought him to that spot at that moment. What then sustains Moss's transformation as something other than Chigurh's contented nihilism is the constancy of purpose in that transformation—which for Moss is Carla Jean. Moss's joyfulness in his constancy thus contrasts with Chigurh's sardonic amusement in the lack of escape from anxiety that he finds in everyone.

The natural response in this existence propelled toward death is to find the saving power in caring—caring about anyone or anything, perhaps, but caring about something creates importance, and, more importantly, the importance of caring itself. Moss separates himself from the ways of people, as does Chigurh. Caring prevails in Moss. The sole vestige of caring in Chigurh lies in his curiosity about his victims' thoughts at the moment of confrontation with death. It won't be enough for that caring to prevail for Moss. It matters what the caring is about—the full spectrum of transcendence and heinous atrocity all lay within the realm of what can give life meaning. Happiness, redemption, and survival aren't guaranteed by transcendence, nor is horror foreclosed. That Chigurh has forged his existence averting caring demonstrates that caring is something to be chosen and created. That it need be so shows the advent of purpose in human nature in an optimistic light.

Emerson describes the inclination of human nature to fixate upon the past while anxiously anticipating the future; but it is only in living exuberantly in the present, *above time*, that happiness is possible (1951, 48–49). The crinkling wrapper perturbs the gas station proprietor because the collapse of all of a lifetime into the moment is terrifying. Wells and Bell both chase *against time*, on behalf of the past and anxiously regarding the future. It is for Moss and Chigurh that living *above time* is possible, both as what separates them from the comprehension of their actions by those they encounter and also for the sake of being devoid of the impingements of either past or future.

Wells and Bell have frameworks of meaning settled deep in lives of professional practice. What Wells never gets to contemplate for more than the brief moment of his mind focused upon it, Bell does confront, in the company of Ellis, isolated in his thoughts, mentored by a man he trusts to understand his needs. The Coens capture this moment with Tommy Lee Jones's head set against the background architectural confluence of walls and windows, trisecting the ambiguous formalist space behind him and rendering it the figuration of his transcendence. For the moment, Bell enjoys the separation from the ways of the world that have always enveloped him, but still he is unable to divert his focus upon the inevitable.

Moss, however, sustained obliviousness to death, not out of vain fearlessness, but for the sake of not letting the inevitability of death dominate. His death results from a miscalculation, not an obsession.[6] Moss shows that orientation toward life that Gilles Deleuze projects as devoid of trepidation in the face of eventual impending death (1990, 268–72, 315–20).[7] What corresponds to Heideggerean resoluteness Deleuze delineates in terms of exuberance in the inventive creation of transcendent meaning. Finding precedence in Spinoza's assertion that "a free man thinks of nothing less than of death, and his wisdom is a meditation on life, not on death" (qtd. in Deleuze 1990, 271). Deleuze articulates the Spinozist emphasis upon the authentic joyfulness that comes from a life lived openly, actively, expressively, and devoid of the enervating fixations upon guilt and death. In contrast, it is superstition, myth, and forms of faith fueled by superstition that divert the passions away from what is imminent in this life. Genuine joy isn't possible for a life governed by faith in the fabulous transference of meaning and purpose to what lies beyond life. We won't have a clear idea of just what Llewelyn thought he could pull off, but it clearly placed him with Carla Jean in joyful escape. There is, needless to say, nothing in that exuberance that guarantees happiness, redemption, or survival.

THE COEN BROTHERS' ADAPTATION

Sheriff Ed Tom Bell arrives at the motel in El Paso just as the shooting commences. Men armed with automatic weapons have Moss cornered. Bell opens fire from behind, and calls in support. Moss exposes himself to draw attention away from the woman by the swimming pool. She is able to scramble away, but Moss is hit before he can retreat back behind cover.

Bell has the assailants pinned down well enough when police arrive and take command of the situation. Some of the assailants have been shot, and the others are apprehended. Bell attends to Moss, who dies in his arms, beseeching Bell to tell Carla Jean that he loves her. Knowing that the unknown man hunting Moss will likely arrive on the scene, Bell sets a trap. Chigurh enters the room. Before Bell can effect an arrest, Chigurh raises his weapon, and Bell fires repeatedly. Dying, Chigurh curses the cracker law man. When Bell visits Carla Jean some weeks later, he explains that the money that was still in Moss's possession when he was killed will go without legal claim and hence will revert to her. She weeps and tells Bell that she's pregnant—the conception must have happened that night in the mobile home when Llewelyn first came home from hunting with the satchel. The next morning, Ed Tom tells Loretta about a dream he had about his father, who was waiting for him next to a warm fire. They embrace tenderly. Poignant, plaintive solo piano music wells up in the soundtrack as—fade to black.

The travesty of a standard Hollywood denouement for the film would derive from more than just the hackneyed action-thriller plot elements of trite heroism, gratification of the need to see evil punished, an "up" ending of hope and optimism, and confirmation that good guys win and bad guys lose. What, moreover, gets obliterated in the trivialization of an adult story into the fairytale requirements of what the industry has conditioned a national audience to crave is the seriousness of the issues of life and purpose that interleave events in McCarthy's novel. Contradicting the strictures of the action-thriller genre, the likeable Moss dies ridiculously, the innocent Carla Jean is killed for no reason, Wells's swagger escapes him once he's cornered, the sympathetic Bell declares he's overmatched and quits, and the dastardly but clever Chigurh wins the loot and survives. It could not be other if the story is to leave the trivial plot gratifications behind, among them the expectation that likeability guarantees virtue, which guarantees victory, which guarantees redemption, which guarantees affirmation of meaning and purpose. It is only the fatuous joy fueled by myth that could find affirmation in this strident retreat from anything serious.

The Coens' adaptation retains elements of the novel that continue what one can find in McCarthy's novels about the West, particularly the Border Trilogy. How Moss instantly recognizes the sudden possibility for transformation to his life in the satchel of money has its parallel in Billy Parham's sudden, though nonmonetary, championing of the fate of the she-wolf and then later Boyd's corpse (*The Crossing* [1994], 58, 393), and also in John Grady Cole's young prostitute (*Cities of the Plain* [1998], 70). Moss's prize will be his burden and his undoing—just as was the she-wolf for Billy Parham and the girl for John Grady Cole. Those two other McCarthy protagonists exhibit the same mold of persistent, enterprising will and precocious worldly wisdom. As is the case with Billy Parham's rescue of the she-wolf, everyone Moss encounters is puzzled to understand the purpose behind his actions—expressed with McCarthyesque wry commentary. "Have you always been crazy?" the old man in the Model A asks Billy (*Crossing*, 59). Llewelyn and Carla Jean exhibit the wry, understated humor typified in many McCarthy characterizations, on the edge of being sardonic yet relishing the intimacy of shared humor. Like Billy Parham's protective pursuit of John Grady Cole, Bell will see in Moss his own esteem for finding meaning on one's own terms, frivolous and romantic as Moss's choice may have been. Like Parham, Bell will arrive too late to intervene against the greater skill and persistence of the administrators of death (*Cities*, 258–62). Bell's second dream is similar to Billy Parham's, which also draws a stark picture that echoes how Homer depicted the netherworld (*Crossing*, 112; Homer 1963, bk. 11). In *All the Pretty Horses* (1992), McCarthy offers a bleaker assessment of how social commerce hardly subdues the readiness to kill as a measure in worth in men (182).

McCarthy's blind wise man in *The Crossing* tells Billy Parham that "most men were in their lives like the carpenter whose work went so slowly for the dullness of his tools that he had not time to sharpen them" (292). This is also the underlying message of the philosophical confrontations that Chigurh has with the man in the gasoline station, with Wells, with Moss, and with Carla Jean. It is also the underlying message in Ellis's conversation with Bell. The old blind man explains to Billy Parham how easily people come to believe that their lives are fully determined by causes and forces beyond their comprehension and command, but that though choices are constrained beyond what people imagine, genuinely free choices are contemplated in terms of what is given (*Cities*, 195). The Coens recreate Parham's absurd full-body embrace with the she-wolf for Moss to have with a dying pit bull (*Crossing*, 58). The unnaturalness of the embrace initiates Moss's separation from the normal order of the world—as it had for Parham. It is Cole's inability to foresee every part of what's coming that will mean his violent sudden death—as it will also for Moss. Like both Cole and Parham, Moss is the romantic—devoted to his commitment to love and inclined to a precipitous pursuit of what transforms meaning in life. Chigurh is also like the wise killer, Eduardo, in *Cities of the Plain*, a man whose lethal power derives in part from understanding human nature, understanding the skills he needs, understanding how to deploy his skills with a weapon (*Cities*, 246–54).

McCarthy populates his novels with wise elders, and some of their thoughts will resonate in this story as well. Maria tells John Grady Cole of the history of men's greed and God's inability to alter it (*Pretty Horses*, 239), which will echo Bell's befuddlement with the transformation of his world. Don Arnulfo tells Billy Parham that when the acts of humanity and God conjoin, God dismantles this arduous achievement (*Crossing*, 47), which will also describe what happens to Llewelyn and Carla Jean. The old man that Parham meets in the mountains tells him that in times of war, the best men are killed. Wells and Moss survived a war, count as the best men in what they have mastered, and they will be killed in this subsequent war for which the lethal Chigurh is emblematic. The old man also understands how Parham no longer belongs to the ways that rule among people, which he takes as a sign of largeness in the boy. People will see that in him and will wish to know him. He also warns that while this is a good thing, like all good things, it was also a danger (*Crossing*, 133–34). Finding himself set apart from the world gains Moss the immediate acknowledgement of the INS border guard, the clothing store salesman, and the woman by the pool. Avoiding the predictable pathways of the world prolongs Bell catching up with him and subjects Moss to the danger posed by those who do catch up with him. The old blind man tells Parham that "that which was given him to help him make his way in the world has power also to blind him to the way where his true path lies" (*Crossing*, 293). Moss underestimates the dangers that surround him, though it is not be clear how he may have avoided them.

This is the first instance of a Coen brothers' film that doesn't derive from their own original script, though there is an affinity among their films for both themes and characterizations in McCarthy's novels about the West.[8] One finds starkly cold-blooded characters similar to Chigurh in the Coens' previous films—Loren Visser in *Blood Simple* (1984), Eddie Dane in *Miller's Crossing* (1990), and Gaear Grimsrud in *Fargo* (1996).[9] Appropriate to the grim terrain of human deeds and endeavors, the austere light and textures of the land captured in just a few transitional images provide significant contrast to the lush cinematography that Roger Deakins provided in his previous work with the Coens and others. It is a land amenable to beauty, but also to the interminable mundane and to horror.

The text of the novel consists of unadorned depiction of things done, things said, and the a posteriori ruminations of Ed Tom Bell. The Coens' adaptation pares away numerous elements of the story that could not congeal into a spare narrative for a feature-film length. The innocent young girl hitchhiker becomes the flirtatious woman by the motel pool, but retaining the impetus for musings about what's coming, while omitting the need to exclude mention of the unknown female victim to Carla Jean. In the novel, Bell's understanding of the expansive socioeconomic basis for the evils he faces is more explicit (*No Country*, 79, 218, 303). The issue of who absconded with the load of contraband dope after the desert massacre is dropped.[10]

Other salient details are original in the film—the pit bull chasing Moss into the desert river and falling dead into his arms, Chigurh's confrontation with the chicken farmer, and Chigurh's presence in the El Paso motel room when Bell looks for him there. More than what can be attributed to the realization as functions of the formulae for effective, if not faithful, adaptation, the Coens compose strictly cinematic textures that build the substance of the central characterizations of the film: Chigurh's demeanor killing the deputy and in his repeated commands, Carla Jean's equanimity with Llewelyn even when complaining about his strange demands, Moss's tempered defiance of Wells and the INS border guard, Bell's sanguinity, Ellis's earnest philosophical mentoring. The careful irony-indulgent treatment of the brief roles of various strangers in the drama also attest to direction of acting that at once pries the story away from the mold of an action-thriller without devolving into farce.

Aside from eliciting the nuances of actors' performances, the Coens invent these important purely cinematic touches: the wavering image of the wounded pit bull in the desert turning back to look at Moss, the raucous roar of the truck chasing Moss, the crinkling wrapper on the counter, Chigurh drinking milk and staring at his reflection in the TV set and Bell repeating the same later, Moss pulling at the tag on his new shirt as he emerges from the riverbank weeds, the color of Bell's uniform bleeding into the glint of light on the inside of the empty lock cylinder in the El Paso motel, Chigurh waiting inside in the darkness, Moss's embrace with the dead pit bull, the playing cards in the spokes of the boys' bicycles, the ironic supplicant gesture of Chigurh to the two boys, Moss's ironic supplicant gesture to the mariachi band, the crow flying upward into the dark night, the long dusty road to Ellis's cabin in the desert, and the last instance of overlap sound in the film—the ticking of the clock after Bell finishes the recitation of his dreams to Loretta. The Coens layer cinema onto the distilled structure of story, character, and meaning extracted from the novel. The film proceeds as the flow of important details to observe and interpret, with humor ever lingering just on the other side of pending mayhem, which exactly reiterates the flow and tone of the novel and preserves its penetrating philosophical pull. The last of those details is the ticking of the clock, which pulls together everything important in the story—and particularly the crinkling cashew wrapper.

NOTES

1. A draft of the screenplay describes the images of this dream, which would have been the only element of the diegesis not set in continuous time (Coen and Coen 2005, 121–22).

2. Bell's voice-over that opens the film derives from several of the first-person brief chapters in italics that McCarthy intersperses in the novel. The reflection about where one puts one's soul at hazard, which is retained in the film voice-over, appears in the very first of these italicized first-person asides. But in the novel, Bell concludes by saying, not how one "would have to be ok with that," but rather, "*I wont do that. I think now that maybe I never would*" (*No Country*, 4). That assertion, along with the preceding description of "a prophet of destruction" whom Bell doesn't want to confront will identify these first-person accounts in the novel, particularly this very first one, as temporally *posterior* to the events of the story, including also Bell's conversation with Ellis, and his description of his dreams to Loretta. But these clues identifying the temporal setting of Bell's reflections are missing in the brief film voice-over. That Bell's voice-over only occurs once and serves to summarize his past will establish those reflections as *prior* to the events of the story as presented in the film, and *prior* to Bell's conversation with Ellis as well. One can thus conclude for both the novel and the film that Bell's views are indeed altered after hearing Ellis out. See *No Country*, 3–4.

3. *The Searchers* features John Wayne (Ethan Edwards), Jeffrey Hunter (Martin Pauley), Vera Miles (Laurie Jorgensen), Ward Bond (Rev. Capt. Samuel Johnston Clayton), John Qualen (Lars Jorgensen), Olive Carey (Mrs. Jorgenson), and Henry Brandon (Chief Cicatrice).

4. In the novel, Chigurh adds, "I'm talking about your life. In which now everything can be seen at once" (*No Country*, 175).

5. As Chigurh lingers upon that look into the mirror, one hears the boys' voices and the fluttering noise of the playing cards at a distinctly *muted* level in the soundtrack. This would reflect how those sounds would be heard from Chigurh's vantage point inside the automobile, or perhaps as they linger in his train of consciousness.

6. In the novel, Moss tells the girl hitchhiker, "Most people'll run from their own mother to get to hug death by the neck. They cant wait to see him" (*No Country*, 234).

7. See also Adkins 2007, 125–208.

8. One may discount *O Brother, Where Art Thou?* (2000) as an adaptation, since how it borrows from Homer's *Odyssey* consists of sparse parallels, variously transposed.

9. *Blood Simple* features John Getz (Ray), Frances McDormand (Abby), Dan Hedaya (Julian Marty), and M. Emmett Walsh (Loren Visser); *Miller's Crossing* features Gabriel Byrne (Tom Reagan), Marcia Gay Harden (Verna Bernbaum), John Turturro (Bernie Bernbaum), John Polito (Johnny Casper), J. E. Freeman (Eddie Dane), and

Albert Finney (Leo O'Bannon); and *Fargo* features William H. Macy (Jerry Lundegaard), Steve Buscemi (Carl Showalter), Peter Stormare (Gaear Grimsrud), and
Frances McDormand (Police Chief Marge Gunderson).

10. Traces of both of these elements stemming from the novel are still to be
found in the November 28, 2005 draft script (Coen and Coen 2005, 58, 80, 105). See
No Country, 97, 141, 152, 241.

REFERENCES

Adkins, Brent. 2007. *Death and Desire in Hegel, Heidegger and Deleuze*. Edinburgh:
    Edinburgh University Press.
Blood Simple. 1984. Dir. Joel Coen and Ethan Coen. Foxton Entertainment.
Coen, Joel, and Ethan Coen. 2005. *"No Country for Old Men*: Adaptation by Joel
    Coen and Ethan Coen. Based on the Novel by Cormac McCarthy. This draft:
    November 28, 2005." Unpublished draft.
Deleuze, Gilles. 1990. *Expressionism in Philosophy: Spinoza*. Trans. Martin Joughin.
    New York: Zone Books.
Dreyfus, Hubert L. 1997. *Being-in-the-World: A Commentary on Heidegger's "Being
    and Time," Division I*. Cambridge, MA: MIT Press.
Emerson, Ralph Waldo. 1926. "Self-Reliance." In *Essays*, 31–66. New York: Harper
    and Row.
———. 1951. *Emerson's Essays: First and Second Complete in One Volume*. New York:
    Harper and Row.
Fargo. 1996. Dir. Joel Coen and Ethan Coen. PolyGram Filmed Entertainment.
Heidegger, Martin. 1962. *Being and Time*. Trans. John Macquarrie and Edward
    Robinson. New York: Harper and Row.
———. 1977. "The Question Concerning Technology." Trans. William Lovitt. In
    Basic Writings, ed. David Farrell Krell, 287–317. New York: Harper and Row.
Homer. *The Odyssey*. 1963. Trans. Robert Fitzgerald. Garden City: Anchor Books.
McCarthy, Cormac. 1992. *All the Pretty Horses*. New York: Vintage International.
———. 1994. *The Crossing*. New York: Vintage International.
———. 1998. *Cities of the Plain*. New York: Vintage International.
———. 2005. *No Country for Old Men*. New York: Vintage International.
Miller's Crossing. 1990. Dir. Joel Coen and Ethan Coen. Circle Films.
No Country for Old Men. 2007. Dir. Ethan Coen and Joel Coen. Miramax Films.
O Brother, Where Art Thou? 2000. Dir. Joel Coen and Ethan Coen. Touchstone
    Pictures.
Plato. *Apology*. 1981. In *Five Dialogues*, trans. G. M. A. Grube. Indianapolis: Hackett.
Salinger, J. D. 1945. *The Catcher in the Rye*. Boston: Little, Brown.
Schopenhauer, Arthur. 1958. "On the Inner Nature of Art." In *The World as
    Will and Representation*, trans. E. F. J. Payne, vol. 2, 406–10. New York: Dover
    Publications.
The Searchers. 1956. Dir. John Ford. C. V. Whitney Pictures.

15

✛

Cold-Blooded Coen Brothers: The Death Drive and *No Country for Old Men*

Jason Landrum

No Country for Old Men (2007) is a film about death. Whether it is death at the hands of a merciless hit man, death from the ravages of an unforgiving landscape, or death from the unyielding march of time, *No Country for Old Men* unflinchingly stares in the face of that one thing that awaits all of us. The certainty of death that fuels Joel and Ethan Coens' Academy Award–winning film, adapted from Cormac McCarthy's novel, is neatly summed up in a conversation between Sheriff Ed Tom Bell (Tommy Lee Jones) and his Uncle Ellis (Barry Corbin) in the dénouement of the film. As Ed Tom and Ellis discuss the sheriff's impending retirement and reminisce over the shooting death of a relative, Ellis intuits Ed Tom's helpless fear of death and says, "What you got ain't nothing new. This country's hard on people. You can't stop what's coming. It ain't all waitin' on you. That's vanity." Ellis's terse explanation of death's relentless and egalitarian pursuit puts a final stamp on *No Country for Old Men*'s cosmic debate over whether the death that awaits us is destiny or the whim of chance. In this hard world, death gets us all, and when we are dead and buried, it does not matter how we get there. We are all headed there no matter what.

Throughout the Coen brothers' impressive cinematic career, the lurking presence of death has featured prominently in all of their films. In *Blood Simple* (1984), murder, blackmail, and a hard-to-bury "dead" body result in many untimely deaths. *Raising Arizona* (1987) features the dream-like presence of the Loner Biker of the Apocalypse (Randall "Tex" Cobb), who symbolizes the death that awaits H. I. McDunnough (Nicolas Cage) if he continues to live the life of an outlaw. In *Miller's Crossing* (1990), the undead Bernie Bernbaum (John Turturro) haunts Tom Regan's (Gabriel Byrne) progress through multiple gangland double-crosses. Madman Mundt (John Goodman), a serial killer living next door to writer Barton Fink (John Turturro), murders two policemen in a Nazi-themed tirade about the "life of the mind" in *Barton Fink* (1991). *The Hudsucker Proxy* (1994) opens with Waring Hudsucker (Charles Durning) jumping out of a window to his death and ends with Norville Barnes (Tim Robbins) avoiding the same fate as time is literally stopped. A kidnapping and ransom scheme goes horribly wrong for Jerry Lundegaard (William H. Macy) in *Fargo* (1996), resulting in multiple violent deaths. Donnie (Steve Buscemi)—often the third-wheel in the Dude's (Jeff Bridges) and Walter's (John Goodman) never ending debates about bowling, life, and politics—surprisingly dies of a heart attack toward the end of *The Big Lebowski* (1998), his ashes spread "at sea" in a hilarious quasi-memorial service. In *O Brother, Where Art Thou?* (2000), death is represented by the diabolical pursuer of the chain gang escapees; his opaque goggles and bloodhound sidekick are at every turn as Everett (George Clooney), Pete (John Turturro), and Delmar (Tim Blake Nelson) struggle to attain their freedom. Ed Crane's (Billy Bob Thornton) blackmail scheme and accidental murder of Big Dave (James Gandolfini) leads to his death-row confession and execution in the electric chair in *The Man Who Wasn't There* (2001). The heart attack that kills Rex Rexroth (Edward Herrmann) in *Intolerable Cruelty* (2003) serves as the crucial turning point in the matrimonial, double-crossing battle between attorney Miles Massey (George Clooney) and Marylin Rexroth (Catherine Zeta Jones). Finally, the many attempts to kill the unwitting Marva Munson (Irma P. Hall) go comically awry in *The Ladykillers* (2004), leading to the deaths of each of the would-be master criminals. While this list demonstrates that death is a constant feature in their films and represented in a variety of ways by the Coen brothers, *No Country for Old Men* removes the metaphors, the comedy, and the Busby Berkeley–inspired dream sequences, in favor of a more direct expression of death's grip on life.

Death is often represented in narrative cinema as an absence or as an excessive presence. In many mysteries and dramas, a puzzling death exists at the center of the story, thus propelling the protagonist toward an answer that fills the absence left behind by the death. In contrast, horror films portray death excessively. Bodies pile up in all types of horror films—zombie, slasher, serial killer, vampire, and so on—but, more importantly, these films identify the many ways that someone or something can die. Instead of situating death as a missing puzzle piece, the horror film shoves gruesome death into the faces of the audience. The horror genre always shows too much when it shows death. While the Coens do not explicitly work within the horror genre, their approach to death has more in common with its excessive display. Whether it is the undead Marty's haunting presence, the pressure brought to bear upon H. I. by a menacing phantasm, a gruesome death by wood chipper, a knife to the jugular, or a bolt to the forehead, the Coens consistently present death's power to unhinge the would-be perfect plans of the desperate, and often hilariously stupid, characters that populate their oeuvre.

Identifying the death current that runs through the Coens' films opens two new avenues for discussing both their filmmaking career and *No Country for Old Men*. First, many film critics have recognized the Coens' investment in excess, especially in character development and visual style, but few have connected the brothers' penchant for excessiveness with their thematic interest with death. Indeed, the Coens' interest in excess has resulted in a surprisingly uneven critical reception, which ranges from effusive praise for their inventive style to charges of being condescendingly aloof. Second, bringing together excess with death and theorizing them using the psychoanalytic conception of the death drive provides a useful launching pad for positioning the Coen brothers within a broader cinematic context, which has been a particularly thorny problem for film scholars since the directing duo started their filmmaking career. Scholars often position their films within larger cultural trends like the independent film movement of the 1990s or late-twentieth century postmodernism's reliance on parody and pastiche. However, theorizing the Coen brothers through the death drive provides us with an opportunity to rethink and regroup how we categorize their films and consider their filmmaking career. While genre, nation, and auteur have been the most common ways of organizing film history,[1] I propose that we can group films by how they manage excess, from its abundance to its elimination, and the Coen brothers' filmmaking career and the critical embrace of *No Country for Old Men* stand at the center such a reconsideration.

VACANT VIRTUOSITY

Although the Coen brothers have been nominated for and won multiple Academy Awards for their films, their critical reception throughout their career remains largely uneven. Moreover, those deeply involved in the aesthetics and politics of the independent film movement have remained ambivalent about their work because the Coens have typically straddled the fence between the independent and commercial filmmaking worlds. Conversely, the Coens have defied many expectations of mainstream filmmaking by refusing to take seriously their roles as directors and writers who work within the establishment. They rarely give interviews that could be defined as "substantive." They have yet to provide a commentary track to DVD editions of their films. They refuse to define their motivation for making their films, choosing, instead, to hide behind enigmatic comments that frustrate interpretation.[2] R. Barton Palmer argues that the divergent views of the Coens rest on their adherence to the practices of parody and pastiche that form the core of postmodern aesthetics: "The divergent response to *Blood Simple*, and to the nine films they have since released, *can* be traced, as I have said, to what some have identified as the Coens' 'postmodern sensibility,' a central feature of which is said to be the transgression of the boundary between high and low culture. . . . No doubt, they are more 'in' than 'of' Hollywood, consistently disdainful of any expectations that they play the role of 'serious' established director and writer" (2004, 33). The "divergent response" Palmer correctly notices in the reception of the Coens' first film, *Blood Simple*, what he calls a "symptomatic response," can be found in the reception of all of their films. Reception to a Coen brothers' film often follows one of two paths. The first lauds their films for their technical virtuosity, shot compositions, and self-conscious approach to genre. The second finds fault with these same virtues and argues that the Coens' approach to filmmaking is a cold, banal exercise that lacks heart and humanity. In both cases, the response to the Coens is guided by a critical aversion to or appreciation of their excessive presence in their films, and the "symptomatic response" to their films often resorts to complaints about how they seem to enjoy themselves too much and refuse to sacrifice that enjoyment for the sake of their audience. Palmer argues that this approach to filmmaking is consistent with postmodernism's recourse to the "blank parody of pastiche" that resists the personal filmmaking championed by the *les politique des auteurs* developed by the critics at *Cahiers du cinema* (2004, 58–9). All at once, the Coens are insufficiently present while also being excessively so; they refuse to personalize their narratives with either autobiography or political commitments and rely too heavily on overly stylized compositions and playful nods to other texts, either literary or cinematic.

As evidence for his argument about the typical response to the Coens' films, Palmer identifies an early review of their first film, *Blood Simple*, by Elliot Stein (1983). Writing in *Film Comment* about the 1983 New York Film Festival and the Coens' impact on it, Stein is the first reviewer to pursue what Palmer calls the "symptomatic response" to their films.[3] Stein frames the debate over *Blood Simple* in terms of the conflict between independent and commercial filmmaking and suggests that the Coens' reliance upon genre conventions disqualifies them from membership in the independent movement. As Palmer explains, the independent film movement often conforms to high-culture, modernist notions of what films should be while Hollywood films emphasize spectacle and easy-to-follow narratives (2004, 28). *Blood Simple,* however, does not differentiate between the two, and many critics in 1983 echo Stein's belief that the film tends to be inauthentic. Palmer argues that early critics of the Coens dismiss their work as a cynical bid for commercial success that favors style over substance (28):

> [*Blood Simple*] is "really about nothing so much as Coen's avidity to earn points on his first big studio project." The result is thus a "callous banality" that has been cobbled together from the genre conventions gleaned from "Prof. Lawrence Kasdan's Film Noir 101 course." Even worse, the Coens have dressed up the emptiness of their story with stylistic excesses that are irrelevant and pointless. Stein fulminates about these at length: "Amplified chunks of face are shoved up close to our dumbstruck gaze, prosaic household objects are given the fisheye and magically attain ominous connotations that don't mean anything in particular." (28–29)

Palmer ultimately concludes that early critical reception to the Coens' excessive style focuses primarily on their perceived "vacant virtuosity," which fails to be either independent or artistic. Film reviewers often find the Coens' excessive virtuosity troubling and accuse them of not caring for or liking their characters. For most reviewers, the Coens are all head and no heart.

There are many examples of this type of review. Throughout their career, the perceived vacancy at the center of a Coen brothers' film has disqualified them from entrance into the canon, relegating them to a kind of oddball status that only hardcore Coen fans could fully embrace and understand. A brief summary of these kinds of reviews is helpful in seeing how this trajectory has affected their critical acceptance. Manohla Dargis agrees with early critics of *Blood Simple,* arguing that it is "about genre and movies; mainly it was about itself. It was a hermetic puzzle, a closed system" that ushered in an era of movies "filled only with death and technique" (2000, para. 6). Roger Ebert accuses them of going too far in their use of dialect in their second film: "everyone in *Raising Arizona* talks funny. They all elevate their dialogue to an arch and artificial level that's distracting and unconvincing and slows down the progress of the film." Moreover, Ebert complains about the film's excessive style, suggesting that it is "shot down by its own forced and mannered style" (1987, para. 4). Jonathan Rosenbaum echoes Ebert in his review of *Miller's Crossing,* calling it "self-conscious and show-offy, with more portent than soul" and arguing that "the film shows some progress over the Coens' earlier efforts—if only because of the allure and energy of the cast. Yet it never fully convinces in terms of period or plot" (1990, para. 1). Terrence

Rafferty finds the same combination of excess and emptiness in *Barton Fink*. He explains that the film is "densely packed with allusions, clever dialogue, ingenious visual jokes, startling plot twists, and imaginative atmospheric effects, yet it feels thin. It's an empty tour-de-force, and what's dismaying about the picture is that the filmmakers . . . seem inordinately pleased with its hermetic meaninglessness" (Rafferty 1991, para. 1). The big-budget comedy *The Hudsucker Proxy* failed in the eyes of many critics because, as explained by Kenneth Turan, "if *The Hudsucker Proxy* is a triumph, it is a zombie one. Too cold, too elegant, too perfect, more an exhibit in a cinema museum than a flesh-and-blood film, *Proxy's* highly polished surface leaves barely any space for an audience's emotional connection" (1994, para. 9). By 1994, the Coens had achieved a good deal of critical success but very little box-office success, and film critics settled on the "zombie" argument as to why. Their films, up to the commercial failure of *The Hudsucker Proxy*, were exercises in extravagant excess that failed to connect with actual human audiences, and the Coens, according to the critics, appeared to be lost in their own enjoyment, refusing to let the rest of us in on their private joke.

Reviewers briefly abandoned the zombie argument in 1996 after the release of *Fargo*. Praised as their warmest film to date—despite the film's setting in freezing cold Minnesota and its gruesome subject matter—*Fargo* was admired by many critics because of its lead character Sheriff Marge Gunderson, portrayed by Frances McDormand, who won that year's Academy Award for Best Actress. Rita Kempley of the *Washington Post* effectively captures the sentiment of many reviewers when she states that the Coens "have been criticized for poking fun at the regional peculiarities of Arizona trailer trash, Texas yuppies and Irish drunks. Cries of Scando-bashing will doubtless ensue. Yet the brothers . . . have never taken quite so overt a stand for life's simple joys: a warm bed, a loving partner and a hearty breakfast every morning" (1996, para. 7). For Kempley, the Coens had moved beyond their sterile examinations of criminal motivation and added some humanity to the mix. Instead of being simply a film designed to amuse its makers, *Fargo* has something that Kempley can identify with through the main character, and she praises the Coens for reaching out to her simple desire for warmth and humanity. However, Desson Howe, writing for the same newspaper, asks "Do these guys ever step outside of themselves" and "Do these guys have a worldview, a feel for humanity?" (1996, para. 10). Even though some warmth could be briefly detected in *Fargo*, Howe continues to advance the zombie argument: "All of their movies, from *Blood Simple* on, seem closed-in. Their stories are basically boxes within boxes: One revelation leads intriguingly to another. But the secret, the point, or the ultimate punch line becomes even smaller" (para. 9). Much of *Fargo's* success rests on the sacrifice made by the filmmakers to reach out to the audience, providing a "true crime" story that takes place in a realistic setting with realistic people. Indeed, the Coens are praised for stepping out of their box and connecting with audiences. For many, this connection appeared to announce the arrival of the brothers as "grownup" filmmakers ready to articulate a coherent worldview. The Coens, however, refused to arrive.

The post-*Fargo* releases of *The Big Lebowski*; *O Brother, Where Art Thou?*; *The Man Who Wasn't There*; *Intolerable Cruelty*; and *The Ladykillers* did not fulfill the promise that critics felt in their award-winning sixth film. Instead, the filmmaking duo continued making films that featured their interest in excess and how it impacts the look of their film and the motivations of their characters. While there are numerous examples of reviewer disappointment with their post-*Fargo* films and various versions of the "symptomatic response," Kent Jones's review of *O Brother, Where Art Thou?* qualifies as what could be considered the typical review of the Coens' failure to arrive. Not only does it traffic in every single complaint about the Coen brothers as auteurs, but it also effectively summarizes the life of their reception. Entitled "Airtight," Jones's review begins by comparing the "mechanical" Coens to the magicians Siegfried and Roy, describing their films as "airless," "tricked-up," "derivative," and "perfectly thought through as to cancel [themselves] out" (2000, 45). Jones argues that the Coens, as directors, "were the first to achieve (or to want) a complete disjunction between style and subject matter" (45). Like the vacant virtuosity recognized by early critics, Jones explains that the brothers' films operate as exercises in mechanical precision: "What makes the Coens' body of work feel so alarmingly coherent is their monotonous syntax, the sense that any given film has been fed through some hitherto unknown image/sound processor, which pre-sets for shot duration, centered framing, emotional tone, and visual handsomeness. . . . You can set your watch by their remarkably uniform editing rhythm, which features a percussive yet deadpan one-two combination: probably intended to surprise, it's become as predictable as the rising sun" (46). Within all of this fussiness for precision, Jones also finds that the Coens have little regard for their characters or their endeavors, arguing that their films "are less than kind to their characters" and that the Coens feel the same way about their characters as a "hunter likes his trophies" (48). In Jones's review, the twin concerns of film critics—the Coens' pervasive formal excess and cold-blooded attitude toward their characters—combine to form a kind of conventional wisdom about the brothers' work. Jones's recognition of this conventional wisdom suggests that the Coens' films demand viewers respond to them via their own attitudes toward seeing "too much," whether that "too much" be the equivalent of cinematic showing-off or visions of gruesome or comic death. For the film reviewers discussed in this section, the combination of too much of both appears to be difficult to endure.

Interestingly enough, the reception of *No Country for Old Men* departs from the established trends of the Coens' previous films. While *No Country for Old Men* features more murder and their most cold-blooded character to date, Anton Chigurh (Javier Bardem), reviewers found the film to be a refreshing new direction for the Coens, a view wholeheartedly endorsed by the Academy Awards, which recognized it with awards for Best Picture, Best Director, Best Writing, and Best Supporting Actor. The outpouring of critical and industry praise stems from a perceived sacrifice that the Coens made in directing *No Country for Old Men*. Lisa Schwarzbaum claims that the brothers have eschewed their "hyper-controlling interest in clever cinematic style" that turned their previous films into "finicky pieces that might as well be viewed under glass" in favor of a movie "that doesn't rely on snark as a backup source of energy" (2007, para. 1, 2). Moreover, she argues that this film is the first to respect "its own characters wholeheartedly, without a wink" (para. 2). Geoffrey O'Brien praises the film for similar reasons. He suggests that the gratification of watching *No Country for Old Men* comes from the Coens' deliberate willingness to repress their desire to "step over the line": "The surpassingly excellent movie the Coens have made of *No Country for Old Men* gets part of its power from deliberately holding in check the invention that flourishes so exuberantly elsewhere in their work. . . . In *No Country for Old Men* the Coens rigorously deny themselves most of the gratifications associated with the phrase 'a Coen brothers movie.' The moments when they seem ready to step over the line . . . gain in power from the firmness with which such gestures are brought back under narrative control" (O'Brien 2007, 30). Similar to Schwarzbaum, O'Brien detects a renunciation of excess in the Coens' award-winning effort, and like previous critics, they both orient their response toward how they feel about seeing too much when they see "a Coen brothers movie."

In many ways, *No Country for Old Men* is typical of their previous work: the comic use of regional dialects, the constant presence of a moving camera, the impact of hostile environments, and the ill-conceived plans of dimwitted characters—to name a few. However, critics continue to regard the Coens as almost childlike because of their inability to demonstrate artistic restraint and to exhibit a properly respectful attitude toward death, both of which require a heavy dose of repression in order to achieve. The Coens, however, often refuse to equate successful art with such sacrifices and, instead, continue making films that challenge viewers to confront how excess and death affect what we watch.

Replaying the critical debates over the Coens' career is crucial to understanding the significance of how the cinema impacts how and why we choose certain things to watch and resist others. At the heart of the Coens' critical reception is a debate over the impact of excess on the spectator's experience, and visual excess—whether it is featured or hidden—remains the political and aesthetic driving force behind narrative cinema. Filmmakers constantly struggle with questions of how much to show, and whether their decision is based on economics, ratings, politics, or aesthetics, the choice to show too much, too little, or something in between is central to our experience as a spectator. While some filmmakers choose to hide excess, the Coens, as the critics have correctly noticed, seek to foreground an encounter with its effect. This encounter, properly theorized, demonstrates how we deal with its impact. More precisely, reception to the Coens' filmmaking style is not incorrect or misguided. Instead, I argue that the recognizable pattern in the criticism of the Coens reveals how they consistently disturb viewers with moments of too much visual satisfaction in order to reveal the power that death—more specifically our need to repress it at all costs—has in shaping our lives.

THEORIZING EXCESS

The previous section established a trend within reviews of the Coen brothers' filmmaking career. Within this trend, we see an evolving fascination with the duo's formal virtuosity coupled with complaints about their lack of narrative heart. For many film critics, the Coens' films are excessively calculated, formal exercises that belie a cold-blooded attitude toward their characters. This critical trend is crucial to understanding how excess affects spectators, and I want to suggest that the effect of excess is a new way to think about how to organize films and filmmakers. In what follows, I explain a psychoanalytic theory of film that takes the Coens' reception as its point of departure. This theory focuses on the spectator but does not focus on an historical or empirical spectator. Instead, the spectator discussed in this section is one that is demanded by the text. In other words, a Coen brothers' film demands that the spectator engage excess, either through formal cinematic conventions or narrative displays of violent death. It is around excess that all Coen brothers' films revolve, and this point is best underscored by the words of movie reviewers because, in many ways, their sensitivity to the concerns of what they might deem "thumbs up" or "thumbs down" helps us identify a kind of hierarchy of mainstream tastes. For movie reviewers, how a filmmaker deploys or obfuscates excess quite often determines the potential success a film might have in the marketplace or during award season.

In film theory, the psychoanalytic concept of the gaze has been used the most often by scholars who seek to explain how spectators identify with narrative film.[4] These theories, however, have incorrectly located the gaze on the side of the subject and not as a visual embodiment of the *objet petit a*; the question for film theorists should not be how a spectator identifies with a film but how a film manipulates a spectator's desire. Hugh Manon argues that the "keystone concept in Lacanian theory is the *objet petit a*, of which the gaze is one 'paramount embodiment.' Although the term resists easy definition, if asked to sum up the structure of the gaze in a single word, we would be hard pressed to find a better approximation than *masked-off-ness*" (forthcoming).[5] The gaze, like the *objet a*, is a partially masked object that sets our desire to "see more" in motion. The gaze is bound up in the subject's dialectic of desire that is constituted by lack, and, therefore, guarantees that what we see is never fully satisfying. The gaze as *objet a*, therefore, is experienced by the subject as an unexplainable absence in the subject's field of vision, and how the subject coordinates itself in relation to this absence defines how the subject experiences its reality.

One way the subject overcomes the disappointing absence of the gaze is through fantasy.[6] To overcome the problem of never seeing exactly what we desire to see, the subject turns to fantasy as a way to imagine itself as satisfied. Through fantasy, subjects project onto the emptiness of the gaze a narrative that represents satisfaction, wholeness, and meaning, but doing so puts the subject at risk of being shocked by seeing "too much" or being bored by the same. Fantasy, moreover, is one way that filmmakers can choose to engage the spectator's desire, and the choice of fantasy involves rendering the gaze as fully visible. In *The Real Gaze*, Todd McGowan argues that films can be theorized based on how they manage the absence represented by the gaze, a process that he believes "is the fundamental political and existential act of cinema" (2008, 18). For McGowan, rendering the gaze as visible, occluding its lack, and presenting the spectator with a cinema of too much satisfaction constitute a cinema of fantasy.[7] Therefore, fantasmatic cinema focuses "on disturbing spectators with moments of too much satisfaction rather than reminding spectators of their dissatisfaction" (McGowan 2008, 25). McGowan suggests that the cinema of fantasy elevates those things we believe to be hidden within social reality and demonstrates how the things we cannot see shape our desire: "By rendering the excess of the gaze visible through fantasy, cinema makes us aware of the hidden enjoyment that silently informs our social reality. In doing so, it confronts spectators with the sources of their own enjoyment and deprives them of the illusion of a neutral social reality. This gives the cinema of fantasy its political, ethical, and existential power" (25). For McGowan, filmmakers like Stanley Kubrick, Spike Lee, Michael Mann, and Federico Fellini exemplify excessive, fantasmatic filmmaking, and I argue that the films of the Coen brothers fit in this category as well.

The primary aim of a Coen brothers' film is to confront spectators with too much satisfaction. According to McGowan, films that satisfy too much seek to exceed our daily experience and allow us to recognize the excess that everyday reality obscures (2008, 70). As the reviews discussed in the previous section illustrate, the Coens delight in an overattentiveness to the plenitude of the image and pack each frame with too many formal innovations: high and low angles superfluously employed, moving cameras disconnected from a realistic mise-en-scène, and wide-angle lenses gratuitously used to distort faces and objects, stretching them beyond recognition. On the level of content, their films often focus on how the excesses of death stain the social reality of their characters. They satisfy the spectator with a vision of death's dismantling of everything from perfect crimes to Southern populist politics and from writer's block to corporate America. Often using a comedic tone, the Coens call attention to the many ways that their characters work against their self-interest. The death drive, as Freud formulated it, does precisely the same, suggesting that we will "often act in complete disregard of our self-interest and instead act out of a compulsion that we do not understand. The concept of the death drive means that we will sacrifice anything and everything (even life itself) for our particular Thing—which is to say, for our enjoyment [*jouissance*]" (McGowan 2004, 5). The death drive operates as a kind of pressure on the unconscious, producing a nagging sense that there is something more beyond everyday reality, and fantasy is a way of screening an encounter with this impossible excess.

Through fantasy, the Coens render the death drive and the "compulsion we do not understand" visible, satisfying viewers with the exploits of dimwitted characters who continually crash into walls of their own making. The effect of such fantasizing confronts spectators with their own willingness to not seek out their own good, and the Coens convincingly challenge viewers to question the notion that we are driven by our own self-interest. In Coen films, kidnapping and murder plots achieve nothing, gangland warfare goes nowhere, and investing in early attempts at dry-cleaning leads to the electric chair. In both formal and narrative concerns, a Coen brothers' film forces the spectator to question the power of excess by exposing its impact on our plans—whether they be noble or boneheaded—for progress.

FIXIN' TO DO SOMETHIN' DUMBER THAN HELL

In the previous section, I explained how we might begin to think about films that confront spectators with excessive satisfaction. Filmmakers eliminate the absence represented by the gaze and produce the hidden *jouissance* that silently informs social reality. They work to excessively satisfy spectators through overstuffed narratives and formal flourishes, demonstrate how excess dismantles our view of society as neutral, and illustrate the never-ending series of threats that might erupt and tear at its fragile fabric. Excess, in the case of the Coen brothers, is not something that resists interpretation or is meaningless. Instead, excess, as represented by the death drive, provides us with the fundamental point underscoring each of their films. Nowhere is the Coens' investment in the death drive and its complicity in our own unconscious sabotage more evident than in *No Country for Old Men*. While many movie reviewers found the film to be a departure from the Coens' previous work, *No Country for Old Men* demonstrates a continuing investment in the same themes and formal concerns, and in many ways, their twelfth film boils down their narrative and visual practices to a kind of streamlined perfection. Many film critics applauded the Coen brothers for sacrificing their penchant for heartless pastiche, going so far as to declare—like Schwarzbaum and O'Brien—that the Coens have found a new level of restraint in their aesthetic. However, I argue that the Coens have not sacrificed any of these things and that *No Country for Old Men* is, without question, the most brutal and heartless film of their career.

Sometimes film theorists launch into their analyses by explaining that they are looking at a particular film through a lens. In the case of psychoanalytic theories of film, we often read articles that analyze these cultural artifacts through a "psychoanalytic lens," producing a moment of insight into the motivation for a character's actions or the construction of the film's ideology. This chapter, however, does not look at the Coen brothers through a lens and, instead, argues that their films actually screen an experience with the death drive, an experience that magnifies how the death drive applies pressure to social reality and operates as a mechanical, compulsive persistence. *No Country for Old Men* screens the death drive in two basic ways. First, the death drive factors into the depiction of the three main characters: Llewelyn Moss (Josh Brolin), Anton Chigurh, and Sheriff Ed Tom Bell. Each offers a different response to the pressure of the death drive, thus demonstrating how it destroys self-interest. Second, the formal and narrative choices made by the Coens elevate excess over absence, forcing the spectators to confront their persistent demand for death to have meaning—to provide, in other words, many answers for the dissatisfactions of life.

Llewelyn Moss is a typical protagonist of a Coen brothers' film. Much like H. I. McDunnough and Ed Crane, Moss thrives on bamboozling himself. This character trait can be found throughout the brothers' career and is probably the one aspect of their films least appreciated by film critics.[8] The typical Coen protagonist is a self-deluded schemer who will always sacrifice his given predicament for an elusive promise of something better. Most importantly, the typical protagonist always fails at achieving the promise of that special thing that he believes will release him from the dissatisfactions of his life. The Coen leading man is probably best explained in Moss's declaration to his wife that he's "fixin' to do something dumber than hell, but I'm going anyways." This dialogue exchange between Moss and Carla Jean—about his decision to take water to a dying drug dealer—sums up what we might consider the protagonist's credo in a Coen brothers' movie. They are always about to do something "dumber than hell," and nothing, not even death, will stop them. The compulsion to chase after an elusive *jouissance* at the expense of everything else drives Coen characters to murder their lover's husband, kidnap a baby, hire criminals to kidnap their wife, and in the case of Moss, steal money from drug dealers. At the end of these dumber-than-hell schemes waits the allure of a life unfettered by dissatisfaction. But these schemes never pay off. They always end in some kind of tragic or comic misery. For Moss, he inherits the wrath of one hit man who is described as being deadlier than the "bubonic plague." Moss's desire for excess—represented in the film by the suitcase of money everyone wants—unnecessarily increases the problems in his life. He must outwit the hit man; he must find a safe place for his wife and mother-in-law to hide; he must avoid being caught by the police; he must out-maneuver the one hit man hired to kill the other hit man chasing him; he has to negotiate the barriers posed by the Texas-Mexico border; and all of these plans are designed so that he and his wife can escape with the money, the reason for which is never fully explained.

Like the Coen protagonists before him, Moss is driven by a compulsion that is dumber than hell, but he proceeds without regard. For his effort, Moss is killed at a hotel in El Paso while waiting for his wife. Adding insult to his death, Moss is not killed by the hit man Chigurh but is, instead, killed by the other thugs in the rival drug gang. The effort he expends in stealing the money and going into hiding ultimately adds up to nothing. In their protagonists, the Coens recognize the allure of *jouissance* and how its excess drives their characters to sacrifice everything they have—even their lives—for its fleeting promise.

If Moss is the typical Coen leading character, Anton Chigurh is, to some degree, the typical antagonist. Chigurh is both typical and the "ultimate badass" version of a Coen antagonist. In Chigurh, the brothers have found a character who perfectly embodies excess and captures the coldness that many reviewers find in their films. Chigurh is an amplified version of the cynical detective Loren Visser (M. Emmet Walsh), the biker bounty hunter Leonard Smalls, and the kidnapper Gaear Grismrud (Peter Stormare). While the Coen protagonist is always caught in the allure of *jouissance*—sacrificing today for the promise of what may come from tomorrow, only to find himself in the end back where he started, arrested, or dead—Chigurh always proceeds forward, much like a zombie, with little regard for enjoyment, murdering those people he has been hired to kill. With Chigurh, the Coens can screen the hidden world of the hit man for the spectator, illustrating how he is excessively human in many ways. They focus closely on his choice of weapons: a bolt shooter designed to kill cattle and a shotgun with an oversized silencer. They show how he out-maneuvers regular people because they fail to see the threat he represents. They demonstrate that he does not need a hospital to clean and dress a gunshot wound. They emphasize the destruction he leaves behind. They highlight his ruthless attitude toward his targets and those who fall prey to the whims of his diabolical coin flips. But Chigurh is also an atypical Coen character because, in the end, he gets away. He simply walks down the street and away from a nearly fatal car crash. His escape suggests that death offers us no compromises, and in Chigurh, the Coens effectively screen the pressure that it brings to bear on life. Had Chigurh died in the car crash at the end, the Coens would have provided some kind of solace for the spectator, providing a kind of karmic rejoinder from the senseless deaths of Llewelyn and Carla Jean, but Chigurh's escape reaffirms the film's commitment to presenting death as an unyielding and excessive presence.

The film's commitment to excess is also found in its clear explanation of what Chigurh wants. Briefly consider how many action films handle chase scenes. The protagonist spends a good portion of the film running from someone or something, the conflict of which is fueled by the inability to determine what the pursuer wants or who they even are; think, for instance, of *Butch Cassidy and the Sundance Kid* (1969) as the title characters flee from the posse led by the man in the white hat, the outlaws constantly asking themselves, "Who are those guys?" These chase sequences often end by answering the question of the pursuer's desire or, more radically, leaving that question open. The Coens, however, leave little doubt about what Chigurh wants. Indeed, his clearly defined desire seems to drive the narrative forward. Chigurh ruthlessly tracks and kills his prey because of his personal code, which demands that he proceed without questions or doubts. The money, as we are often reminded, has nothing to do with it. The money is for those who are dumber than hell and cannot resist its lure. Chigurh kills because fate demands it of him. The creepiness of Bardem's portrayal of Chigurh revolves around his assured, cold-blooded attitude toward others, and the spectator knows that, no matter what, Chigurh will not fail in his pursuit. Killing Carla Jean firmly cements for the spectator that he will not compromise his drive to fulfill his promises. He is, in effect, the embodiment of the death drive, persisting in his demand without hesitation or regard to pleas that he does not "have to do this."

Sheriff Ed Tom Bell serves as the conscience of *No Country for Old Men*, commenting on the nature of violence, death, and time's uncaring forward march. In the film's voice-over narration, Bell reflects on his inability to understand the violent struggle between Moss and Chigurh, and he futilely works throughout the narrative to encourage Moss to give up the money and come home. Much of Bell's dialogue centers on the nature of death and, more specifically, on whether death has any meaning. For example, in the opening voice-over Bell describes a death-row case in which he was the arresting officer, his testimony ultimately convincing the jury of the suspect's guilt. Bell's opening voice-over introduces the questions surrounding death's meaning:

> He killt a fourteen-year-old girl. Papers said it was a crime of passion but he told me there wasn't any passion to it. Told me that he'd been planning to kill somebody for about as long as he could remember. Said that if they turned him out he'd do it again. Said he knew he was going to hell. "Be there in about fifteen minutes." I don't know what to make of that. I surely don't. The crime you see now, it's hard to even take its measure. It's not that I'm afraid of it. I always knew you had to be willing to die to even do this job. But, I don't want to push my chips forward and go out and meet something I don't understand.

Bell's description of the suspect's attitude toward death accurately reflects the power of the death drive. The death drive is passionless, unyielding, and repetitive. To avoid its pressure, the subject gives way to repression, which allows the subject to avert the death drive, keeping it partial and limited. Moreover, repressing the death drive is necessary for full membership into social reality, and this exchange is clearly represented in the film whereby Moss and Bell are full members and Chigurh, who is often described as a ghost, is not. Moss does not understand how someone can do something dumber than hell like steal money, sell drugs, and murder people. For the sheriff, death does get us in the end, but he does not seem to understand why everyone around him is in such a hurry to find out what it is like.

While each one of the main characters perform various responses to the death drive's destabilizing presence, the narrative also reflects its cold presence. *No Country for Old Men* is ostensibly a mystery. A detective sifts through various crime scenes in order to find the missing link between each, all the while hoping to secure Moss's safe return and the capture of Chigurh. While many elements of the crimes and their motives remain a mystery for Bell, the spectator is never misled about the central elements of Moss's flight and Chigurh's murderous pursuit. In other words, the Coens do not organize the narrative around lack and, instead, overwhelm the spectator with excess.[9] *No Country for Old Men* is more of an antidetective story than it is a detective story because there are too many satisfactory answers as to why and how Moss dies and Chigurh gets away. Imagine how another director might handle this material in a more traditional way, one that posits lack as its central concern. If this new version were more about Bell's investigation, Moss would steal the money, a faceless pursuer would track him, and the detective would be responsible for identifying the killer, eliminating him at the climax of the film, rescuing Moss, and recapturing the money. Moreover, Moss would be given a light prison sentence in the dénouement in order to reestablish the rules of social reality, namely that crime does not pay. But *No Country for Old Men* is primarily about Chigurh, his excessive presence, and our capacity for doing something against our self-interest, the consequences of which are death. As a detective, Bell moves from scene to scene without identifying any evidence to help bring this case to an end. Instead, he cycles somewhat helplessly through the remnants left behind by Chigurh, ultimately failing to identify the hit man or rescue Moss. The culmination of Moss's drive to forgo his life in order to chase the allure of more money, Chigurh's radical embodiment of the death drive, and Bell's inability to fill in the blanks of the mystery result in a film that forces spectators to consider how much time we spend fending off thoughts about death and the shape that it gives to our decisions about life.

CONCLUSION

By creating characters who embody certain aspects of the death drive and crafting an antidetective narrative that does not pursue lack, the Coens have effectively made a film that highlights the unbearable presence of death. The elimination of lack and the addition of too much satisfaction exposes how often Hollywood portrays death as a meaningful fantasy, thus showing us how much this fantasy gives shape to our conception of death. In many ways, we conceive of life and death like a Hollywood movie. Our lives have acts, there is often a central conflict that drives our lives forward, there are persistent lacks that need filling, and toward the end, our life will be revealed to us to have meant something. *No Country for Old Men* confronts this fantasmatic conception of death and portrays it, instead, as unstoppable and meaningless. The silence that runs throughout the film—the Coens offer no musical score to accompany the on-screen action—underscores this final point. In the film's final scene, Bell recounts two dreams he has about his father, one where he meets him in town to get some money and the other where he and his father ride horses in the snow, his dad passing him by without saying a word. The film ends, rather abruptly, on Bell's final line that "I knew that whenever I got there he would be there. And then I woke up," which is followed by a silent, black screen. Regardless of evidence to the contrary, Bell still shares in the fantasy of death's meaning, that lack can ultimately be filled. Rather than experience loss, Bell continues to fantasize about his dead father waiting for him in heaven with all of the answers; he "woke up" and has moved on. Doing so allows him to regain the silence of his social reality and to forget the noisy and meaningless death left behind by Chigurh and Moss.

The Coens have consistently pursued this theme and produced many films that explore the impact of death on life. In effect, their films fill some spectators with the same feelings that death does. For many movie reviewers, the Coens' films are cold, formal experiments that refuse to grant the warmth of the human condition to their characters. These movie reviewers find the filmmaking brothers to be mechanical and without passion, almost as if they "pre-visioned"—to steal a term from Carla Jean's mother—the directing duo as sharing qualities with Anton Chigurh. It is an odd point of comparison, but reception to a Coen brothers' film often mirrors the responses many of the characters in *No Country for Old Men* have toward the cold-blooded hit man. Theorizing the critical response to the Coens' penchant for excess shows us that they are intent on exposing the shape that excess gives to our lives. If their depiction of the death drive is right—as that thing that is dumber than hell that we insist on having even though it may threaten our lives—the Coen brothers have shown us that we must be willing to resist our drive for that elusive *more* that often derails more lives than it enhances.

NOTES

1. In *The Real Gaze: Film Theory after Lacan*, Todd McGowan (2008) argues that film history can be rethought based on how a film (or films) approaches the Lacanian conception of the gaze. McGowan's argument will be explained in later portions of this essay and rigorously engaged in order to show how the Coens deploy the gaze through their thematic interest in death and their excessive visual style.

2. The Coens typically evade providing "serious" answers to the motivations behind their craft, resorting, instead, to humorous responses. An example of this evasive maneuver can be found in an interview the brothers gave to a London online magazine. Asked by the interviewer to explain the process they used to adapt McCarthy's novel, Joel said, "Well, Ethan pointed out that it's really not that difficult but it takes two people—I hold the book open while he types the text into the computer" (Carnevale 2007, para. 4). In a way, the Coens have perfected the "nonanswer answer" to questions that most "auteurs" take seriously, thus confounding those critics who would like to elevate the Coens into the highest pantheon of filmmakers but refuse to because of their unwillingness to reveal anything personal about

themselves. The interview can be found at www.indielondon.co.uk/Film-Review/ no-country-for-old-men-joel-ethan-coen-interview.

3. In this section I am using Palmer's description of the Stein review deliberately. I want to both highlight the significance of Palmer's discovery of this foundational review and his coining of it as symptomatic of all Coen reception. I also want to use Stein's words in the same way that Palmer does. My aim, however, is to theorize this symptomatic review using the psychoanalytic conception of the death drive.

4. This article assumes that there is a great deal of familiarity with the gaze, especially as it has been characterized by Laura Mulvey and her conception of the "male gaze." For an explanation of the history of film theory's engagement with the gaze and how the concept has been misused, see McGowan 2003, 27–47.

5. Manon (forthcoming) effectively explains how the concept of partial masking of the gaze, or its *masked-off-ness*, informs Haneke's opening shot and its three formal lacks—editing, sound, and movement.

6. *Fantasy* is a term often associated with films like the Lord of the Rings trilogy or the Harry Potter series. However, I am employing the Lacanian notion of fantasy, which suggests that fantasy is how subjects project a satisfying image of themselves onto the dissatisfactions of symbolic reality.

7. McGowan employs four categories for how films deploy the gaze: (1) cinema of fantasy, (2) cinema of desire, (3) cinema of integration, and (4) cinema of intersection. The first two adhere to the specific aims of fantasy and desire, the third shows how fantasy solves the problems of desire, and the fourth shows how fantasy and desire collide. For McGowan, *Citizen Kane* (1941) fits in the desire category, *Schindler's List* (1993) fits within integration, and *Blue Velvet* (1986) operates as a supreme example of intersection.

8. Film reviewers often claim that Coens do not like their characters, and it is my contention they feel this way because of the Coens' investment in the death drive. The Coens consistently feature characters who act against their self-interest and seem trapped by the death drive. Hollywood films, however, often depict characters caught in this trap but deliver them to some kind of moment of clarity in which they learn a lesson. The Coens often avoid these types of moments.

9. A film organized around lack would be something like *Citizen Kane*. The spectator, through the reporter, chases clues to the meaning of Rosebud, which promises to unlock the meaning of Kane's life and death. The spectator follows the lure throughout the film only to find the answer to the question frustrated by the revelation of the sled. Its meaning is never fully clarified. *No Country for Old Men*, actually, has more in common with horror films, especially those featuring clearly defined monsters like zombies. What they want is never in question, and their excessive presence pressures their prey into making less than helpful decisions.

REFERENCES

Barton Fink. 1991. Dir. Joel Coen and Ethan Coen. Circle Films.

The Big Lebowski. 1998. Dir. Joel Coen and Ethan Coen. PolyGram Filmed Entertainment.

Blood Simple. 1984. Dir. Joel Coen and Ethan Coen. Foxton Entertainment.

Blue Velvet. 1986. Dir. David Lynch. De Laurentiis Entertainment Group.

Butch Cassidy and the Sundance Kid. 1969. Dir. George Roy Hill. Campanile Productions.

Carnevale, Rob. 2007. "*No Country for Old Men*: Joel and Ethan Coen Interview." IndieLondon. www.indielondon.co.uk/Film-Review/no-country-for-old-men-joel-ethan-coen-interview.

Citizen Kane. 1941. Dir. Orson Welles. Mercury Productions.

Dargis, Manohla. 2000. "Too Simple." *L.A. Weekly*, July 5. www.laweekly.com/2000-07-13/film-tv/too-simple.

Ebert, Roger. 1987. "Raising Arizona." *Chicago Sun-Times*, March 20. rogerebert.suntimes.com/apps/pbcs.dll/article?AID=/19870320/REVIEWS/703200302/1023.

Fargo. 1996. Dir. Joel Coen and Ethan Coen. PolyGram Filmed Entertainment.

Howe, Desson. 1996. "In Cold Blood in Cold Climes." *Washington Post*, March 8. www.washingtonpost.com/wp-srv/style/longterm/movies/videos/fargo.htm#howe.

The Hudsucker Proxy. 1994. Dir. Joel Coen and Ethan Coen. PolyGram Filmed Entertainment.

Intolerable Cruelty. 2003. Dir. Joel Coen and Ethan Coen. Universal Pictures.

Jones, Kent. 2000. "Airtight." *Film Comment*, November/December, 45–49.

Kempley, Rita. 1996. "Coen's *Fargo*: How Swede It Is." *Washington Post*, March 8. www.washingtonpost.com/wp-srv/style/longterm/movies/videos/fargo.htm#kempley.

The Ladykillers. 2004. Dir. Ethan Coen and Joel Coen. Touchstone Pictures.

The Man Who Wasn't There. 2001. Dir. Joel Coen and Ethan Coen. Good Machine.

Manon, Hugh. Forthcoming. "'Comment ca rien?': Screening the Gaze in *Cache.*" In *On Michael Haneke*, ed. Brian Price and John David Rhodes. Detroit: Wayne State University Press.

McGowan, Todd. 2003. "Looking for the Gaze: Lacanian Film Theory and Its Vicissitudes." *Cinema Journal* 42, no. 3: 27–47.

———. 2004. *The End of Dissatisfaction? Jacques Lacan and the Emerging Society of Enjoyment.* Albany: State University of New York Press.

———. 2008. *The Real Gaze: Film Theory after Lacan.* Albany: State University of New York Press.

Miller's Crossing. 1990. Dir. Joel Coen and Ethan Coen. Circle Films.

No Country for Old Men. 2007. Dir. Ethan Coen and Joel Coen. Miramax Films.

O Brother, Where Art Thou? 2000. Dir. Joel Coen and Ethan Coen. Touchstone Pictures.

O'Brien, Geoffrey. 2007. "Gone Tomorrow: The Echoing Spaces of Joen & Ethan Coen's *No Country for Old Men*." *Film Comment*, November/December, 30.

Palmer, R. Barton. 2004. *Joel and Ethan Coen.* Urbana and Chicago: University of Illinois Press.

Rafferty, Terrence. 1991. "*Barton Fink.*" *New Yorker*. www.newyorker.com/arts/reviews/film/barton_fink_coen.

Raising Arizona. 1987. Dir. Joel Coen and Ethan Coen. Circle Films.

Rosenbaum, Jonathan. 1990. "*Miller's Crossing.*" *Chicago Reader*. onfilm.chicagoreader.com/movies/capsules/6165_MILLERS_CROSSING.

Schindler's List. 1993. Dir. Steven Spielberg. Universal Pictures.

Schwarzbaum, Lisa. 2007. "*No Country for Old Men.*" *Entertainment Weekly*, November 7. www.ew.com/ew/article/0,,20158940,00.html.

Stein, Elliott, Stephen Harvey, and Harlan Jacobson. 1983. "The 21st New York Film Festival." *Film Comment*, November–December, 60–74.

Turan, Kenneth. 1994. *Los Angeles Times*. www.metacritic.com/video/titles/hudsuckerproxy.

16

✛

"Just a cameraman": An Interview with Roger Deakins

Lynnea Chapman King

Notable partnerships in the film industry are not uncommon, particularly between directors and cinematographers—Oliver Stone and Robert Richardson, Frank Capra and Joseph Walker, Jonathan Demme and Tak Fujimoto, Martin Scorsese and Michael Ballhaus—collaborations such as these, given their longevity and familiarity, yield remarkable films, and the pairing of the Coen brothers and Roger Deakins is no exception. Deakins has served as cinematographer for ten Coen projects and has received three nominations for his contributions to their films, including *Fargo*, the Oscar winner for the best film of 1996. Deakins' excellence, however, is not limited to his work with the Coens, as he has earned a total of eight Oscar nominations to date, becoming one of the most lauded and prominent cinematographers in the film industry.

Raised in Torquay in Devon, England, Deakins initially attended Bath Academy of Art, where he developed an interest in photography, which in turn led him to the National Film School. His earliest work was on documentaries, shooting in Ethiopia, India, Sudan, and Rhodesia, following which he worked with such directors as Michael Radford and Mike Figgis. His role as cinematographer for *Barton Fink* (1991) marked the onset of his collaboration with Joel and Ethan Coen, a partnership that has continued for almost two decades. Roger Deakins was kind enough to correspond with me in the spring of 2008, weighing in on his work, that of the Coen brothers, and the role of the cinematographer in filmmaking.

219

Those issues raised at the Coen Forum in Albuquerque are ever-present here, as they have been throughout this collection—fate, morality, responsibility, myth, influence, antecedents, genre—serving as a reinforcement to the conclusions the contributors have drawn. The perspective of the cameraman and the academic vary in many ways, but the central issues of the film and novel resonate in such a manner that they are evident to all spectators.

LCK: Did you read the Cormac McCarthy novel prior to production? How did your reading of the text affect your perspective of the film?

RD: I read the book before it was published. Joel told me they were adapting it and would, maybe, direct the film. I like Cormac McCarthy's writing, and I was very keen to shoot anything that was based on his work and especially so with Joel and Ethan attached. I don't know how that "changed my perspective" at all. The script is close to the book. The book certainly gave me ideas about the visuals, but when you are shooting a film it is the director who is most influential in the way you see something. It is first and foremost the director's interpretation of a story you are helping bring to life.

LCK: To which of your previous projects, with Joel and Ethan Coen or otherwise, would you compare *No Country*?

RD: They are all so different. *No Country* is a cautionary tale and in that way similar to *Fargo*, although that is the only real similarity. We were to do *To the White Sea*, based on the James Dickey novel, at one time, and that was closer, in many ways, than any film I have worked on with the brothers.

LCK: To many viewers, *No Country* seems to be a logical project for the Coens, very much in keeping with their previous films. To others, *No Country* is a complete departure, as it lacks the "quirky" elements present in many of their films. Do you see this film as a departure from their oeuvre or as a natural continuation?

RD: Who would not want to make a film from such an interesting piece of writing? Who cares if it was a so called departure from their other films—their oeuvre, whatever that is. Who decides what their oeuvre is, by the way, marketers and advertising executives?

LCK: The Coens often make very stylized films that fit loosely into specific genres—mistaken identity caper, noir, gangster films—but *No Country for*

Old Men is more challenging to classify, as viewers have characterized it alternately as a thriller, a crime drama, film noir, a Western . . . Is this challenge a result of a strategy as you filmed—a deliberate challenging of generic conventions?

RD: I don't see the problem. Marketers and advertising executives might want to characterize a film as one thing or another but I don't see what that has to do with the film itself. A film is a film! In this case one that was based on a very well-regarded novel, which I'm sure those same people couldn't categorize either. Sure, it was a blend of ideas about the Old West, the rise of violence in society, border drug dealing, and the search for any meaning to it all. That is the world Cormac was writing about.

LCK: In reference to the Western elements of the film, how would you characterize its cinematic heritage—were there particular Westerns that influenced your camera work as you approached the project?

RD: I love many of the films of Sam Peckinpah. For myself, the script of *No Country* brought to mind *Guns in the Afternoon*, *Bring Me the Head of Alfredo Garcia*, and *Pat Garret and Billy the Kid*. I love those films but I wouldn't say they influenced my cinematography in any conscious way. I never thought of any other film or image whilst I was shooting *No Country*. There is never time to contemplate such things whilst in production. I don't think films are made in such a cerebral way. Certainly not the films I have worked on. I just get on and shoot the script.

LCK: The landscape of *No Country* seems to be a character itself. Was this a conscious goal as you filmed, or do you think that this presence is inherent in the New Mexico and Texas locations themselves?

RD: The setting or at least a visual interpretation it, whether it be a coal mine, a motel room, or a desert, is important to any film. The landscape that acts as a backdrop for *No Country* was no exception. Its presence is referred to by the characters who seemed very much a part of it and whose actions are in some way dictated by it. It is a recurrent image throughout the film but the environment that *No Country* is set in is about more than just the landscape. Probably, the bulk of the story takes place in motels, hotels, gas stations, and on the street, all of which were very evocatively described in the book.

Joel and Ethan both had very clear ideas of the kind of environment they wanted for the film, and so we spent many days scouting that part of Texas described in the book, and locations, mainly in New Mexico, that were more realistic financially for us to use for the shoot. The landscape was very important to them and the look of the film was very consciously created by their choice of locations. We eventually shot for about six days out of Marfa in Texas so that we could establish a more distant horizon than that available to us from where we were based in Santa Fe.

LCK: The Coen brothers' approach to storyboarding is well documented; were there any significant spontaneous moments you would like to share, instances in which the filming departed from the storyboards?

RD: The storyboards are continually developed as we prep a film and usually incorporate what the locations have to offer by the time we get to shooting. There were some spontaneous changes to the storyboards based on the light and so on, but not many. Quite often we shoot fewer shots than are boarded as we see how one shot can work for more than might have been intended. We played a scene between the two sheriffs in a different shot to the ones boarded. It was raining that night and, partly to save time and because I liked the idea of the two profiles in silhouette, we shot the scene in the one angle against the rear wall of the coffee shop. I think that if and when something changes it is, most often, to connect or simplify the coverage.

LCK: The motel-room scene with Ed Tom and Chigurh invites multiple viewings and much speculation as to the literal, physical presence of Chigurh behind the door when Bell walks into the room. Would you care to comment as to your reading of this scene? Is the viewer to see Chigurh as the "ghost" Ed Tom references, or is there a more practical answer to this mystery?

RD: I think the book is as elusive as the film on this point, but Chigurh is evil and, perhaps, the devil. Whether he's something or someone who we ourselves have created or just a reflection of our own fears, we don't know.

LCK: You stated in a 1995 interview that "if you could show people what life is like for their neighbors, it could only help change things for the better. . . . That is what great filmmaking is—an exploration of ourselves." Seeing ourselves in Bell or Moss is certainly possible for many viewers, but I wonder if you see Chigurh as an opportunity to explore ourselves as well?

RD: I'm not sure that quote is strictly accurate. Of course film has the power to help break down prejudice and inform people. Certainly, I still believe that, and I believe most truly great films do explore the way we are as "human" beings in some way. Sadly, these films don't seem to make money any more.

To me, Chigurh represents the dark side of our nature, our basest fears and a loss of human decency. He is as much a part of the world we are creating as Moss. We live as individuals and by our own individual codes. Even Chigurh lives by a code. It's one that most of us would be repelled by but it is a code nonetheless, and without a "God," it is as justifiable as any other. Ed Tom has been waiting for God to come into his life to make sense of it all but he seems to realize that the concept of God and "goodness" is just a human creation, as is the devil, personified by Chigurh.

LCK: The entire quotation read: "If a film creates a world that you can go into as though it's an entity to itself, you have succeeded. A successful film should create a feeling of place and time, and a sense of how the people in the story live their lives. I always thought that if you could show people what life is like for their neighbors, it could only help change things for the better. I still believe that. That is what great filmmaking is—an exploration of ourselves" (*InCamera Magazine*, Winter 1995).

How would you characterize Chigurh's code? Is his code his sense of fate or destiny or something else entirely?

RD: The quote in the fuller version I would still agree with, but I wouldn't say that Chigurh qualifies as one of the neighbors! Ed Tom might be our neighbor whilst Chigurh is really more of a symbolic figure. Chigurh might see the rest of humanity as being bound to their fate, but I'm not so sure he sees himself that way, even if the story implies that he is. Evil personified and bound by fate!

What is a code anyway? A belief in God? The Law? Humanity? The toss of a coin? Who is to say which is more valid? That depends on the individuals beliefs in the first place. Can morality exist without religion? Dawkins says yes. Ed Tom is a moral character but he is beginning to have doubts. In losing his faith in the existence of God he is also losing faith in there being any guiding principal. Chigurh has a strong belief and a code he lives by, which to him is just as valid as one tied to the idea of morality, God, or goodness and that is chance—the toss of a coin.

LCK: You have commented on the voyeuristic nature of documentaries and the moral dilemmas which accompany that kind of filmmaking; does *No Country* strike you at all as voyeuristic, perhaps because of the rather graphic violence therein?

RD: The two are in no way connected. As a documentary filmmaker you are often an intruder in other people's lives and sometimes their misery. You take your trophies, in the form of your filmed images, and then you return to your own, and often more comfortable, life. There is an awkward moral dilemma attached to the work that needs to be considered. *No Country* certainly contains scenes of some very realistically staged fictional violence, but I wouldn't say it was in any way gratuitous or voyeuristic. Without this violent depiction of evil there would not be the emotional "pay off" at the end of the film when Ed Tom bemoans the fact that God has not entered his life.

LCK: You've cited cinematographers such as Conrad Hall as influences on your work; do you also have literary influences? Are there current directors or cinematographers that you find influential to you?

RD: Influences? I don't know. I loved Conrad Hall's work and I loved him as a person. Did he influence me? Probably, but in what way I don't know. He inspired me for sure because of who he was as a person. Directors? Writers? I love the work of Cormac, of course. I tend to read history and science books more than fiction, but I have read most of the novels of Bradbury, Philip K. Dick, J. G. Ballard, Malamud, Kafka, Camus, Melville, Coetze, Richard Morgan, Marquez, Le Carré, Naipaul, William Boyd, Russell Banks, Patrick White, Walter Tevis, Theroux, Conrad, Joyce, Mailer, Koestler, Matthieson, Ian McEwan, and so on. Have they influenced me? No more or less than anything else my senses come up against. I don't see how you can make a direct connection. I watch other films. Do I copy them? No! Do I think about any of them when I am working? Almost never! It's chicken and egg. I love reading those writer's work because of who I am, but I am who I am because I read those writer's books, see the photographs of Bresson, Salgado, Mayne, McCullen, Riboud, Lartigue, Ray-Jones, Kudelka, and so on; the paintings of Munch; the films of Huston, Peckinpah, and Melville; the landscape of Devon, the Southern Ocean, Africa, people and cities, and so on; had a father who . . . And then there is genetics!

LCK: Projects on which you have worked seem to bear your signature, in terms of visual language, even before the credits appear on the screen. How would you characterize this "signature"? Can you describe your own techniques or style of cinematography that contribute to the look of your films?

RD: If I have a signature, as you say, the word for it would be simplicity. I like to help tell a story without distracting the audience and without any superfluous camera "style." There is always a temptation to create dramatic visuals because there is so much technology out there today to help you do just that. But why? If you have a good script you may just be distracting the audience instead of drawing them in to the film.

LCK: How would you characterize *No Country* within the context of your larger body of work?

RD: That is a question for Joel and Ethan—and good luck with it!!!! I'm just a cameraman.

Deakins's style is indeed distinct, and even in films he shoots with different directors, his fingerprints are evident: the vertical shot upward through the bare branches of trees in the Coens' *Miller's Crossing* reappears in M. Night Shyamalan's *The Village*; the warmth of light in an internal nighttime shot in *The Village* is very similar to that of the scene in which Professor G. H. Dorr, played by Tom Hanks, reads aloud Poe's "To Helen"; the camera movement in an external shot of Jessie James, walking through tall, golden grass in *The Assassination of Jessie James by the Coward Robert Ford* is immediately identifiable as the work of the same cinematographer who shot the prison yard scenes in *The Shawshank Redemption*. In speaking about the Coens' storyboarding, Deakins notes his contributions to shooting the film, input that arguably impacts the viewer's interpretation of the narrative, "connect[ing] or simplify[ing] the coverage," offering his vision for a setup, lighting the shot—decisions that help to create a film that is clearly a part of the Roger Deakins oeuvre. Perhaps his role as "just a cameraman" speaks more to his humility than to his ability, both of which are considerable.

Index

About the
Editors and Contributors

Lynnea Chapman King teaches literature and film at Butler Community College in Andover, Kansas. She has served on the governing board of the National Popular/American Culture Associations and is chair of the Film Adaptation area for the Southwest/Texas Popular/American Culture Associations Conference.

Rick Wallach is a founding member of both The Cormac McCarthy Society and *The Cormac McCarthy Journal* editorial board. He taught literature, critical writing, and American studies for twelve years at the University of Miami and is the editor of *Myth, Legend, Dust*, an anthology of McCarthy criticism, as well as a two-volume anthology of McCarthy criticism, *Sacred Violence*, with Wade Hall.

Jim Welsh (James M. Welsh, PhD) was educated in Bloomington, Indiana, and Lawrence, Kansas. Besides founding the Literature/Film Association and coediting *Literature/Film Quarterly* for thirty-two years, he has authored and edited more than sixteen books dealing with drama, literature, and film. In 1973 he hosted a television series *The Films of the Gatsby Era*, originally broadcast on East Coast PBS stations from Boston to Miami, and for seven years thereafter he was arts editor for the CBS affiliate in Salisbury, Maryland, where he now writes as professor emeritus of Salisbury University. He served two terms as Fulbright Lector of American Studies at the Universitatea "A. I. Cuza" in Iaşi, Romania, in 1994 and 1998.

John Cant is a retired mathematics schoolteacher. As a student of "the third age" he completed his PhD on McCarthy at Essex University in 2002. He has contributed to *The Cormac McCarthy Journal*, *Comparative American Studies*, and *The Journal of American Studies*. His book *Cormac McCarthy and the Myth of American Exceptionalism* was published in 2007. He teaches American literature and film part time at Essex.

Scott Covell is an associate professor of English at Antelope Valley College in Lancaster, California, where he teaches composition, literature, film, and pop culture. He has written numerous essays and coedited *Living in America: A Pop Culture Reader* with Patricia Murray. He lives in Lake Balboa, California, with his wife, two kids, dog, and turtle.

David Cremean is associate professor of humanities and English at Black Hills State University, Spearfish, South Dakota. He is the 2009 president of the Western Literature Association and a member of the Cormac McCarthy Society. A resolute Cormackian introduced to McCarthy's writings in 1994 who later on learned he is likely descended from the McCarthy clan (the McCruimmen sept), he has a son named Cormac.

Dennis Cutchins teaches American literature at Brigham Young University. He won the Bode award for "'So That the Nations May Become Genuine Indian': Nativism and Leslie Marmon Silko's *Ceremony*" and the Butler Young Scholar Award in Western Studies. He is working on an essay concerning the influence of George Stevens's *Shane* and coediting two books on film adaptations.

Steven Frye is professor of American literature at California State University, Bakersfield. He is the author of *Understanding Cormac McCarthy* and has published essays, articles, and reviews in such journals as *American Studies*, *The Centennial Review*, *Leviathan, A Journal of Melville Studies*, *The Southern Quarterly*, *American Literary Realism*, and *Modern Fiction Studies*.

Robert Jarrett is professor of English and chair of the Department of English at the University of Houston–Downtown. He is the author of *Cormac McCarthy* (1997), in the Twayne United States Authors series. He teaches courses in professional writing, American literature, and Dickens.

Erin K. Johns is a second-year PhD candidate at West Virginia University. In addition to pop culture, her main area of research concerns intersections between British and American modernism and theoretical conceptions of the sublime.

Jason Landrum is assistant professor of English at Southeastern Louisiana University, where he teaches courses in film and specializes in psychoanalytic film theory. Recently, he has published an article theorizing Hollywood's depiction of the criminal profiler in the *International Journal of Žižek Studies.*

Pat Nickell is assistant professor of English at Webber International University in Babson Park, Florida. She teaches media; technical, creative, and legal writing; and freshman composition and rhetoric. She earned a PhD from Texas Tech University in 1999 and has taught at Webber for five years.

Stacey Peebles (PhD, The University of Texas at Austin) is assistant director of the Lloyd International Honors College at the University of North Carolina at Greensboro. She has published articles on Cormac McCarthy, Terrence Malick, and Michael Herr and is completing a book titled *Battle Rattle in the Suck: Narrating the American Soldier's Experience in Iraq.*

Dennis Rothermel is professor of philosophy at California State University, Chico. His recent publications include an essay on *The Piano, Crouching Tiger, Hidden Dragon, The Pianist,* and *Hero* in the *Quarterly Review of Film and Video* and book chapters on *Mystic River* and *My Darling Clementine.* His forthcoming essays include "Slow Food, Slow Film" in the *Quarterly Review of Film and Video* and a contribution to a collection of essays on adaptation, "Julie Taymor's Musicality."

Sonya Topolnisky is a PhD student at the Bard Graduate Center in New York City interested in mid-century America and the intersections between fashion, art, and popular culture. Her master's thesis, "What That Hillbilly Cat Dragged In: Elvis Presley's Transgressive Self-Fashioning 1954–1958," focused on the relationships between dress, music subcultures, and identity construction. Sonya is also a senior editor and contributor to Worn Fashion Journal (www.wornjournal.com), an independent publication that emphasizes the historical and artistic components of dress.

Pat Tyrer is associate professor of American literature at West Texas A&M University, where she teaches American literature, film studies, and creative writing. She has published in *The Southern Literary Journal,*

The Houston Literary Review, Quiet Mountain Feminist Essays, and *The Journal of the College Conference of Teachers of English.* With cowriter Pat Nickell, she recently completed *Maddie's Crowd,* a novel, and has begun work on a second.

John Vanderheide is a PhD candidate at The Centre for the Study of Theory and Criticism, University of Western Ontario, Canada. His work focuses on the idea of apocatastasis and the modern transformations of allegorical expression in literature, philosophy, film, and television. He plays the blues guitar like the reincarnation of Roy Buchanan.

Linda Woodson is professor of English at the University of Texas at San Antonio, where she teaches courses in Southwestern literature and rhetoric and composition. She has published a number of articles on McCarthy and a wide range of other authors and literary topics.